LYNN SCHOOLER is a two-time winner of *Alaska* magazine's grand prize and winner of the *National Wildlife* grand prize for wildlife photography. He has lived in Alaska for more than thirty years. *The Blue Bear* is his first book.

An Imprint of HarperCollins*Publishers*

The
Blue Bear

》》》 A True Story of Friendship
and Discovery in the
Alaskan Wild

LYNN SCHOOLER

The excerpts reprinted on pages 239–243 from
"The Final Days of Michio Hoshino," by George Bryson
(*We Alaskans,* October 13, 1996), are reprinted here by permission of the author.

The excerpt reprinted on pages 261–262 from *Nanook's Gift,* by Michio Hoshino,
translated by Karen Colligan-Taylor, is reprinted here by permission
of Cadence Books.

HarperCollins books may be purchased for educational, business,
or sales promotional use.
For information please write: Special Markets Department,
HarperCollins Publishers Inc., 10 East 53rd Street,
New York, NY 10022.

First Ecco paperback edition published in 2003

Designed by Kate Nichols
Map by Jackie Aher

Library of Congress Cataloging-in-Publication Data has been applied for.

ISBN 0-06-621085-2
ISBN 0-06-093573-1 (pbk.)

04   05   06   07   BVG/QWF   10   9   8   7   6   5   4   3

For Michio Hoshino

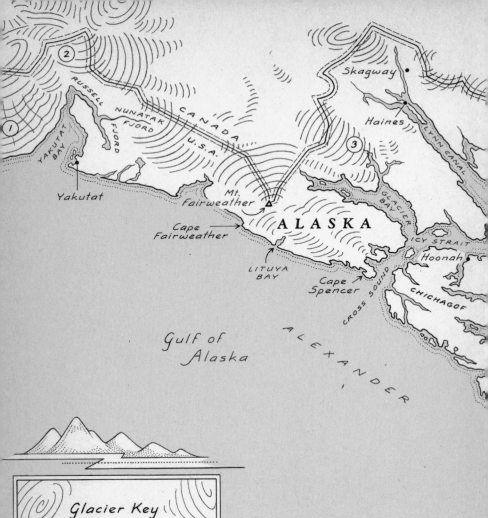

Skagway

Haines

RUSSELL FJORD

NUNATAK FJORD

CANADA

U.S.A.

LYNN CANAL

YAKUTAT BAY

Yakutat

Mt. Fairweather

ALASKA

GLACIER BAY

ICY STRAIT

Hoonah

Cape Fairweather

LITUYA BAY

Cape Spencer

CROSS SOUND

CHICHAGOF

Gulf of Alaska

ALEXANDER

Glacier Key

1. Malaspina Glacier
2. Hubbard Glacier
3. Muir Glacier
4. Mendenhall Glacier
5. Taku Glacier
6. Dawes Glacier
7. Le Conte Glacier

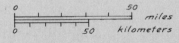

0   50   miles
0   50   kilometers

Contents

Author's Note

In the interest of brevity, I have taken a novelist's license with certain passages in this story by compressing events which took place over the course of several journeys into one, and in others, where time has faded my memory of the exact content of conversations, by reconstructing the spirit of those moments as best I could.

Acknowledgments

I owe a debt of gratitude to the numerous people who contributed to the completion or integrity of this book.

I want to thank Gladi Kulp at the Alaska State Historical Library for retrieving numerous documents during my research, and Kurt Dunbar of Bellingham, Washington, for steering me clear of several glaring mistakes. Wayne and Marie Ivers of Yakutat, Linda Daniel of Juneau, and Bruce Dinneford with the Alaska Department of Fish and Game did me the kindness of reviewing portions of the manuscript. I'm also indebted to John Hyde and Kim Heacox for sharing their memories of Michio with me, and to Curtis Hight for helping me to better understand the circumstances of his death.

Among the numerous naturalists, biologists, researchers, and scientists whose work has contributed to my own small understanding of Alaska's natural systems, special mention must be made of Richard Carstensen, Robert Armstrong, Greg Streveler, Fred Sharpe, and Beth Mathews for their ever present willingness to teach.

A special appreciation is owed to Warren Frazier, who as a boxer makes a pretty good midwife, and to Dan Halpern, whose encouragement was critical.

Last but not least, I want to thank Leta Schooler and Schooler Farms of Hawaii, for paying the bills.

The
Blue Bear

Prologue

I LIVE ON A BOAT in Juneau. As I write this, the ship's radio is muttering the weather forecast for the next three days. Outside, a cold wind pries at the windows and whispers down the stovepipe. It is December, a few days before the winter solstice, and a thin skim of green-and-black ice covers the surface of the harbor. It has been snowing for several days, and the droning voice on the radio warns of an impending gale that will bring strong winds, warmer air, and rain.

Juneau, home to fewer than thirty thousand residents, is more than merely remote. Tightly wedged between the sea and the mountains, it is accessible only by air or water. No roads connect it to the outside world; the mountains here rise abruptly from shoreline to timberline, and above that is the alpine. Beyond the pale colors of the alpine are naked stone peaks, and behind the peaks lies a vast, broken field of ice thousands of feet deep.

The icefield is not visible from the downtown area of the city, but it is always there, looming just beyond the ridges, sending its cold breath down in gusts that swirl among the homes and businesses in a

constant reminder that ice is to Alaska what Shiva is to the Hindu pan-
theon—it is the god that creates and the demon that destroys. Advanc-
ing and retreating through the millennia, glaciers dug relentlessly at
the bedrock of the continent, runneling a thousand miles of coastline
with a winding pattern of ice-carved mountains and inlets that mim-
ics the intricate, serpentine joint that binds the bones in a skull.

The mountains are clad along their lower slopes in dark green
forests that protect a dense understory of blueberry, alder, and devil's
club. Moist winds sweeping in from the Pacific Ocean and the Gulf
of Alaska often blanket the land in heavy clouds. Steep-walled fjords
slice deep into the body of the mainland at regular intervals, and at
their heads the long blue tongues of tidewater glaciers lap at the sea.
A rosary of islands decorates the coast and divides the intruding ocean
into a warren of long, narrow waterways. The gravitational pull of the
passing moon sometimes raises sea level here by as much as twenty-
five feet in six hours, subjecting these passages to some of the world's
most extreme tides and currents.

Along the crescent of coastline between the Aleutian Islands in the
west and the mouth of the Stikine River near Wrangell, over twenty-
five thousand square miles of land are still buried in ice, forming eight
major icefields and numerous smaller ones from which dozens of pale
blue glaciers flow slowly downhill to the sea, where they feed icebergs
into the water with a sound like thunder. Here, the Ice Age still lingers.

The front page of yesterday's newspaper carried a story of a missing
hunter, a twenty-one-year-old Tlingit Indian man from the village of
Hoonah, lost somewhere in the heavily forested islands to the west.
Even now, boats are scouring the shoreline, a search party combs the
tangled woods, a helicopter has been dispatched to peer down from the
gray and ragged clouds. The missing man's name is familiar but I cannot put a face to it. This does not mean I have no connection with
him—I almost certainly do. People are spread thin in Alaska, but our
trails loop and intersect together in odd, predictable patterns. We recognize each other by our connections through friendships and families,
or by where a man hunts and with whom. We know each other by our

boats—their silhouette, color, and name—and we know which child belongs in which house. This is a neighborhood a thousand miles long.

My connection to the lost hunter evades me until I remember his father—a soft-spoken, broad-chested man with a shock of black, carefully combed hair and the slow, cautious movements of someone who spends a lot of time outdoors. We've sat together in the sauna at the community swimming pool, sweating away the chills of winter, listening to fishermen bemoan the low prices being offered for winter king salmon.

I think of the father pushing his way through the thick underbrush, the smell of wet wool and worry clinging to him as he looks for his son. If it rains, his son will probably die, if he is not already dead. The combination of rain and wind is far more deadly than snow, because a wet man denied food or shelter will lose body heat twenty times as fast as one simply exposed to cold air. The boy has been missing for two days, and the odds against his survival are dropping as steadily as the needle on the barometer.

Tlingit legend sometimes lays the blame for such disappearances at the feet of the Kushtaka, a pitiless half-human, half-otter spirit that takes on the form of a siren or loved one to lure the unwary to their doom. The Kushtaka is a ravenous snatcher of souls, and its sinuous, twisting shadow flickers through the forest and melds with the fog.

The Otter-man takes to the water as easily as he travels across the land, and when he swims, he sometimes develops an appetite that can swallow ships whole. This can make the sea, like the forest, a gray and frightening thing.

Recently, a fast-moving storm pounced on a fishing vessel from Haines—a small port north of Juneau—that was working its gear a few miles offshore. I had just seen the *Becca Dawn,* perhaps a month ago, heading southbound in calm waters, steaming along with what mariners refer to as a "bone in her teeth"—the full white wave curling away from her bow, a trace of engine smoke hanging in the still air of her wake. I was northbound on my boat, the *Wilderness Swift,* and as we passed, a hand reached out of the *Becca Dawn*'s window and gave a casual wave.

But two weeks ago, word came that there was trouble—the weather was bad, the Coast Guard had launched a helicopter. By nightfall the seas had grown to forty feet tall and a shrieking seventy-knot wind tore at the frothing crests. As the last of the deep-winter daylight paled away in the west, black walls of water broke and tumbled from horizon to horizon, cloaking the world in a chaos of thunder and spray. One after another, furious waves avalanched out of the darkness, falling on the *Becca Dawn* and twisting her frames. Battered and weakened, the *Becca Dawn* foundered and began to sink.

In the confusion a floating emergency radio beacon and life raft were launched over the side before being secured to the vessel. When the life raft failed to deploy, the strongest swimmer among the crew— an athletic young fisherman with a fondness for whitewater kayaking—tied a line around his chest, fastened the other end to the boat, and swam for it while his two older brothers worked frantically by the silver glare of a floodlight to stay afloat. Hammered by the huge seas, the *Becca Dawn* lurched, yawed, and began to sink faster as the hatches carried away and the hold filled with water. Three times the older brothers struggled to cut the line tying the swimmer to the boat; three times a wave broke over the deck and tore the knife from their hands.

When the *Becca Dawn* finally sank away beneath their feet, leaving them to fight their way through a wrack of floating lines and fishing gear to the tenuous shelter of the tiny life raft, the swimmer—their brother and friend—remained tethered to the vessel. The survivors later reported that the glow of the *Becca Dawn*'s floodlights remained visible for a long, long time as the boat slipped farther and farther away beneath the dark waters.[1]

---

1. The crew of the Coast Guard helicopter involved in the rescue were later awarded the nation's highest peacetime aviation award for what Coast Guard admiral Tom Barrett called "extraordinary airmanship and tenacity." Lieutenant Commander Robert Yerex, Lieutenant James O'Keefe, Petty Officer First Class Christian Blanco, and Petty Officer Third Class Noel Hutton were presented with the Distinguished Flying Cross for their heroism in overcoming pitch darkness, nausea, snow, blowing spray, and low fuel to pluck the survivors from the sea.

The *Becca Dawn* went to its grave near Lituya Bay, a storied place and one I know very well. It's a T-shaped fjord that lies directly on a geological trip wire called the Fairweather fault, and according to the legends of the Tlingit Indians, it is home to Kah-Lituya, a great, angry bear-god who deeply resents the trespass of strangers. When aroused, Kah-Lituya sends one of the dark, lavishly muscled grizzlies that roam the glacier coast to grasp the landscape in its terrible jaws and shake it until landslides fall from the mountains and whirlpools boil in the sea.

Forty-odd years ago one of Kah-Lituya's earthquakes centered within the bay generated a massive tidal wave that annihilated two and a half square miles of forest. The wave struck with such force that it stripped the mussels and barnacles from the beach and surged up the side of the mountain to an altitude of 1,720 feet, tearing away every living thing in its path and stripping the thin, acidic soil down to bedrock. It also destroyed two fishing boats anchored in the bay.[2]

When I first visited Lituya Bay twelve years ago, it was still licking its wounds. The beach was littered with chunks of fiberglass, splinters of planks, and rusted metal parts scattered between boulders of granite and schist. A crude cenotaph of stones had been erected near the entrance to the bay. A tattered yellow raincoat emblazoned with the name of a fishing vessel hung, arms akimbo, on a crucifix of driftwood, and an offering of beachcombings—eagle feathers and pot buoys, box slats decorated with faded Asian writing, bits of netting and twine—lay strewn at its feet. Listed in rough, fading red letters on the back of the raincoat were the names of four crewmen.

It was a calm day. Seabirds and harbor seals bobbed contentedly on pans of ice calved from the face of a glacier at the head of the fjord. Crossing a strand of smoothly packed sand to enter the forest, I came

2. Shipwreck has been a constant there ever since the French explorer La Pérouse became the first Westerner to sail into the remote bay and promptly lost twenty-one men to a maelstrom of fierce surf and strong currents in the entrance. In the two hundred years since, the souls of more than one hundred mariners have been given up to the cold waters of the fjord and the treacherous entrance barred by the cobbled spit that La Pérouse named la Chaussee and local fishermen call "the Chopper."

upon a platter-sized footprint left by one of Kah–Lituya's servants. The edges of the print were crisp, deep, and fresh. Bending down, I measured the span of the bear's track against the spread of my fingers—fully as wide and longer by half.

I watched the edge of the forest for a few minutes, listening for the alarm calls of squirrels or jays. My scent would drift into the forest ahead of me, borne by the cool breeze playing along the back of my neck and lifting the hair above my ears. Hearing only my heartbeat thumping in the quiet, I walked across the sand and into the trees.

The line of demarcation between the wave-ravaged and undamaged sectors of the forest was clear. Beneath the canopy of the unscathed old growth, sunlight fell in broken patches through trees of uneven age and size. Ancient, scarred veterans towered over limber green saplings, and the ground was littered with the rich, rotting detritus of windthrow and deadfall. An impenetrable, chest-high tangle of blueberries and devil's club rioted and fought for supremacy in the tatters of light streaming through breaks in the trees.

Comparing the old-growth forest to the younger trees colonizing the wave-ravaged ground revealed a stark difference. The new timber was uniform and even, each tree similar in height and diameter to its neighbors. The branches overhead merged into a thick green roof that blocked all direct light. The ground was in shadow and the understory sparse. Weighed against the storm of plant life taking place beneath the old growth, this was a desert, with none of the lush riot of shrubs, ferns, and low-lying plants that grew in profusion beneath the older forest.

But life, being what it is, was forcing its slow, insistent way back in perfectly suitable forms. Twisted stalk and bunchberry struggled to form a low carpet of vegetation, and the first rambling strands of lycopodium moss had begun to arch tentatively across low stones and root swells. In time—fifty or a hundred years, maybe more—a tree or two would outgrow their neighbors, reach into the wind, and fall, tearing a gap in the closed canopy. Light would enter, and the higher, thicker forms of plant life would break out in a frenzy of growth.

A draft of cool air stirred the forest around me as I stood quietly, listening carefully for any sound that might alert me to the return of the grizzly. A single loud *boom* echoed off the mountain wall above me as the glacier at the head of the fjord dropped another chunk of ice into the bay.

The wind howls, the earth quakes, the tides rise and fall. People step into the landscape and vanish without a trace. And all the while, the ice is there—massive, sterile, and cold—waiting to return.

But when the ice is in remission, life floods back into the valleys and bays, reaches up into the mountains, and sends roots down into the earth, just as it was doing in the aftermath of the cataclysmic wave. Forests grow, animals breed, birds remember the migratory flyways that take them from season to season. As the ice retreats, salmon and steelhead discover newly sprung rivers that will shelter their fry and become traditional spawning grounds for generations to come. An entire ecosystem evolves, spinning the elemental strands of sunlight, energy, and rainfall into the dynamic, whirling interplay of creation, procreation, predator, and prey.

It is for this that I love this place. I love it fiercely for its power of recovery after being scalped down to bedrock by ice or violent tsunamis, for the intricate play of forces as the convalescent earth unfolds its wealth of indomitable life. I love it for the power it shows us in the weight of its rain (which in many places along the coast approaches two hundred inches a year). I love it wildly for the songs it sings in the voice of a whale's breath or the rusty tracheal trumpetings of a flock of cranes. I love it for its turbulence and eagerness, and I love it when it storms or is calm. Sometimes in the spring, when the new green leaves and first delicate blossoms are aching into bloom, I love it the way a dog loves to ride in the back of a pickup truck, and I want to run side to side barking and flapping my tongue.

Spring is also the time of year when bears first emerge from their winter dens, and since I make my living as a wilderness guide helping wildlife photographers find and capture images of them, it marks the beginning of my year more precisely than any calendar event. In April the days grow rapidly longer, and the deep snow on the upper slopes begins to rot in the flood of sunlight. Trickles of meltwater work beneath the snow cover and the crust begins to sag. Grizzlies asleep beneath the surface stir and twitch, prodded by the intrusion of new smells into their moss-lined caves.

The first to emerge are the single bears, solitary boars and sows that squint into the sun and lift up their noses to the new world around them. Females with cubs to feed will come later, after food becomes more readily available. Uncertain and addled with sleep, they pace and loll at the entrance, soiling the snow with mud from the den. With good binoculars, an observer on the beach below can spot the alpine smudges and know that winter has finally relaxed its grip on the land.

Down in the forest, the noses of the grizzlies' smaller cousins poke tentatively from beneath root wads and blowdowns. *Ursus americanus,* the American black bear, prefers to winter in the holes and cavities of the forest, worming its way into small openings beneath living trees or a lucky crack between boulders, where it weathers the cold, hungry season by retreating deep into dreams.

But there is a third creature here that comes alive in the spring— a wary, elusive animal that spends its life sheathed in mystery but seems to linger in the periphery of my vision like an afterimage of the Ice Age. It is the color of winter skies, a pale blue-gray hue that matches the bare granite boulders left behind by the retreat of the glaciers and it exists nowhere in the world outside of a five-hundred-mile stretch of coast between Prince William Sound in the northwest and Ketchikan in the south. The only official effort ever undertaken to count its numbers estimated that fewer than one hundred roam this wildly tangled piece of map. The aboriginal people, believing it was the result of a union between the clan of the bears and that of the mountain goats, called it *klate-utardy-tseek*—"white," or "snowlike," bear. But it is also called the blue or glacier bear, and a person may easily spend a lifetime searching the fjords and icefields of Alaska and never lay eyes on one.

As I write this, I've sometimes paused to look at a photograph taped to the bulkhead beside the bunk where I sit. The subject of the photograph stands four-square and broadside to the camera in the shadowy light of dusk. It is by most measures a poor image—the light is flat, the focus blurred, its elements weakly composed—yet I number it among the most precious of my material possessions.

The picture is valuable to me not because it is an image of a glacier bear (though it is and there are far fewer pictures of glacier bears than there are twenty-carat canary diamonds in this world) or because I hope its rarity will bring me money or fame. It required only 1/60 of a second for light to enter the lens, play across the prisms and mirrors, and snatch up the image forever. But it took nearly a decade of searching for the glacier bear before the shutter could fall, and before that, an entire lifetime before I came to the place where the search could begin. Most important of all, at the moment my shutter clicked and captured the bear, a decade of friendship with an uncommon man was whittled down into a single small fraction of time.

The picture holds the story.

1 » Severance

I WAS BORN in 1954 on the edge of the Llano Estacado in West Texas, a desert so vast and featureless that the early Spanish explorers drove a line of stakes across this land to avoid losing their way. The German, Dutch, and Russian immigrants who scattered across West Texas at the turn of the century stringing barbed wire and sinking windmills in an effort to subdue the sunbaked land were a generally mule-headed people, averse to quitting *anything* once begun, but by the time my father was a young man things were changing, and he became the first of our line to leave our ancestral home—a small, flinty ranch nestled into the mesquite-covered hills near Robert Lee, Texas, where his own father and grandfather had been repeatedly ground down and bested by unending droughts and tightfisted cattle buyers. When I was born he took to the road as a modern-day drummer, driving a blue Plymouth Fury a thousand miles a week across Texas and New Mexico to peddle electrical supplies and hardware to the steadily declining oil and construction industries.

One afternoon in 1969 (my fifteenth year), Dad's Plymouth rolled into the sunburned yard in a cloud of biting alkali dust. The driver's-side door swung open as the car skidded to a halt and one booted foot swung to the ground. My father cocked his slender frame on the seat, draped an arm over the steering wheel, then sat there looking at me for a moment before waving me over.

"Look at this," he said, unfurling a newspaper in my face. "What do you think of that?"

Dad ran a hand through his thinning hair while I studied the paper.

"Well, what do you think?" He was smiling. "They've found oil in Alaska. Lots and lots of oil."

I wasn't sure where Alaska was, but it was pretty far away, I knew that. It was much farther than El Paso or even Colorado, where my friend Jimmy went elk hunting with his father. Jimmy was gone for a week when he went to Colorado. If they had oil in Alaska, it probably meant Dad would be gone much longer.

"You gonna be gone some more?"

Dad smacked me on the shoulder with the paper, a small web of smile lines crinkling in the corners of his eyes.

"Well, I guess I might," he said, starting toward the house. He seemed in a hurry, didn't even close the door to the car. I could smell the Camel cigarettes he smoked lingering in the interior.

"Will you?" I hollered after him. "Be gone a bunch more?"

"Don't worry, son." He was already to the open garage, disappearing into the cool darkness, taking the shortcut into the kitchen. "You're coming with me."

I squinted into the glare of the sun as I looked around at our home—an acre and a half of hard-packed Texas dirt with a cinderblock house set square in the middle of it; an oil refinery a half mile away that flared off so much waste gas at night that its burning made it possible to read without turning on a lamp; the scrubbed, level horizon of mesquite brush and caliche dirt, the fan of a windmill in the distance. When I spoke it was to myself and out loud.

"Sounds pretty good to me." Anyplace, I thought, was probably better than this.

DAD TRADED and wheedled, made a deal with a busted wildcat driller for a thirdhand, two-ton Chevrolet oil field truck, then got busy converting it into a makeshift moving van. Barrel-sized saddle tanks straddled the cab left and right.

"Fuel's expensive, especially in Canada," Dad said, unscrewing the pipe cap that covered the fill spout and peering into the hollow darkness of one tank. "These'll give us plenty of range. It's a long damn road to Alaska."

A swiveling crane the previous owner had made of steel pipe welded into the shape of an A-frame and mounted above the bed to lift welding machines, drill heads, and other heavy objects crashed to the ground as the pins were knocked free. A skeleton of wooden slats went up in its place to support a skin of aluminum in the shape of a box, and Dad showed me how to cut and slide Styrofoam sheets between the boards as insulation. "We might have to live in here," he said, and I wondered if he was joking. Taking off for Alaska was such a wild idea that living in the back of a truck didn't seem so far-fetched.

Mother watched with her arms crossed, shaking her head and smiling, then went back to packing. Her best friend dropped off a tub of peanut butter the size of a bucket, and then Jimmy's mother phoned to ask where we were going to get vegetables once we were living in Alaska. My parents put their arms around each other and laughed at that, but Mother's mouth tightened up when she thought no one was looking.

Everything we owned was carefully wedged, packed, and padded into the back of the big truck and the door bolted shut. My eyes dazzled and danced from the sparkling blue glare of the welder a friend of my father used to build a tow bar onto the front of our old Ford pickup. With the pickup in tow behind the moving van, Dad drove carefully, double-clutching the overloaded rig up the long, slow rises, and I sat beside him, absorbed in a stack of magazines (*Argosy, Outdoor Life, True Tales of the Old West*) to spare myself the incessant boredom of the plains. My mother and two sisters crept along behind in the family car, playing Otis Redding's "(Sittin' on) The Dock of the Bay" (the only music they could agree on) over and over on the eight-track tape player as we said good-bye to West Texas.

Our slow-moving caravan swung north through the mountains of Colorado, pointed itself toward the Pole star beneath the wide skies of Montana, and lurched across the border into Canada.

Three weeks after leaving Texas we came to the end of the pavement and drove off the power grid onto the Alcan Highway, a thousand miles of washboard gravel road that wound through the Yukon's endless forests of birch and stunted spruce until it reached Alaska's border. Through the thin plywood walls of the rough roadhouses we stayed in at night, I could hear the murmur of my father answering questions my mother asked in a rising voice. The strain of leaving everything we knew nibbled and gnawed, chewing its way into the journey, with a bite as sharp as the ever-deepening chill in the air.

It was January and we had never imagined such cold. Hoar frost clung glittering and white to every surface, and the smoke of my breath hung without moving in the air. The temperature plummeted to seventy degrees below zero, and in the morning it was necessary for Dad to apply a blowtorch to the gears and axles of the pickup before we could get under way. The farther we went, the deeper the furrows in his forehead grew.

After thirty days of driving we crossed into Alaska. The dividing line between America and Canada was delineated by a wide swath chainsawed into the dense trees on both sides of the road, and a line of tree stumps marched into the ice-rimmed distance, climbing into the forest until it disappeared. A few miles past the border Dad slammed on the brakes as a wolf burst at full gallop from the willows bordering the road. Truck and wolf skidded to a simultaneous stop. The slanted yellow eyes in its lean black face stared unblinking into my own for a long, frozen second before the wolf spun on its heels and disappeared back into the brush.

We sat unmoving and silent, listening to the idling of the engine, staring at the spot in the brush that had swallowed the wolf. I realized

I was holding my breath. Dad leaned forward, resting both forearms on the steering wheel for a moment. Finally, he turned to me, a curious look on his face.

"We did the right thing," he said. "Didn't we?"

I couldn't say anything, but I knew exactly what he meant.

I HELD HIS HAND as he died. That cancer was like an execution: first there was the sentence and all of the small humiliations of no longer being free to fend for himself or make everyday decisions. Then came the hopeful stays of chemotherapy, diet changes, and radiation, until the final realization that it all had not meant much and time spent struggling against the sentence had left more important things unaddressed.

The hand I held was work hardened and strong and felt like carved oak under the papery leather skin. Even as the cancer finished its final feast on my father's muscles and organs, his hands looked as if the fingers could still grip a frozen, rusted bolt head and turn it without benefit of a wrench.

As I held my father's hand that final time, it bothered me that it had required this disaster to put his hand in mine. The only remembrance I had of him ever taking my hand before (other than a handshake) was when the twisting of my spine by a congenital disease called scoliosis first came to the attention of doctors. Scoliosis twists the spine into curves and kinks and, if severe enough, can distort and interfere with the function of organs, cause constant, racking pain, and result in a hunchback.

It was our second year in Alaska. I was barely sixteen and beginning that spurt of gangling growth that leaves boys' hands and feet too large and in the way. The hunchback gene had put its weight on my shoulder and was trying to hold me down even as my body grew taller, like a weed trying to grow out from under a board thrown aside in a field. My grandmother's spine had been arched and troubled her, and it was clear that mine, too, intended to grow in any direction except straight up.

A stout, gruff doctor with silvering hair and a scowl offered me a choice. "We can remove slivers of bone from the femurs in your thighs," he said, making a slicing motion along his own leg with his fingers. "Those can be grafted to your spine and that will prevent the curvature from developing any further." He folded his arms across his chest, crossed his legs at the ankle, and leaned back against the examination table beside me before continuing.

"Of course, when it's over, you'll be a bit stiff. And we'll have to put you into a body cast for a while after the operation." He looked at me from beneath his shaggy eyebrows.

"Body cast?" I said.

"Neck to waist." He glanced at my parents and nodded. "He'll be on his back in bed for about a year. Takes that long for the bones to grow together."

I imagined lying flat on my back for a year, swathed in a cocoon of plaster. No school. No football. No girls. The prospect of staring at a ceiling for a solid year while my bones grew around each other was unthinkable, and I felt myself coming unhinged just considering it.

Dad lit a cigarette and offered one to the doctor, who took it and examined it, avoiding my eyes.

"There is . . . ," the doctor began, then paused to light the cigarette from the match my father cupped toward him in his hand. He blew a draft of blue smoke toward the ceiling. ". . . an alternative."

IN A CONCRETE-FLOORED workroom the doctor had me step up onto a plywood box and place my forearms on rests at my side while he swathed my torso in plaster for the mold that would be used to form the leather parts of a brace. I was to be strapped into a framework of chromed steel bars spanning my body between chin, underarms, and hips. My neck and hips would be encased in the leather parts being molded to fit my slender teenage body. The bars could be expanded so that the tension would keep spreading my shoulders and waist farther apart, like an Inquisitional rack stretching the kinks from my spine. This process would take two years, during which I would be allowed to remove the contraption once a week for a brief bath. He smoked a cigarette as he worked, wiping the plaster from his fingers with a towel before each puff.

My father stood beside me as the doctor bent to his work. My mother sat at the back of the room in a straight-backed chair and was silent. I sobbed while I stared straight ahead.

"Crying and jerking like that, you'll crack this plaster before it sets up." The doctor dabbed with the towel at a spot on the front of his smock before reaching for his cigarette. "If I have to start over, I gotta charge your folks twice for the job."

Dad shuffled awkwardly from foot to foot, then reached over and carefully worked my hand loose from its grip on the armrest. He took my hand in his, squeezed, and did not let go. Thirty years later, when it was his turn to stare straight ahead and try not to sob in front of the oncologist, the walnut-hard joints and rasping calluses of his hand still felt warm and strong in my grip.

The brace did straighten my spine over the next two years—to a degree. Looking at my body from any angle there is still a lack of symmetry. Straight on, my head appears mounted off center on sloping shoulders. From the right side I appear thicker than I do from the left. My body reflects the topography of my life; normal at first glance, but on closer inspection scoured by cataclysm and upheaval, flash floods, and hurricane winds.

When I look back, unrolling my life like a bolt of used cloth—stains and all—I can mark the day that brace was strapped onto me as the point the dismantling of any innocence I had was begun. It seems to me now that as surely as the leather and metal around my neck and body locked my head and gaze straight ahead, my future was locked on its course. The nine pounds of steel bolted and strapped around my body was as magnetic as a compass needle, pointing me toward the wild parts of Alaska and a quiet alienation that would always be there, like a bad tooth waiting to be bitten down on. From my early teens on I stood at a strange angle to the rest of the world.

The February day two years later that I shed the brace from my body was a disappointment. I had looked to that emancipation to free me from all that seemed wrong with my life, imagining that—surely—once I walked away from the metal and rotting leather husk of my estrangement the arms of the world would open for me, with girls rushing to take me in their embrace and boys reaching to pat me on the back, full of admiration for my endurance of the prolonged torture.

I was wrong. The hulking, forward-leaning silhouette of the brace, which I had tried to hide under too-large coats that did little to cover the ripe odor of an adolescent body bathed only once a week, and the strange, top-heavy lurch that had become my habitual stride stayed with me, even after the brace itself was gone. My strangeness had isolated me from my fellow teens, and I was to find that my isolation was permanent, my hermitage ongoing. The years of hiding had made me different from other youths, and throwing away the brace had no impact on my standing. It was the last half of my junior year, and there simply was not enough time left in my youth to learn how to fit in.

What divesting myself of the brace did do, however, was enable me to strap on an encumbrance of another sort—a backpack—and escape into the freedom of the countryside. As the last bright days of August faded the leaves of cottonwoods and aspens along the rivers, I began exploring the road that ran south from Anchorage down to the Kenai Peninsula. Thirty minutes after leaving the house I could be alone, away from the city. The highway wound forty miles along the turbid waters of Turnagain Arm, dipping and winding through stone cut-banks where the roadbed had been chiseled from the flank of the Chugach Mountains before it turned south onto the peninsula, leaving the hurly-burly of the city behind and entering a beautiful world.

There were wide spots in the winding road where I could pull onto the shoulder and watch white beluga whales search the muddy waters for salmon and eulichon, a smelt that spawns in the silty, glacier-fed rivers that run into the sea along the arm. An hour of climbing would take me into the mountains to look down on the backs of white-coated Dall's sheep. Looking the hills over with binoc-

ulars, I learned to see moose by spotting the darkness of their huge
bodies against the pale olive walls of willow brush and alder.

Once, while sitting on the gravel shore of a small lake listening to
the complaining voices of a flock of sandhill cranes high overhead I
felt something behind me. Turning around, I froze at a pair of deep
yellow eyes looking into mine from a few feet away. A lynx sat on its
haunches, completely still except for diamond pupils that seemed to
expand as we stared at each other. A pattern of silver and gray dappled
its face. The way the big cat sat revealed an underbelly of white fur
that spread up the chest to a rim of brown so delicate my hand ached
to stroke it.

The cat moved its head slightly toward me, pushing its nose delicately into my smell. The yellow, unblinking eyes seemed to open
wider briefly before the cat sat back and looked to the side. The animal stood without looking at me again and padded off along the shore,
twisting its body into the willows and ferns, flickered gray among the
leaves for a moment, then was gone. I never heard a sound, either in
its approach or in its leaving.

I hiked and climbed at every opportunity, searching out the places
where I was least likely to encounter other people. I learned how to
tell chum salmon from sockeye salmon by the patterns of their mark-
ings and the color of the flesh beneath their bright skins. River holes
that held king salmon as long and thick as my thigh were deep secrets
I kept to myself. At night I camped in meadows of fireweed or rolled
a sleeping bag out in the back of the Ford.

In the fall I shot snowshoe hares and spruce hens with a .22 rifle.
The lean meat of a rabbit was tender when cooked slowly in a
saucepan of salt and butter, but I preferred to spit the small body onto
a limber switch of green alder and roast it slowly over a fire. The result
was often stringy, raw near the bones and cooked dry on the surface,
but it fit some image I held of life out of doors. And when I was outside, beneath all of the sky and in the embrace of the wind, I found
the solitude I craved, without feeling alone.

2 » First Encounters

THE SLATE-COLORED BIRD crouched flat to the ground and spread its wings in a threatening pose. One of the crows gathered in a circle around the disabled kingfisher darted forward, stabbed at its head with its bill, then retreated as the injured bird spun to meet the threat. Mouth agape, the kingfisher reared back and lunged, only to be mobbed by more crows rushing in from the side.

I stooped to pick up a stone, intending to hurl it at the crows, but stopped when my companion held up his hand. I hesitated, cringing as another, then another of the crows stepped up to jab at their weakening prey. It could take hours for the crows to peck and savage the kingfisher to death—a cruelty that stung too much to watch.

"They're just being crows, Lynn," he said.

The kingfisher is a crevice nester, digging into steep cut-banks or lining an existing cavity with feathers and grass to create a home for its eggs. It's a peculiar-looking bird, with a head that appears much too large for its body and feet that seem too small, but somehow the kingfisher's pure white breast collar and sharp, raucous call combine with its rapier bill and the obsidian glint in its eye to give it an unassailable, pompous dignity like that of an antebellum southern senator—a sort of gray-feathered John C. Calhoun. Kingfishers perch on snags and limbs along meandering rivers and on the edges of calm saltwater coves, plunging headfirst into the water in pursuit of minnows and fry. They are a common sight along the forested streams I love to wander, and it seemed odd to find one in an environment so dire: all around us the ground was naked and lunar, with the exception of a thin band of beach greens struggling along the shoreline and a smattering of grass and young alders clinging to the bottom of a draw. My boat, the *Wilderness Swift*, lay at anchor in a small bight a half mile away, and from our present altitude it looked like a small toy snuggled against the shore.

My companion kicked at the ground, sending a cascade of small, smooth stones clattering down the slope, and shifted his weight into the new foothold. He was a small Asian man, with a round, open face, an easy smile, and the high color of someone who spends a lot of time outdoors. His pack weighed half again as much as my own, and as he paused to watch the drama between the kingfisher and the crows, he reached up to straighten a Greenland-style cap that sat askew on his head, then raised a hand to point behind me and made a small sound of alarm.

Spinning around, I glimpsed a large, mottled brown form rushing through the air and instinctively ducked as it passed overhead. The immature eagle seemed to hurtle out of nowhere, dropping into a gliding attack that rocked it back on its talons as it cleared the ridge. In one smooth, snatching moment it plucked the kingfisher from amid the circle of crows. Perhaps one of the eagle's sharp talons pierced the kingfisher's heart or the sudden shock of the attack killed it instantly, but in either case, when the eagle rose in a circle and flew back the way it had come, I could see the kingfisher dangling, lifeless and fluttering as a ribbon in its grasp.

I winced, imagining the stab of the talons. The circle of crows cawed and argued among themselves, then dispersed with a great deal of fluttering.[3] Michio (for that was my companion's name) watched as the eagle disappeared, then looked pensive for a moment and said, "Everything always gets what it needs"—meaning, I imagined, that the raptor had gotten fed, the kingfisher had been released from its torment, and the crows . . . well, the crows would just have to return to foraging as best they could.

Turning to me with a serious look on his face, he continued: "We only have so much time. I think this is what Nature is always trying to tell us—that we are going to die someday, too, and that's what makes us want to really *live*."

It was a theme I was to hear him reiterate many times over the coming years, but at the moment, I didn't give it much thought. I was still disturbed by the crows' needling of the kingfisher and the unpleasant memories that echoed from the scene. I shrugged, settling the weight of my pack onto my hips, and took a step down the bluff.

I had first met Michio Hoshino only a month before, when he had telephoned out of the blue and asked to charter me for a month to work on a film for a Tokyo-based broadcasting company. Now we were in Glacier Bay National Park, a few days from the end of a five-week trip. We'd stopped off in this small cove to document a phenomenon left behind by the retreat of the Ice Age and stumbled onto the small, dark drama of nature and life.

Below us, a great blue heron drifted across the steep face of the hill, skimming in to a landing at the water's edge before flaring its wings and folding itself into an elegant pose. Small rocks and gravel slid away from our feet like water flowing downhill as we made our way across the face of the bluff. All around us stumps and tree trunks the color of driftwood protruded from a surface of loose till.

Michio paused to wipe a hand across his face, then reached out to feel the smooth surface of a stump: "Hard to believe it's so old, isn't it?"

---

3. In Old English, the proper phrase for a flock of crows was a "murder," but under the circumstances, perhaps an "unkindness"—as a gathering of ravens was called—would have been more apt and poetic.

At the base of the incline I could see the three-man camera crew making their way toward a small point of land to set up a shot. Yamanushi Fumihiko, the junior member of the trio, stepped carefully along behind the others, burdened under an immense pack and an unwieldy thick-legged tripod. Maeda Yasujiro, the cameraman, walked ahead of his assistant, pointing out possible shots and discussing angles of lighting with the producer, a tall, slender man named Eiho Otani.

"Some of the interstadial wood has been carbon-dated at seven thousand years," I explained, using a glaciologist's term for the shattered remains of a pre–Ice Age forest that surrounded us. "These trees were saplings two thousand years before Cheops started sketching out his ideas for the Great Pyramid."

Michio probed ahead with his folded tripod, using it as a staff to stabilize his footing, then stopped beside a stump and braced his hand against it before swinging his heavy pack to the ground.

"Please say again how this happened?" he asked, unfolding the legs of the tripod and working it level into the ground. This was, I'd quickly discovered, Michio's favorite kind of question: very complicated (at least for me) to answer, but posed with the innocence and simplicity of a child. I hunched my shoulders to settle the straps of my pack and braced my hands on my uphill knee before answering. The chance to grandstand a bit by showing off some of my knowledge pushed the crows to the back of my mind.

"Well, during the last ice age, the glaciers advanced very rapidly," I said, sweeping a hand before my chest to indicate the flow of the ice coming down from the head of Muir Inlet below us. "And a tremendous amount of water was flowing along the sides, washing all this gravel and sand down from back in the valleys. The outflow just buried the forest alive. The gravel covered it this deep"—here I pointed to the top of the splintered stump, level with my head—"and the ice rode forward on the new surface, shearing off the trees as it went."

Michio dug a camera body from his pack and snapped it onto the tripod. "And when the glacier started to melt, water washed everything away?"

I nodded, then shrugged out of my pack. "Right. Washed all the sand and gravel down the fjord and left the forest behind. It's not petrified, just preserved for thousands of years by a lack of oxygen during the time it was buried."

Michio looked thoughtful for a moment, then stroked the platinum smooth face of the stump. "Seven thousand years." He sighed. "It makes life seem so short."

Time was a popular subject with Hoshino. Its passing seemed to burn brightly before him at all times, creating an awareness of the importance of moments, hours, and ages. Earlier that morning, while watching the newly de-glaciated ridges and mountains flow by outside the windows of the *Swift* as we motored deeper and deeper into Glacier Bay, he'd told me that our lives were "like a stack of calendars."

"When we are born we are given this many." He held out his hands, one above the other, as if passing me a stack of calendars a foot high. "Already we are to the middle of our life and have only this many left." He moved his hands until they were only six inches apart.

"Or maybe only *this* many." Two inches. "You never know."

Now the burial and reemergence of the interstadial forest seemed to fascinate him. He adjusted the camera while we talked, dusted the lens with a small brush, made a minute adjustment of the focus, and attached a shutter cord. "So," he finally said. "The forest is like a bear, going into sleep in the winter and coming up again."

I nodded in agreement and arched my spine to let the breeze cool the skin beneath my pack. Over the course of the days and weeks since we had left Juneau, I had begun to fathom why this small, soft-spoken man was such a gifted photographer. He had an intense way of looking at things, often noticing details and minutiae that escaped me. A bead of sweat itched its way down my ribs and I took a deep breath.

"Michio . . ." I hesitated, fiddling with a pack strap. There was something I wanted to ask him, a favor I'd been chewing on for days, but the words were uncomfortable in my mouth. Asking another person for *anything* had always seemed like a violation of the arm's-length treaty I maintained with the rest of the world.

But there was something in Hoshino's manner that made it feel safe to plunge ahead. Perhaps it was his gentle consideration of larger issues and images (such as time's effect on the land) or some recognition I had even then that he possessed little or no ego of the sort that threatens others with its shadow. Besides, the trip's end was quickly approaching, and one of the harsher realities of the guide business, I'd learned, is that most friendships are temporary. Contacts with clients, no matter how companionable, dissipate quickly after the customary end-of-trip dinner, drinks, and handshakes, sometimes a postcard or two. This might be my last opportunity.

I motioned to his camera, trying to sound casual. "Would you teach me a little something about photography?"

Michio didn't reply as he snapped the picture and rewound the camera, then glanced at the lowering sun and clicked the shutter again.

He's ignoring me, I thought. I was hurt, I suppose. Over the course of the last month, I had come to admire him enormously, and this made the slight all the more painful. Guess you can't ask someone to give away his secrets for nothing.

Michio squinted into the viewfinder a few moments more, nodded, and then stepped back, motioning toward the camera: "*Dozo.* Please, do you want to see?"

Giddily, I bent low to the camera and put my eye to the viewfinder. I pulled back—amazed—and looked at the stump, then lowered my head again to the camera. What I saw in the camera was not like *anything* I had seen with my eyes. The stump, framed to pass from the top of the picture, formed a perfect balance with a composition of varicolored stones jumbled at its base. The sweeping lines of the roots drew my eye along the grain of the ancient tree to the edge of the frame and seemed to suggest that something outside of the picture—perhaps the soul of the tree—was standing and looking down on the perfect waiting stillness of the stones cradled in the curve of its roots like an infant in the arms of its mother. Where I had seen only a random arrangement of rocks and deadwood, Michio had seen a pattern that told a whole story.

"How did you see that?" I asked, shaking my head. "How'd you *find* it?"

"Camera is . . ." Michio shrugged and pursed his lip to show that he was thinking deeply. "Camera sees only a small piece of what your mind sees." He peered at me sideways, waiting to see if I understood.

I blinked, then hunched my shoulders to show I was drawing a blank, and he tried again. "If you look into the camera, your mind fools what you see. Maybe . . . maybe look at what camera *really* sees."

"But you've made something from *nothing* here."

"No, no. This is . . ." He paused to get the words right, then carefully pronounced every syllable: "A picture should make you think about a story."

An inkling of his meaning began to worm its way into my understanding: finding the elements of a story—in this case the remains of a tree seeming to embrace the very stones that had killed it—then consciously looking at what was *actually* in the viewfinder rather than what my mind, with its preconceived notion of how the scene *should* look, presumed the camera would see. It was a straightforward concept that explained the number of truly bad photos I always got back from the developer—pictures of mountain ranges that had seemed overwhelming and awesome went ho-hum and boring; moose and bear that had been thrillingly close when their picture was taken were somehow reduced to tiny, hard-to-tell brown spots that could have been collie dogs or stumps.

Later, I'd realize Michio's explanation was a simple extension of a method used to spot camouflaged or partially concealed wildlife: look at what *is* there, not what you hope to see. Many people go into the forest expecting to see an entire deer or bear striking a pose like those they see on a calendar. After a time, though, you learn to look for the out-of-place line of a leg standing motionless behind a screen of brush, a patch of color just slightly different than the rest of a shadow, or the twitch of an ear in tall grass. Once the preconceived search image is abandoned, the ability to spot wildlife increases exponentially.

But now Michio bent to his pack, nodding to himself as he

replaced the camera. The sun was moving quickly to the west and the light was fading. I steadied the pack as he grunted it onto his back, struggled to retain his balance, then stood up straight, cradling the tripod in the crook of his arm.

I bent to pick up a scrap of film wrapping that fluttered from Michio's pocket. The images he created as he wandered the countryside absorbed in the pink origami of a delicate Sitka rose or the patterns of sunlight flooding a cathedral of mountain peaks and ridges might be magnificent, but picking up after this absentminded genius as he left behind a trail of forgotten gloves, film canisters, and even expensive camera lenses was becoming a bit exasperating.

"Look, Michio," I said, pointing to a faint concavity pressed into a hollow of wind-driven sand behind a boulder.

Michio bent to peer at the ground. "*Brack* bear, I think." As for many Japanese, even those proficient in English, the *ell* sound remained an obstacle to his tongue.

I nodded agreement. The track had the small, almost-human shape of a black bear's rear foot, and the indentations left by the claws were close to the pad. The track of a grizzly is shaped more like a spade, and the claws, which extend farther ahead, are better suited for digging.

"Odd place for a bear," I said. "Nothing to eat around here."

Michio shrugged under the weight of his pack and smiled. "Maybe just *cruising* around," stretching out the word, then laughing at his use of the slang.

"Yep, like us," I replied. "Going up to look at the glaciers."

Michio stared across the valley at the stupas of rock laid down by the glacier's passing, then waved to Otani and the others, who were waiting on the beach by the skiff. Before taking the first glissading stride down the shifting gravel slope, he turned to me and in a tone that meant it was a joke, said, "Yes. A bear really knows how to *rook*."

I smiled and slid after him, laughing as he flailed for balance in the down-flowing loess, skidding out of control all the way to the beach below.

MY FIRST ENCOUNTER with Michio Hoshino took place in the spring of 1990. The solstice had passed without its usual stormy bluster, and the weather had settled into a pattern of bright, rain-free days of the sort that boat owners think of as painting weather. The harbor was abuzz with the sound of power tools, and the chandler across the road was running low on sandpaper and turpentine as fishermen hurried to catch up on long-neglected chores before July plugged the rivers with salmon.

I was doing a small remodeling job on the *Wilderness Swift*'s galley, sprucing up the existing woodwork and building a few drawers. The phone rang just as I'd begun varnishing a cupboard door. I slipped a piece of newsprint under the door, balanced the wet brush across the can, and stripped off one glove to pick up the phone, hurrying to catch it before the answering machine kicked in.

"Hello?" The voice of the caller was hesitant and foreign. "My name . . . ah . . . my name is . . ."

My clients come from all over the world—Germany, Singapore, Argentina, France, even once from Mongolia—but still I couldn't quite catch the wavering rhythm of his speech when he said his name. In fact, I wasn't even sure if it *was* a name; it sounded like he was sneezing and I had to ask him to repeat it. The second time around, I understood: *Michio Hoshino*.

I could hear him digging for words as he tried to clarify his thoughts: "I am a . . . a pho*to*grapher," and went on to explain in halting English that he was working with a producer from Tokyo's TV-Asahi on a piece about Alaska, with segments on both humpback whales and Glacier Bay, and that they needed a guide with a boat. He asked to hire me for a month.

I was wary at first. The *Wilderness Swift* is thirty-two feet long with a ten-foot beam. She's a work boat, built on the lines of a Pacific Northwest fishing boat in what is called a "bowpicker" style by fishermen who work their gear from the front of similar boats, picking salmon from a net as it is reeled in over the bow. The house is aft and consists of a single small cabin with a broad lower bunk over the engine, a narrow, tight shelf above that which can serve as a bunk for a small person (unless claustrophobic), and a table which can be folded down into a third bed. There is an enclosed head—a toilet to the landsman—on the port side, with an oil stove and sink opposite, and the helm forward of that. All squeezed into a space eight feet wide and fourteen feet long.

The *Swift* was built to provide transportation and support for climbing expeditions, researchers, kayakers, and others going into the wilderness with more gear than can be fitted into a floatplane. With the house aft, an outside steering station installed well forward, and the foredeck clear of obstructions, it is an ideal design for edging carefully up to an unknown beach or rock face to unload people and gear, but not for carting four passengers around for a month. I'd never intended to provide extended living and sleeping accommodations for my clients; I liked being alone, enjoyed waving good-bye to people as I pulled away and headed for a quiet anchorage somewhere else for the night.

But I also had a daunting mortgage, absurdly expensive insurance premiums, and operating costs that never seemed to go down. And the number of blank pages in my charter schedule was causing me spasms of anxiety. The prospect of a solid month of business was enticing.

"Come see what you think of my boat," I said. "I can sleep on the floor."

THE NEXT MORNING as I waited on the deck in the sunshine, enjoying the feel of the warmth and light on my face and splicing a new eye into the end of the anchor line (live on a boat, you'll never run out of tasks), I saw four Asian-looking men making their way down the ramp into the harbor. I quickly tucked the last yarn of the eye into the line, rolled the back splice between my palms to smooth it, and watched as the quartet approached.

The first to clamber aboard was a smallish man wearing a baggy, roughly knit sweater and denim pants that were beginning to tear at the knee. His head seemed slightly large for his body, and when he swung one leg awkwardly over the rail, he had to grope for a hand-hold to retain his balance as the boat rocked under his weight. He introduced himself with a soft handshake and a broad smile that revealed two prominent canines.

"I am," he said, removing his peaked knit cap and revealing hanks of unruly dark hair that sprouted from his head, "Michio Hoshino."

Next was a big man with the long, muscular build of a climber who made the three-foot step from the dock up onto the boat with-out effort. Hoshino held his knit cap behind his back and gave a slight bow as he introduced us.

"And this is Eiho Otani."

A quick intelligence showed in Otani's eyes as he looked me up and down from behind dark-rimmed glasses, measuring me just as I was measuring him. His parka was faded and worn from hard use, as were the boots on his feet—a good sign, I thought. I pegged him instantly as the boss, Hoshino as a hired hand taken on for his ability to speak English.

"Captain-san," Otani said, and ducked his head in a marginal bow. I fumbled an attempt to return the bow, settled for bobbing my head and shaking his extended hand, then tried to ease the formal begin-ning by asking him not to call me captain.

Eiho Otani's name was vaguely familiar, and it took me a moment to place him: he was an accomplished mountain climber–cinematographer and had climbed many of the world's more difficult peaks, including the west ridge of K2 in the Himalayas in 1981, where he had been forced to bivouac in a snow hole at eighty-three hundred meters with no oxygen, sleeping bag, food, tent, or bivy sack. In Feb-ruary 1984, Japan's premier adventurer, Naomi Uemura, disappeared in a storm on Alaska's Mount Denali after becoming the first person to summit the 20,300-foot mountain alone during winter. Otani had been producing a film on Uemura's climb and was camped lower on the mountain when the storm struck. Jim Wickwire, an American climber who joined the search for Uemura, later referred to Otani as "tireless" throughout the unsuccessful effort to find the lost climber.

Maeda (pronounced with a long *i* sound) Yasujiro was the camera operator, and in the manner of someone familiar with nautical etiquette, he waited on the dock until being invited aboard. He was a stocky, strong-looking man with steel-rimmed spectacles and a square, honest face. He wore light nylon running pants, a hooded pullover of windproof material, and a billed cap that showed a good deal of wear. He glanced at the new eye splice in the anchor line and gave an approving nod before extending his hand for a handshake that was firm, but without the conscious demonstration of strength squeezed into the greeting by many Americans.

Yamanushi Fumihiko, the slender, smooth-faced boy who acted as assistant cameraman and technician, came aboard last, wearing new-looking Levi's and a pressed cotton shirt, shook my hand shyly, then stepped back to position himself unobtrusively behind the others.

All four men were deeply red with windburn.

"Where'd you all get the nice tans?" I asked, hoping to break the ice.

Michio brightened immediately. "We are filming in Denali National Park before coming here and we have very good weather," he said. "And before, they have been in Amazon for nearly one year," Michio said, encompassing the film crew with a sweep of his hand. "Living with Yanomami Indians."

Michio was rightly enthused by the fact that his three companions had spent time among the primitive Yanomami Indians of the Amazon Basin—a fierce, war-loving people who shave their heads with razor-sharp slivers of bamboo before painting their scalps red and setting out armed with blowguns and poison-tipped arrows to do battle against gold seekers and loggers armed with shotguns and rifles.

I was impressed, as well.

We stood in awkward silence for a moment before I finally took a step to the side, sweeping out my hand, miming an invitation to look over the boat. Michio instantly made a move toward the foredeck, but he stumbled just as he stepped from the hatch cover, recovering only at the last minute by grabbing at the rail. The little finger of his right hand was stiff, stuck out at a slight angle, and seemed to interfere with his grip. He asked several questions about the amount of room in the cargo hold and various storage spaces and translated my answers to the others. Then he moved into the galley and poked around there for several minutes.

"Refrigerator?" he finally asked.

I shook my head. "I carry a couple of ice chests. We can get plenty of ice from the glaciers while we're traveling."

"Vegetables okay in the hold?" He peeked inside a drawer. "You have enough pots and pans?"

I nodded to reassure him, wondering at his obsession with food and its preparation. After he quizzed me intently on the oil stove and peered into the oven, it finally struck me why he was preoccupied.

"So you're the *cook* as well as translator?"

Maeda laughed lightly at my question; his understanding of English was better than I had thought. The cameraman shook his head and labored to explain in hesitant, broken English. "Hoshino-san is . . . ah . . . subject."

"Subject?" I asked. *Subject to what? Fits?*

Hoshino blushed and became overly interested in the workings of a small one-burner gas stove gimballed above the galley counter.

"Subject of film," clarified Otani. "*Shashinka-dobutsu.* Famous wildlife photographer."

"No, no." Michio shook his head. "Subject of film is A*las*-ka."

I was dead wrong. Michio was not a freelance photographer hired to translate, cook, and do chores: he was the centerpiece of the film we planned to spend the next month working on, and I'd just been too dense to see it.

"So. Whales, Lynn-san?" Michio wanted to steer the conversation away from himself. "Can we find humpback whale to photograph?"

THE HUMPBACK WHALE is an endangered species and came close to being eradicated before an international ban on commercial whaling was imposed in 1986. Now the worldwide population hovers around ten thousand animals and may even be increasing—

slowly—as the moratorium on the slaughter takes effect. Approximately two thousand humpback whales make their home in the North Pacific and only a quarter of these spend their summers in Alaska, drawn north from wintering grounds in Hawaii and Mexico by the enormous banquet of herring, sand lance, and krill that enriches the northern waters every year.

Less than a week before, I had motored carefully around a group of a half dozen animals feeding in the waters of Seymour Canal, a long narrow waterway that penetrates Admiralty Island fifty miles south of Juneau. It was a clear, calm day and the spouts of the humpbacks' salty exhalations were visible for miles. I slowed the *Swift* to an idle and watched as a calf practiced standing on its head, holding its tail erect above the surface and flailing its pectoral fins, until the dark reef of its mother's broad back rose from the sea in a gush of foam and the pair swam slowly away to the south.

"Absolutely." I nodded. Yes, I was confident, but I also don't like making guarantees. "We'll find some whales."

Unrolling a chart on the galley table, I weighted the edge down with an empty coffee cup and pointed to a body of water eighty miles south of Juneau. "Frederick Sound is probably our best bet. It's an important feeding ground for the whales."

Frederick Sound is a basin of salt water a thousand miles square and twelve hundred feet deep, squeezed between the hulking bodies of Admiralty Island in the north, Kuiu and Kupreanof Islands in the south, and the mainland to the east. It is surrounded by files of forest-clad mountains that rise up like green waves and are crested along their tops with glittering white snowfields and glaciers.

I drew a finger along the chart as I explained how the tide enters Frederick Sound between Kingsmill Point on Kuiu Island (pronounced *q-u*) and Point Gardner at the southern tip of Admiralty Island. From there it sets northeast to the mainland, where it divides at Cape Fanshaw to flow either north for seventy-five miles until it reaches Juneau or east for forty miles until it meets the outflow of the Stikine River at the head of the sound.

"Where the tide crosses the ridges and valleys of the sea bottom it boils," I said, rolling my hands to demonstrate the motion. "This throws up a tremendous amount of nutrients from the seabed below." I explained briefly how this rich soup combines with the near-endless daylight of summer to nourish a splendid biomass of plankton and krill, which in its turn feeds a million tons of herring.

I paused after describing how the herring flow silver and shining over the contours of the bottom, waited for Michio to translate, then illustrated how the swarming mass of herring attracts millions of salmon, seabirds, killer whales, eagles, and porpoises by scooping my hands toward my chest. Yamanushi's eyes grew large when I said more than three hundred humpbacks, ravenous from months of fasting in subtropical seas, rely on the herring of Southeast Alaska for the oils and proteins critical to the laying on of blubber that will take them through the seasonal famines of their lives.

"The whales dive below a school of herring and begin circling," I said, as I drew a large downward spiral with my hand. "And one whale releases a steady stream of air from the blowhole on top of its head."

My audience was politely attentive as I pantomimed bubbles rising from the top of my head. Maeda toyed with a spoon, drawing circles that mimicked the whales' method of surrounding their prey. Otani looked at the chart, fingered the area where all of this was supposed to happen, then nodded for me to go on.

"The bubbles form a 'net' around the fish that keeps them from escaping," I continued. "And when herring feel threatened, their initial response is to hide behind each other and hope the predator catches the other guy first. With each fish trying to get into the middle of the swarm, the school condenses into a compact mass. An easy target for the whales."

Michio translated, rolling his hands in the shape of a ball.

"Then the whales rush to the surface with their mouths wide open." I placed my wrists together and spread my fingers as far as they would go to imitate the rush of gaping mouths.

"We might get some spectacular footage," I said, envisioning the coordinated rush of five hundred tons of whales exploding from the water: "But the main thing," I continued, "is to stay out of their way."[4]

I peeled out of my sleeping bag before five o'clock the next morning, then sat at the galley table with a cup of coffee and watched the eastern sky turn white, then blue, as the promise of sunrise was fulfilled. By six thirty the breakfast dishes were washed and I was down in the engine room tightening a water pump belt and checking the oil. At seven, I got my first lesson in the Japanese language when there was a rap on the hull and I looked out to see Michio standing on the dock beside an immense stack of gear.

"*Ohayo*, Lynn-san!" The way he pronounced it, the greeting sounded like "Ohio!" and I knew that it could only mean an enthusiastic *good morning*. Behind him, I could see the others shuttling more bags down from a rental van in the parking lot.

The equipment came aboard in heaps and piles. A beer cooler—dry, airtight, and impervious to temperature extremes—made a perfect protective container for packs of film and video supplies. Maeda babied the video camera—a solid chunk of machinery that used beta tapes to guarantee footage of broadcast quality and cost roughly the equivalent of my boat—by placing it carefully into the bunk and tucking it in with a bolster of pillows. Yamanushi worked hard toting a generator to the boat to ensure a supply of electricity for recharging the camera batteries. A two-man kayak was strapped to the cabin top, an outboard and inflatable skiff stowed on the deck. Each of the film crew stowed a duffel bag of clothing and rain gear in the hold alongside a dozen large boxes packed with the bulk of our food. Michio's personal gear was a loose heap of clothes, a sleeping bag, notebooks, a Walkman and music cassettes, and odds and ends piled at random

---

4. Accidents are extremely rare, but in 1998 a sailboat was holed and sunk while at anchor near Sitka. The vessel was unoccupied at the time, but salvage efforts revealed baleen from a humpback whale's mouth imbedded in the hull.

into a backpack. But his 35-millimeter camera gear came aboard carefully sorted and stowed in padded bags.[5]

At the fuel dock a grimly able man in gray overalls wiped his hands on an oily rag and pumped two hundred gallons of fuel into the *Swift*'s tanks—enough to carry the five of us and all of our gear for four hundred miles. Water for drinking and washing was limited to a single twenty-five-gallon tank, but the forest that spans Southeast Alaska is the largest temperate rainforest in the world, with uncountable numbers of creeks, springs, and rivers. It was not likely that we would suffer a shortage.

Maeda came on deck to help as I untied the *Swift* from the dock, taking in the mooring line and coiling them neatly. The clean, sure movements of his hands as he clove-hitched the coils to a cleat showed a sailor's dexterity with lines (only a landsman would call them "ropes"), and I was pleased to know that I was not the only seaman aboard. Mariners have a culture of their own, where an understanding of the physics specific to a world of wind, water, and tides can be more valuable than words. Should all nautical hell break loose during bad weather, rough seas, mechanical failure, fire, or any of the other plagues that thrive on the sea, it would be far better to have another experienced seaman aboard—even a Japanese-speaking one—than an inexperienced landsman with a perfect command of English.

From Juneau to Frederick Sound the weather and tides were with us, and the *Swift* skimmed across an ocean of glass. Sixty miles south,

---

5. Professional photographers carry a tremendous variety of equipment—wide-angle lenses used to encompass expansive views, telephotos for bringing distant subjects close; two or more camera bodies on which to mount the lenses; hundreds of rolls of film; a stiff, heavy tripod with a finely machined head to hold the camera steady for long exposures; and a miscellany of filters, batteries, hoods, straps, tools, and cleaning materials to keep it all working.

Michio's assortment of photography gear was larger than most. When photographing wildlife, he favored the popular 35-millimeter format for its relative ease of handling, but also carried a full set of medium-format equipment. Medium-format photography uses film several times larger than its smaller 35-millimeter cousin to capture more of the fine details in a scene. This allows a photograph to be enlarged without sacrificing clarity and is ideal for set shots and landscapes, but the cameras are slow, bulky, and awkward to hold.

the white tower of the Five Finger light station passed along the port side as we crossed into Frederick Sound.

Easing back on the throttle, I slowed the boat to an idle, took the engine out of gear, and went on deck with a pair of binoculars. Yamanushi followed, leaned his back against the wheelhouse, and shaded his eyes.

"*Kujira?* Whale?" he asked, putting a lot of breath into the *w*.

"There." I pointed to the south, where a faint plume of spray spiked low against the horizon, then faded rapidly away. I raised the binoculars to my eyes and caught a flicker of black as the humpback jackknifed into a dive.

"I guess," I said smiling, "this is a good place to start."

3 » Eruption

"NATURE PHOTOGRAPHY." Michio shrugged. "Always lots of waiting."

By evening of the second day out of Juneau the sea had given up only a few brief glimpses of isolated whales, and I was becoming concerned by the lack of activity. Maeda said something to Otani, who smiled at me and shook his head. *Don't worry*.

The galley was littered with the detritus of cooking and the "warm" smell of a pork roast came from the oven. All around us the sea was beginning to reflect the pale, golden light of evening. A range of green-and-white mountains marched patiently past the cabin windows as the *Swift* drifted in a slow circle on the tide. Yamanushi gathered a stack of plates from a cupboard, squared each plate precisely to its neighbor, then prepared silverware for duty by folding paper towels into perfect isosceles triangles and placing each knife and fork in flawless alignment atop the improvised napkins.

Michio stood at the stove, prodding a saucepan with a spoon. "One time I wait nearly one month for the northern lights to come out." The words came out *nor-zern rights*. Laughing, he caught himself and beat time with the spoon, laboring at the *l* as he corrected himself: "I mean . . . *nor-thern lights!*"

I twisted the top off a bottle of beer, handed it to Maeda, and cracked another for Otani. Michio never drank alcohol.

"You were in Fairbanks?"

"No, no." Michio swung the spoon as he answered, flicking droplets of sauce about the galley. "Tokositna Glacier." The stiffness I noticed in his fingers, he explained, was the result of the frostbite suffered when he spent that month alone in temperatures that ranged to thirty degrees below zero, camped in a tent high on a broken river of ice that flows down the flank of Mount Denali—all for the chance to photograph the northern lights dancing above the twenty-thousand-foot mountain on the one night they appeared.

"You get lonesome up there by yourself for so long?" I asked, mostly in jest.

"Oh, sure," he replied, matter-of-factly. "The wind . . ." He held out his hands and rattled them to imitate the buffeting of a tent in a gale. "Sometimes I felt really alone."

"Was it worth it? All that cold for just one night of northern lights?"

"Oh, sure," Michio answered without hesitation, rubbing his frostbitten fingers against his thigh. "It was a *beautiful* experience."

"Well," I said. "Guess we can be patient with the whales then. Sooner or later, they'll come."

There were nods and reassuring smiles from the others as we crammed around the small galley table and set to on the pork roast. While we ate, we kept a close watch out the windows—whales appearing in the red-and-gold light of sunset would be a photographer's dream. An occasional seine boat or private cruiser appeared on the horizon, passed at an even, stately pace, then disappeared again, but for the most part, we kept our vigil alone or in the spare company of seagulls drifting across the darkening, cloudless skies.

A cruise ship the size of a small city lumbered into view, glittering with spotlights, and altered course to pass close to our stern. The liner charged, cleaving the sea with the black cliff of its bow, sending a dark, rolling swell surging toward the drifting *Swift* and its perilously loaded dinner table.

Michio, Yamanushi, and Otani leaned toward the window, oohing and aahing at the beautiful bulk and partylike atmosphere of the light-strung ship as Maeda and I lunged for the dinner ("Hang on! *Tsukete!*"), grabbing at the roast, plates, and bottles just as the wave struck and threw the *Swift* into a wild gunnel-to-gunnel roll. A dish pan clattered to the deck, Michio's horde of spices shifted and spilled into the sink, a book left unsecured on a shelf thumped to the floor. But the evening meal was saved.[6]

"We better head for an anchorage," I said, flicking on the running lights. "I'm sure we'll find whales tomorrow."

FOR THE NEXT SEVERAL DAYS we crisscrossed Frederick Sound, hoping to spot the tightly clustered spouts that are usually the first sign of humpbacks engaged in cooperative feeding. I stared through binoculars at the shimmering horizon until my eyes swam in my head and my vision grew blurry. It became difficult to stay focused, to avoid drifting into daydreams as a way to escape the tedium and frustration of miragelike images that lured us on false chases across miles of disappointingly empty ocean.

We drifted for hours, listening to the sharp cries of Bonaparte's gulls, marbled murrelets, and pigeon guillemots while we glassed for some sign of the whales. I kept an eye on the depth sounder as I

---

6. I'd learn later that Maeda's supper-saving instincts were hard-won, when he described (through Michio's translation) having been a crewman in an offshore sailboat race that encountered a terrible storm. At the time, Michio's English was insufficient to fully translate the details, but from Maeda's description of the storm and the time frame in which it took place, I've always wondered if it wasn't the 1979 Fastnet race in the Irish Sea, when faulty weather forecasting led a group of racers (many of them professionals) to charge offshore into one of the worst hurricane-force blows to sweep the coast during this century. The result was disaster. Boats were capsized, holed, dismasted, and swamped, and nineteen people were drowned in the worst yachting tragedy of the twentieth century. If this was so, the fact that Maeda Yasujiro was alive and sitting on the *Wilderness Swift* was a testament to ability, courage, and—above all—good fortune.

steered long, fruitless transects of the sea bottom, searching for the tightly massed blips that could signal a large school of herring. My passengers cleaned and organized their equipment as we traveled, and when nothing remained to be done, they began to trade jokes and stories to pass the time. All were great laughers. When Otani smiled, he grinned so broadly his eyes disappeared into his cheeks, and Yamanushi's shy giggle often exploded into belly laughter. Michio always went out of his way to include me in the conversations, translating as best he could the subtleties of another culture's humor. I was grateful for his consideration of my isolation, then learned that he understood very well what it was like to be isolated among other people. He had first come to Alaska before learning to speak English with any fluency.

In 1971, when he was nineteen, Michio said, he saw an aerial photograph of Shishmaref, a small village nearly lost in the sweep of Alaska's wide arctic plain, and immediately became infatuated with the idea of such an immense, open space and the lives of the people who lived there. He immediately sat down and wrote a letter, addressing it simply to "the mayor of Shishmaref village, Alaska, USA," asking if he could come for a month and live with a family in the village in order to experience the Eskimo way of life. The mayor, Clifford Weyiouanna, responded by inviting Michio to stay in his own home.

"Really nice people," said Michio, grinning broadly. "Wonderful people. I planned to stay one month, but stayed three."

After returning to Japan and finishing a degree in economics, Michio apprenticed himself to Japan's leading wildlife photographer, Kojo Tanaka, and began to perfect his technique. In 1978 he returned to Alaska, living in a tiny, ramshackle log cabin in Fairbanks while he attended a nearby university to study wildlife management. During breaks in his studies Michio wobbled along Alaska's few lonely roads in a barely-running Volkswagen bus, exploring the countryside and searching for wildlife to photograph as he made the first inroads into his new career.

Maeda and Otani conveyed to me in broken sentences that Michio was arguably the most accomplished wildlife photographer in the world. He had won the prestigious Anima Award for his book on grizzlies; had seen his photos and writings published in dozens of prominent journals, including *National Geographic* and *Audubon* magazines; and was respected in his own country in a way that no American photographer (with perhaps the exception of Ansel Adams or Edward Curtis) has ever been.

He was persistent, perhaps even obsessive, when it came to his photos. He was willing, it seemed, to endure anything—to wait for days among swarms of mosquitoes or outside in lung-searing cold for the right weather or light to capture a beautiful image, just as he had when he spent a month alone on the Tokositna Glacier for a single chance to photograph the northern lights dancing above Mount Denali—and often did so at great risk to life and limb.

He reaggravated his frostbitten fingers in 1988 when three gray whales became trapped in a tiny crack of open water in the sea ice off Point Barrow, the northernmost point of land in Alaska, four hundred miles above the Arctic Circle.

The trapped whales quickly became the focus of world concern, and Barrow was flooded with reporters and television crews from around the globe as an effort was made to free the animals from their prison. Michio had flown north from his home in Fairbanks in such a rush that he neglected to pack adequate gloves and landed in Barrow only to find every available helicopter and snow machine already taken. Rather than give up and go home, he simply hoisted seventy or eighty pounds of gear onto his back and walked three miles across the frozen Arctic Ocean to the whales.

"Halfway out, I start thinking about polar bears." Michio smiled. "How many there are around Barrow.[7] First time I ever saw polar bear

7. In December 1990, twenty-eight-year-old Carl Stalker was killed defending his pregnant wife from a polar bear that attacked the couple on a street in Point Lay, a small village southwest of Barrow. Three years later, another bear smashed through the window of a dormitory at a radar station and badly mauled a worker inside.

was in Canada, with my friend. We looked for polar bear all day. Nothing." Michio spread his hands to show how empty luck can be.

"But at night we are sleeping in a trailer and it starts shaking," he said, pushing back and forth with his hands. "So we have to take flashlight and go outside to see. And there," pointing at his feet, "right there, polar bear, knocking our trailer."

"What happened?"

"Polar bear went away. Very beautiful."

"How about in Barrow? What did you do when you started thinking about polar bears when you were out in the middle of the ice?"

"I got *shimpai shite* . . . really afraid."

"Too afraid to go on?"

"Yes, too afraid. But I keep walking." Michio smiled ruefully. "I was halfway."

I admired Michio's perseverance in the face of high-altitude winter gales and polar bears, but our current search was frustrating me badly. Day after day, the whales continued their shell game, shuffling their forty-ton bodies among the warren of islands around us, and as I stared at the endless horizon, feeling appalled by how enormous and empty the sea had begun to seem, I listened with one ear to the incomprehensible exchanges between my passengers.

What are they really saying? I wondered. Why can't this goofball that calls himself a guide find something as big as a pod of whales?

Otani and the others maintained an implacable, Asian equanimity, lounging about as if on vacation while I worried. Theirs was the patience of the professional, a Buddhist sort of waiting, which I could not find in myself as time stretched out, became an elastic, variable thing, and ceased to be a meaningful measure.

Our fuel supply, however, was a finite, material thing, and after so many fruitless days at sea the gas tanks had begun to ring hollow. I hauled out a chart, plotted our position, and estimated our remaining range. When we departed Juneau the tanks had held nearly fifteen hundred pounds of fuel, but now the boat felt light and nimble under the helm and the water line had risen several inches as we burned off the weight of the fuel. We had just enough remaining to reach Angoon, a Tlingit village thirty miles away.

Angoon is the only year-round settlement within the two thousand square miles of Admiralty Island. The village of six hundred people lies at the mouth of Kootznahoo Inlet, an intricate system of fingers and coves that pierces inland from Chatham Straits into the foot of a mountain range that runs for a hundred miles along the backbone of the island. Oral tradition holds that the Tlingit Indians have occupied the town site since before the last ice age—a claim lent credence by archaeological evidence that suggests the site has seen almost continuous use by a society of hunter-gatherers for more than ten thousand years, making Angoon one of the oldest continuously occupied sites in the New World. An ancient tribe's sense of themselves as a people is often inseparable from a sense of *place,* and the original inhabitants of Admiralty called themselves Hutsnuwu after their name for the island, which translates as the "Fortress of the Bears."

The Hutsnuwu laid claim to 150 miles of Chatham Straits north and south of the village, including all of the bays, islets, coves, rivers, and streams that feed into it, and the land on either side, excepting the Kuyu territory on the western shore of Kuiu Island to the south. The Hutsnuwu claim included all of the fish, seals, sea lions, and otters that swam in the waters; all of the trees, berries, and edible plants that grew in the forests or on the shores; and all of the animals, be they feathered or furred, that walked the mountains, the valleys, or the shores.

At the fuel dock a slender, twentyish Tlingit man with a mutinous complexion, mirrored sunglasses, and a ball cap advertising a popular brand of chainsaw made no move to help with the mooring lines as I maneuvered the *Swift* alongside the floating pumps. A stout current running crabwise to the dock set the boat in at an angle, and I leaped off, took a turn around a cleat with a breastline, and let the tide swing the boat flush.

"Can I get some gas?"

He met my query with a silver-eyed stare and dismissed it with a one-shouldered shrug.

I felt myself growing irritated by the studied indifference, but I jumped when a disembodied voice blared from an intercom speaker mounted on a pole above the pumps. "Pump's on. Pay in the office when you're done."

The pump hoses lay in a greasy pile on the float. Untangling the stiff, oily hoses was like wrestling a dirty anaconda, and the lounger steadfastly ignored me. I moved to undo a snarl near his feet—"excuse me"—and walked into a sour fog of liquor fumes. Boozy vapors and silent animosity flowed from the drunk like a heat wave as he thrust out his chin, grunted a single glottal syllable, then resumed staring at something to the right of my shoulder.[8]

Liquor has been a problem in the villages of Alaska since the first Boston trader swindled an otter hunter out of a canoe load of pelts with a bottle of cheap whiskey. It was once common practice to ply an entire village with liquor until the inhabitants were completely besotted, then commence dealing in stiff trade until every pelt available had been taken aboard ship. The villagers invariably awoke to find the trading schooner gone, taking with it the wealth of the village and leaving nothing behind but the taste of bad liquor, a few useless trinkets, and venereal disease.

Not all early visitors looked down on Alaska's inhabitants or took advantage of their naïveté. In his 1789 account of his voyage around the world, Captain Nathaniel Portlock noted of the Tlingit: "They have a great number of curiosities among them [perhaps referring to the exquisite craftsmanship of steam-bent boxes and carvings] many of which shew them to be a people of great ingenuity and contrivance."

But liquor did hold great attraction for the people of the coast, and being the creative, inventive people that they were, as soon as iron kettles became common they quickly developed distillery skills of their own, based on readily available trade ingredients of molasses or brown sugar, potatoes, and hops. If no coil of copper tubing or tin was available

---

8. Inebriation is extremely rare in Angoon. The village is "dry," with possession or use of alcohol strictly prohibited as the result of a community referendum.

for use in their homemade stills, the innate cleverness of the villagers
sometimes exhibited itself in the conscription of a long, hollow stem of
bull kelp packed in snow and pressed into service as a condenser.

"Hootchenoo" was as close as the first whites in Alaska could
come to a proper pronunciation of Hutsnuwu—a village famous for
its home brew and stills. Corrupted, the name of the village was shortened to "Hootch," and a new word signifying powerful, poor-quality
liquor was introduced into American slang by traders and sailors
returning home from the Inside Passage.

The result of this newly acquired skill, as Captain Howard of the
USS *Lincoln* wrote in the ship's log while on a tour to show the flag
throughout Southeast Alaska during 1867, was a clear, strong liquor
that "made the natives wild, and thus caused many quarrels and
killings at the feasts where it was consumed."

Captain Howard's description bears no resemblence to the modern village, where I've found the people to be almost unfailingly generous, good-hearted, and kind, but nonetheless, I kept my eyes on the
nozzle as I filled the starboard tank, then dragged the hose across the
deck to top off the port tank. After taking on 180 gallons of fuel, I
returned the hose to the dock, maneuvered around the seething
drunk, and climbed a long flight of stairs through a stand of moss-
girdled trees to the office. The air was sharp with the astringent scent
of spruce sap, and the shade of the trees felt good after days of staring
across sun-dappled water.

While the office manager fingered a calculator and tallied the bill,
I studied the design silk-screened onto his red T-shirt. Emblazoned on
a circle that spanned the width of his chest were the dates 1882–1982
and words commemorating the centennial of what in Angoon is
known simply as "the bombing." Angoon had suffered a visit by the
U.S. Navy that left a bitter taste in the mouths of the residents and
their descendants for more than a hundred years.

A paymaster named Frank H. Clark, stationed in Sitka aboard the
warship USS *Adams* at the time, described the incident in his Christmas
letter home and made no bones about his personal feeling toward the

arrogant young commander of the ship who caused the tragedy. Clark referred to Captain E. C. Merriman as "a perfect d—— f—— . . . and . . . an infernal liar," then went on to describe what took place as his glory-hungry young captain took charge of quelling an apparent insurrection among the natives:

A few days ago a man came down from Kenasloo [Killisnoo, an inlet just south of Angoon] and said the Indians there had seized their steam launch and some nets and boats and two men and held them as security for the payment of two hundred blankets on account of the accidental explosion of a bomb lance in one of the whaling companies boats. To go back a little, I will state that when an indian is killed, either purposely or accidentally, they always expect a settlement and if not made they will kill someone for the death, but it may be two years after and two hundred miles away. This case was as follows: The North west trading company have a post at Kenasloo and also have a whaling establishment and send out boats to get whales that run near there. One of their boats was chasing a whale when the bomb lance that they fire at the whale, exploded and killed an indian in the bow of the boat. They immediately put into a lagoon where the indian village is and the indians probably knowing by experience that the company was not very liberal, seized their launch, boats, nets, etc. and the two white men in them. They then sent word over to the works to Vanderbilt the agent that they wanted 200 blankets (a blanket is $3.00, and everything is valued in blankets). Instead of making a settlement with them as he probably could have done for 20 or thirty blankets, he took a tug they have there and came down here [Sitka] for help. This was the first chance our skipper has had for glory this cruise and it was too good to lose. He took 40 men in charge of Lt. Bartlett and 20 marines in charge of Lt. Gilman, and, he went up on the "Corwin" a Revenue cutter that happened to be here at the time. He took the collector of customs here along with him and a couple of marines for orderlies. Lt. Bartlett went on a steam tug belonging to the North West Trading Co. He took besides his sixty men and rifles a howitzer and Gatling gun. All this preparation against a lot of indians half of whom were unarmed.

On their arrival at Hoochenoo [Hutsnuwu/Angoon] the indian village where the property was seized they found the two white men released and the property all restored. The Captain then notified the indians they must pay him four hundred blankets as a penalty for their unlawful conduct and gave them until the next day at noon to raise them. The next morning they had raised only a little over a hundred and at noon only a hundred & twenty he then burned and bombarded a few houses that were at our side of the village and at the same time raised his demand to 800 blankets which is $2400. This they did not comply with and he then gave orders to shell the town. After firing thirty or forty shells into the town he sent the sailors and marines and burned about forty houses which cannot be replaced for $3000 and only left five houses standing. Besides the dwellings there were a large number of store houses filled with smoked salmon and other winter supplies. All this was burned too. Many of the indians were away at the Harrisburg [Juneau] mining and their houses contained everything that they possessed and were all burned up. Of course the indians that were there saved what they could before the burning. Mr. Vanderbilt who is prejudicial against the indians estimated the loss to the tribe at 30 or 40 thousand dolls(ars). This of course does not include the suffering to women and children who will suffer from want of shelter and food during the winter. As the weather there is much more severe than here it will undoubtedly cause much suffering. Most of the officers including myself consider it a brutal and cowardly thing and entirely uncalled for. It would have been well enough to have arrested the ring leaders and punished them, but in this case many innocent people suffered more than the guilty, and a large number of helpless women and children. It is estimated that there are about 800 people in the village.

We are all anxious to see the account the papers will give of it

and the report the Capt. will give of it. In other words how big a
lie he will tell in order to justify himself.

Six children died in the shelling. There is no record of how many
Hutsnuwu died from insufficient food, lack of shelter, and medicine
during the ensuing winter.[9]

Now the Angoon Oil and Gas Company was reclaiming what it
could of the blanket price owed the Hutsnuwu for the hundred-year-
old killings by practicing a fair form of piracy at the fuel dock: gasoline was forty cents a gallon more than I had paid in Juneau. The
office manager smiled as he handed me the bill, gave me a tip on
where the king salmon were biting—"I got one big as my leg yesterday"—and wished me a good day.

Back at the dock, I was surprised to see Michio had made friends
with the surly drunk, and both were hunkered over a book splayed
out on the deck while Maeda and Otani looked on. *Alaska Geographic*
is a quarterly publication that focuses each issue on a different facet of
Alaska's geography, wildlife, or various cultures, and as the drunk
spoke he was stabbing a finger at a page of an issue titled "Admiralty;
an Island in Contention."

"That's right, seen it myself a hundred times." Michio's new friend
gave an emphatic, exaggerated nod. "*Hundreds* of times." The page
under his finger showed a photograph of a carved stone bear.

As we followed the inebriate's murky directions—turning left at
the Angoon Trading Company store, then wandering vaguely southeast for a moment or two until making a right near a carving of a killer
whale mounted atop a short pole and becoming befuddled until asking
further directions from a grandmotherly woman standing in the open
doorway of a small, unpainted house—Michio tried to explain why he
wanted to photograph the statue.

9. A court case in 1973–74 awarded Angoon $90,000—the estimated value of the village
in 1880 dollars—and the navy issued a written admission that the incident occurred but
made no apology. Angoon elders lobbied the Clinton administration for an apology but
were rebuffed and ignored.

"Bear is a . . . *shocho* . . . a symbol." He squinched his eyes closed as he tried to find the right phrase. "Bear goes to sleep every winter, then again in spring comes out."

Michio folded his hands together near his chest, then curled them outward like a flower blooming. "It's like life. Seeds . . . or . . . ," his explanation shuffled to a stop. The image grabbed me—the bear emerging triumphant into a tabula rasa of clean, untrodden snow after surviving the raging storms of winter; the passage from darkness into light; the inevitability of the cycle drawing a perfect circle of rebirth and life—and I moved to fill in the gaps with a leap of logic: "You mean resurrection? Life and death, the bear going into hibernation, then emerging again?"

"Yes," he said, looking a little unconvinced. "Maybe."

More and more I had noticed over the course of our journey that communication between Michio and me was taking such a course—an exploration of broad ideas in short sentences that sometimes catalyzed previously vague thoughts and images. Having few words between us required precise, explicit choices and allowed little of the aimless chitchat that often supplies an easy path around the difficulties of true communication.

The statue was overgrown, lost in a swirl of underbrush and salmonberry bushes. After pushing aside an overburden of grass and inspecting the carving—a pug-nosed, waist-high figure of a bear sitting on its haunches—Michio decided no composition for a photo was possible. On the way back to the boat, the grandmother was still standing in her open door and gave a warm, gap-toothed smile backed up by a long-armed wave as we passed.

THE *SWIFT* SLIPPED out of the harbor, bucking the inflooding tide. The curling white wave of our wake lipped away behind us as we passed the kelp-girdled channel marker at Danger Point, then came left until the lubber line of the compass settled on 160 degrees, my course for Point Caution. From there we would head south to Point Gardner and again enter Frederick Sound.

The surface of the sea was slick and laminar, smooth enough to reflect the white bellies of cumulus clouds tumbling slowly in from the west. The radio crackled to life with the voice of the Coast Guard station in Juneau advising mariners to shift to VHF channel 22—"Two-two alpha"—for the regularly scheduled broadcast of weather reports, notices to mariners, and other alerts.

I spun the knob until the screen on the face of the radio glowed "22," then took out a pencil and notepad to jot down the forecast.

Beneath the surface, the depth sounder showed blankets of what fishermen call "feed"—krill, plankton, and herring lumped together into a single substance notable primarily for its ability to attract hungry salmon. Below the feed there was no bottom; the depth sounder read to twelve hundred feet, then went blind, bouncing erratically through numbers from one to a thousand. The chart contradicted the instrument's lunatic readings, showing a sloping bottom that declined rapidly from 40 fathoms to well over 350—deep enough to block all light and swarm with blind, undiscovered forms of life.

I jotted down the details of the weather forecast as the voice on the radio continued: winds light and variable, becoming north to fifteen knots, seas less than three feet—perfect for traveling. I was about to cap the pen and put away the notebook when the next words arrested my hand.

"The fishing vessel *Gretel* is reported overdue and missing while en route from Sitka to Petersburg.[10] The *Gretel* is white in color, forty-five feet in length, and reported to have three persons on board. Mariners transiting the area are asked to keep a sharp lookout for signs of distress and report all sightings to Comstat Juneau.

"This is United States Coast Guard Communications Station Juneau, out."

I scribbled *Gretel* on the pad and underlined it. *Overdue* and *missing* are ominous words on the water under any conditions, but in many ways the calm, settled weather made the call more alarming. If it had

10. My memory may be faulty here; I am not certain this was the vessel's name.

been rough and stormy, there would be a decent chance that the vessel was simply holed up somewhere out of radio range, waiting for the weather to break. In good weather, with plenty of boat traffic to spot a vessel in trouble, the only reasons for a sudden disappearance were all bad: an explosion, a fire, a sudden capsize from a poorly arranged load—perhaps a nighttime collision with a large ship or a barge.

Traveling south from Angoon down Icy Straits, the *Swift* would be following the missing boat's likely line of travel between Sitka and Petersburg. I felt my scalp prickle and my stomach turn as I considered what I would in truth be looking for rather than a white forty-five-foot fishing boat: debris; fishing floats adrift in splinters of fiberglass or wood; an oil slick; a swatch of orange neoprene floating just at the surface that would turn out to be a "survival suit" or life jacket that some sudden emergency had denied an unlucky fisherman time to don.

Announcements like this are a regular occurrence in Alaska. The worst part is not the regularity of such calls, but the often-unresolved nature of the tragedies: if, as in this case, I did not know the boat or the people involved, I might never know the outcome. The Coast Guard would issue the advisory for a day or two, then fall silent. Rumor and dock talk might hold on to the missing vessel for a few weeks, or perhaps there would be a short column of newsprint dedicated to the event if wreckage or a body were recovered, but often it is as if the missing boat simply sailed into another dimension, leaving nothing behind but memories, the tears of their families, and a faint, musty whiff of the soul-snatching Kushtaka.[11]

Watching the shoreline to starboard move by as the *Swift* skimmed south in the calm, I studied the skyline, where a rag of cloud writhed in the thermals rising from a hillside littered with the slashed remains of a clear-cut forest. In the twenty-something years since I first tran-

---

11. In downtown Juneau there is a memorial wall inscribed with the names of lost mariners. Every spring a service is held during which the names are read aloud and the preceding year's fatalities are added to the list. This year it took seven long minutes to read the names on the wall—and there are already more casualties waiting to be added.

sited the Inside Passage between Seattle and Alaska, the wholesale removal of timber from the land has scabbed and scarred almost a half million acres of land within the Tongass National Forest. An equal or larger portion of the land deeded over to Native ownership under the Alaska Native Claims Settlement Act of 1971—an act of Congress that rendered the traditional values of the Natives obsolete by "reorganizing" the villages into corporations and designating the inhabitants as "shareholders"—has been cut down as well. By 1990 many of the villages in Southeast Alaska were surrounded by stump fields, and their inhabitants were split down the middle between those lamenting the demise of the old ways and those struggling to make good in a system where such phrases as "cash flow" and "asset development" suddenly meant more than clear running streams and a strong run of salmon.[12]

Michio stared at the scarred mountain through a pair of binoculars and a flicker of worry drew a small vertical line between his eyes. "How long before the forest comes back?" The question was rhetorical, one I could answer only with a shake of my head.

Fifty miles behind us a landmark named Point Couverden split the sea at the junction of Icy Straits and Lynn Canal. In 1794, when George Vancouver (whose original Dutch name of van Couverden was now attached to the landmark) had sailed into Icy Straits, Glacier Bay did not fully exist: a wall of ice 150 feet high filled the gap that is now the entrance to the bay and spilled across the land on both sides, dropping huge icebergs into the now-eponymous Icy Straits.

The Hoonah Tlingit still refer to Glacier Bay as "home" and tell how their ancestors lived "up-bay" until a foolish woman insulted the glacier and caused it to rampage down from the mountains, driving all of the people out of their hunting grounds and across the straits to the current site of their community. Since then the ice has been placated and withdrawn, grumbling and complaining, more than sixty-five miles back into the mountains, and the rich ecosystem of what is now

---

12. This is an exceedingly simplistic description of a very complex situation—a full description of which is best left to the Tlingit themselves.

a national park has been exposed to the forces of recovery that follow the flux and reflux of an ice age.

Surely, I started to say to Michio, if the forest is able to reinvest the land with its abundance after the slow cataclysm of an ice age, it is vibrant enough to survive the ravages of industrial-scale logging. I thought about it, then held my tongue. Recovery would take a long, long time—perhaps several generations—and in the interim, the clear-cuts would remain an ugly, lifeless scar.

LATE IN THE EVENING we hove to off the mouth of Pybus Bay while I stared at the chart and tried to turn my imagination to the pursuit of our quarry. I envisioned a horde of silvery fish adrift on the tide, whorling into back eddies among the islands and channels, filling the sea with their scent. I tried to imagine tendrils of the rich, oily taste of herring curling like smoke through the water, reaching tentatively into a group of whales and coating their tongues, and I imagined the whales' excitement as they followed the smell to its glittering source and began to circle, churning the sea into foam with their fins and broad tails.

I passed a hand over the chart's two-dimensional sea as if I could dowse the location of the whales through my skin. "They've got to be here somewhere," I muttered.

Yamanushi looked up from a lens he was cleaning, nodded in agreement, and looked out the window as if a group of hungry whales might choose that moment to arrive. Otani, weary of the endless watching, had turned to administrative chores and was sorting receipts, then making careful notes in a binder. Maeda and Michio lounged on deck, completely attentive to the sun as it lowered itself to the horizon.

A lone sea lion appeared fifty yards off to port, chuffed once, then rolled away, leaving a bright ring of disturbed water as the only sign of its passing. Scattered bits of conversation from the salmon fleet working the currents forty miles away near Kingsmill Point crackled over the marine radio, broken into static by the distance.

The voice of a fisherman hailing another vessel that answered from somewhere out of range of my receiver broke into my reverie. At first I paid no attention: many fishermen work alone throughout the summer and the ether is alive with constant, aimless chitchat as they fend off the boredom and loneliness that comes with the life.

I continued my divination over the chart, listening with half an ear as the voice said, "Arne's headed back into Petersburg."[13]

An unintelligible crackle and buzz met this news as the other half of the conversation came over the horizon.

"No, he's okay, but it scairt him some when them whales took his poles."

I jumped for the radio and turned up the volume. The voice chortled and launched into a description of how Arne let a "buncha damn whales" become entangled in the fishing gear trolled from his stern.[14]

I guessed from the strength of the radio signal that the audible fisherman was within twenty-five miles of our position, then from the rest of the one-sided conversation learned that a number of whales ("Musta been a dozen!") had been feeding on the same school of herring that had attracted the luckless Arne.

I stepped out on deck and looked to the west, calculating the amount of daylight remaining before the sun dropped behind the saw-toothed spine of Admiralty Island, then measured off the distance to our night's harbor on the chart. It was too late to pursue the lead today, but the conversation had given me a good idea which way to go tomorrow.

A RAGGED FORMATION of mew gulls skimmed past, flying low to the water and piping encouragement to each other as I hauled in

13. Such eavesdropping is not considered rude: to the contrary, most mariners monitor the radio at all times, in case an emergency occurs or a friend calls.
14. Trollers drag strings of lures from thin stainless-steel wires attached to an array of tall, limber poles. The wire is not strong enough to be a threat to a whale but is stout enough to allow a briefly entangled whale to snap one or more of an unfortunate fisherman's poles and deprive him of an expensive amount of gear.

the anchor line hand over hand. A cold dew had settled over the *Swift* during the small hours of the morning, and the predawn air felt good against my skin. Inside the cabin, a kettle shrieked to a boil. By the time I had the anchor line coiled and stowed in its locker, Michio was pouring coffee into a Thermos and was putting out bowls of cereal for a quick breakfast.

Rubbing his eyes, Otani came on deck to inspect the day's weather. Pink fingers of cloud streaked the eastern sky, and the windless surface of the cove was a green-and-black mirror that gave back the ragged skyline of the forest as a wavering, obsidian line. Humming a simple, diatonic tune, Otani stepped to the rail, dug himself out of his pants, and saluted the morning with a stream of water over the side. Inside the cabin I could see Yamanushi, Maeda, and Michio going through the intricate, wordless waltz of sleepy-eyed men waking up, stowing gear, and getting dressed in a small space.

I took the cup of coffee Michio handed me as I went back inside, glanced at the temperature and oil pressure gauges, and thumbed the power switch to the radar. A low band of fog hugged the water across the entrance to the bay, but the bands of high clouds and clear sky overhead promised that it would dissipate as the sun rose higher and warmed the air.

I laid the chart out flat on the table for the others to see. "I know the trollers are working the coast south of here at this time of year," I said, and fingered the map. Otani leaned in and looked where I was pointing, sipped from his cup, and nodded.

"That boat we were listening to last night was coming through pretty clear, so I figure he was somewhere in here." I pointed at Turn Island, where boats and ships crossing Frederick Sound must make a decision to alter course for Juneau to the north, Petersburg to the east, or the Tlingit village of Kake fifteen miles to the south.

"We'll work our way across to the island, then turn west and just keep looking until we find them."

There was no guarantee the herring or whales would still be

where they had been last night, but it was the best plan I could muster.

AT ELEVEN O'CLOCK I killed the engine, adjusted the focus of my binoculars, and began scanning the horizon. Michio plugged his ears with the headphones to his Walkman and hummed tunelessly to himself as he poked at the contents of a pot simmering on the stove.

The sea was flat as a platter and stippled here and there with congregations of birds. The water reflected the blue of the sky and the track of the sun burned a broad, bright line across its face.

Whales were scattered loosely around the arc of the horizon: one to the west, two or three a few miles to the north, another, widely separated pair off our stern. We had been in the middle of a wide-spread community of whales for over an hour but had seen no sign of cooperative feeding. Here and there in the blue distance the pale plume of a whale's breath burst suddenly into the air and lingered, dissipating slowly as the whale rested on the surface and hyperventilated in preparation for its next descent into the lightless, krill-rich zones below.

Michio stepped out of the cabin with a bowl of hot soup in each hand as I lowered the hydrophone over the side. "It's a long shot," I said in answer to his questioning look as I took one of the bowls. "But if we hear the sounds the whales make when they're hunting, we'll know we have a chance."

I closed my eyes and held the soup bowl beneath my nose, inhaling the rich toasted-sesame smell of rice broth seasoned with nori (dried seaweed) while I listened for the light, hissing static that can signal the presence of herring. The clicks and pops emitted by millions of tiny gills create a distinct underwater "signature" that can sometimes be heard for miles and—if we were lucky—might be accompanied by the baritone rumbles and high-pitched squeals of hunting whales.

The hydrophone chortled and whispered in the myriad voices of the ocean: a ratcheting whir—the voice of a porpoise using echolocation to feel its way through the depths; the hiss of strong currents stirring sand along the bottom; the innumerable tiny crackles and snaps that rise from hordes of crab, shrimp, bivalves, and unnameable bottom-crawling creatures; the rapid pulsing of a distant ship's propeller; and numerous odd, indecipherable sounds that added to the depth of mystery in the black world beneath the *Swift's* keel.

Michio listened to the squealing and burbling of the hydrophone with his eyes closed for a moment, slurped at his soup, then turned to me with a soft, absorbed smile.

"*Totemo ki-re,*" he said. *It's beautiful.*

The hydrophone emitted a single low chuckle that resonated and echoed like a noise in a cave. A faint, high ringing tone followed, wavering and climbing, piercing the world beneath the surface with what I recognized as the "stun song" of a whale. Prior to lunging into the massed bodies of a school of herring, a humpback will often emit a high-frequency cry such as the one we were hearing, a cry biologists say serves to stun the fish and makes them easier to capture. But to my ears, the cry seems to be something more, perhaps a scream of excitement, like the ecstatic blood-cry of a goshawk or the crying of a wolf pack on the trail of a moose—a frenzied ululation that serves as much to vent the enormous emotions of a predator awash in an ocean of prey as it does to simplify the act of hunting.

The song we were hearing was distant and weak, and sounded as if it were being sung somewhere beyond the rim of the world.

Otani peered around the horizon, shading his eyes with his hands and muttering as if to himself: "*Kore wa nan desuka?*"

Through the forced intimacy of a small boat, I had begun to grasp a phrase or two of simple Japanese, but I was not sure if he was asking *what* made the noise or *where* it came from, but my answer would do for either question:

"Kujira," I replied, and swept my hand across the horizon: *Humpback whale. It could be anywhere out there.* Sound travels faster and farther through water than through air, ricocheting and bending as it passes through thermoclines and salinity bands, reaching out across incredible distances. The hydrophone is omnidirectional and listens in a complete circle. The song could be coming from anywhere.

The thin, wavering voice of the stun song broke out again, tantalizing us with a single faraway trumpet note, then stopped. I hauled in the hydrophone, coiling the wet black cable into a bag, and stowed it away. The engine snapped to life at the touch of the key, and I motored in a small circle, trying to decide which way to go. The compass card spun like a roulette wheel under its glass cover, passing through all of the possible directions the feeding might lie. Falling tide, I thought to myself, imagining fish pouring down the river of the current into the waiting mouths of the whales—Go with the flow.

The ebb poured west from Turn Island as if the earth had been tipped on its edge, creating a stately rush of water that flowed downhill to the confines of Chatham Straits, where it bent south and ran for the gulf seventy miles away. In the distance the blue smudge of Cornwallis Point stood guard over Saginaw and Security Bays, which had once been the boundary of the territories shared by the Kake and Kuyu bands of the Tlingit.

Like all Tlingit, the Kake and their Kuiu Island neighbors were highly skilled seamen, taking to the sea in immense war canoes carved from the trunk of a single giant tree up to seventy feet long and capable of holding more than a hundred warriors to conduct piratical raids as far as a thousand miles away.

The reputation of the Kake and Kuyu Indians was particularly fierce, even among the other bands of Tlingit, and the whites settling and trading up and down the coast of the North Pacific recorded troubles with the them as far back as 1857, when a party of Kakes traveled to Puget Sound to take the head of Colonel Isaac Ebey as revenge for the death of two of their clansmen the year before when the U.S. Navy brought ashore a howitzer and Gatling gun to break up a debauchery of epic proportions.

The troubles, which came to be referred to as the Kake Wars, lasted more than ten years, and the clash between cultures escalated in 1868

when Brevet Major General Jefferson C. Davis took command of the
U.S. forces in the newly acquired Alaska Territories and imposed a
rigid new civil code intolerant of traditional Tlingit law. F. K. Louthan,
a trader with several years of experience dealing with the Tlingit and
their unforgiving, reactive civil code, described what followed next:

> Last New Year's eve a difficulty occurred at the market-house in
> Sitka, between a Chilkhat chief and a soldier, a sentinel, which
> resulted in the imprisonment in the guardhouse of the chief, and
> through some unaccountable manner the death by shooting, in a
> day or two afterward, of three indians. . . .
>
> Among the indians killed was one Chilkhat, one Kake, and one
> Sitka. The Kakes very promptly sought the usual remedy (com-
> pensation in blankets), but, failing to satisfy themselves, adopted
> their extreme remedy, "an eye for an eye, a tooth for a tooth";
> meeting two white men near their village, promptly dispatched
> them, [and] thereby lost all their village, burned by order of the
> general commanding.

General Davis also refused to meet with a delegation of Chilkhats
demanding payment for the death of their kinsman. Louthan paid the
indemnity himself in order to avoid further trouble and the disruption
of trade that would have followed. The price Louthan paid for peace
with the Chilkhats was three blankets.

The price the Kake and their Kuyu neighbors paid was much
higher. Captain L. A. Beardslee, the senior naval commander who
took over in Sitka after General Davis's reign, described the military's
side of the story in a report to Congress on the affairs of the territory:

> In January, 1869, they [the Kakes] murdered without provocation
> two white men named Ludwig Madger and William Walker, who
> were encamped for the night at a small cove [since named Mur-
> der Cove] near Point Gardner, the southwest point of Admiralty
> Island [in territory frequented by the Kake], and, after murdering

these men, mutilated the remains. For this offense they received prompt punishment, for on the 14th and 15th of January, Lieutenant-commander Meade, commanding the United States steamer *Saginaw,* burned and destroyed one town and three villages (thirty-five houses in all) and a number of their canoes, at Saginaw and Security Bays, Kou [Kuiu] Island [thus destroying the villages of the unoffending Kuyu, not the guilty Kakes].

An hour after leaving Turn Island, just below the bluffs where the log stockades and villages destroyed by Captain Meade moldered back into the forest, we spotted a circle of bubbles a half acre wide just as it erupted into a volcano of whales. A dozen huge black heads exploded simultaneously from the water, tight and violent as a rugby scrum, with flashing rivers of silver herring spilling from their cavernous mouths.

The whales gulped, gasped, thrashed, and rolled on the surface, bellies extended as they forced mouthfuls of water out through the layers of fibrous, mustachelike baleen that line the inside of the whale's toothless upper jaw and acts as a strainer, trapping krill and fish in its mouth. The whales circled, breathed deeply, and dove in close order, one after the other, spinning down into water that sparked and glittered with the scales of their victims.

The depth sounder mounted above my steering station glowed with electronic light, describing the scene fifty feet under our keel, where a large school of herring showed as a glowing, amorphous band of light and a solid, brighter line tracked the firm body of a whale as it passed directly beneath us, then moved out of range of the sounder.

Maeda shrugged into the video camera, bracing it on his shoulder and gripping it near the lens. Michio raced for his cameras. Seagulls spun piping and calling overhead, folding their wings and plunging headfirst into the sea in pursuit of herring crippled in the attack.

I turned the boat broadside and took it out of gear. With so many whales moving around us, I wanted to take no chance of one encountering a spinning propeller. Whales often feed in a pattern, moving methodically and rhythmically along a specific track governed by the line of the tide, the contours of the bottom, and other navigational factors known only to themselves. There was no need to try to second-guess them or pursue them too closely and risk interfering with their task. Telephoto lenses would bring the whales close enough. All I had to do was watch carefully to discern the pattern of their feeding, position the boat correctly, and let the pod come to us.

They cooperated wonderfully. Time after time the piercing note of the stun song vibrated through the hull of the *Swift,* alerting us of an upcoming eruption. The bubbles rose, breaking through the mirror of the surface as the pod encircled the doomed herring, and the slaughter went on for hours.

Michio loaded roll after roll of film, the motor drive of his camera whirring and clicking through frame after frame as he captured the consuming frenzy, the boiling rush, and the awesome physical presence of the whales.

The rhythm of the hunt settled into a continuous, powerful throb: the explosive surge followed by the lolling of great black bodies on the surface as the prey was consumed; the coordinated dive of the whales, one after the other, so close together they formed the immense, rolling coils of a serpent; the water swirling from the thrust of their powerful tails long after the last whale had disappeared beneath the surface; the silence moving in again, broken only by the calls of circling gulls waiting for the first bubble to rise; and the single, stinging note of the song to announce the imminence of the next rise of the whales.

After an hour of nonstop feeding, the whales dove a hundred yards away from the boat, the sea stilled, and it seemed the attacks must have stalled as minute after minute passed with no sign of their return.

"Doko wa kujira desuka?" Maeda muttered, camera to his shoulder. *Where are the whales?*

The answer came in the form of a shimmering puddle of air the size of a basketball that *ploomped* to the surface five feet from the bow. Another, then another, then another bubble appeared, curving in a line that paralleled the shape of the hull. The hunting whales had found a ball of herring directly under the *Swift*'s line of drift, and we were *inside* the bubble net. The hull began to ring with the shrill, electric piping of the stun song so sharply that the note transformed itself from an audible sensation into a tangible, tactile thing vibrating up through the soles of my boots.

I shouted "Hang on!" and dove for the wheel.

The engine screamed as I threw it into reverse and slammed the throttle wide open to back the boat out of the line of attack before a dozen speeding humpbacks could ram us and spill us into the water, where we would be crushed by the melee of flailing fins and forty-ton bodies that would follow.

The whales exploded to the surface a few feet off the bow, slathering a spray of fish breath and salt across the deck. I looked *up* at the black pyramid of a vertical whale's head towering above the boat and saw clearly the dark combs of baleen and the stiff pink board of its tongue inside the mouth before the enormous jaws slammed shut on a cubic meter of seawater and fish.

The boat rocked, slopping side to side in the maelstrom. A black pectoral fin studded with barnacles the size and texture of wild walnuts scraped along the hull, scratching the paint with a grating, tearing sound while the roar of fifty-gallon lungs boomed through the air. A fine, oily mist settled across the deck from the breath of the whales, coating everything in a frieze of warm, slippery droplets that stank of old herring and krill.

I counted my passengers—*four, no one knocked overboard*—and began to hope we had survived. Michio was crouched with his back to me, covering his cameras from the spray. Yamanushi was gripping Maeda, helping protect the video camera, and Otani stood spraddle-legged and braced at the rail.

"Is everybody okay?" I asked.

Michio straightened up, threw back his head and crowed: "That was *great!*"

THE WHALES BLEW, the herring died, and the sun looked down on it all for hours, until the whales' immense appetites were replete, the school of fish shattered, and we human observers limp from our part in the orgy. Near sunset the pod slowed, groaning over huge, distended bellies, broke into disorder, and began drifting apart, moving lethargically away into the cardinal directions. A slick of herring scales and oil floated on the surface of the water, glittering in the low red light of the sun.

The deck was littered with the wrappings of film. Maeda busied himself packing the video camera while Yamanushi labeled several reels of tape, but Michio remained in the bow of the boat, staring after the departing whales. As a broad fluke slid below the distant horizon, he took a deep breath, then lifted his camera in a slow salute. When he whispered a thank-you to the whale—*"Arigato, kujira. Arigato"*—I wanted to put my hand on his shoulder to show that I, too, was grateful for everything we had been given that day; instead, I busied myself with steering the *Swift* toward the night's harbor.

A half hour later the anchor chain rattled over the roller and disappeared into black water. The silhouette of the forest ringing Murder Cove formed a torn line against the last maroon in the sky as I reversed the engine and backed down, using the thrust of the propeller to drag the anchor slowly across the bottom until the flukes bit deep into the mud and secured us from drifting in the night.

On the beach a shadow detached itself from the black wall of the forest and wandered slowly into the tide zone. I thought of Madger and Walker, the traders murdered and mutilated in this anchorage by the revenge-seeking Kakes, and peered closer at the moving shadow, looking slightly to the side, using my night vision to catch the movement of darkness-within-darkness. A gnawing sound drifted across the obsidian water. The shadow was not a spirit roaming the site of a century-old murder, but a grizzly, peacefully foraging intertidal delicacies on the beach.

A pale green smear of light spread across the sky, took on the form and shape of a curtain, and began billowing and blowing as the aurora borealis danced in the solar winds. A small anchor light at the masthead of the boat scribed a slow, careful arc across the constellations as the current spun the *Swift* on her anchor and the tide pulled away, gathering its strength for tomorrow.

THE NEXT MORNING was crisp, with streamers of vapor rising from the surface of the water and a rim of new, golden light crowning the trees alongshore. Michio held the bowline as I slid the kayak over the side, then I steadied the boat while Michio climbed in and adjusted the fit of his life jacket. As I followed, a raven *klock-klocked* to the dawn from the forest.

"There." I pointed with my paddle to the tide flat at the head of the bay. "If we go ashore there, we can work our way along the beach and maybe spot a deer."

Sitka black-tail deer abound on Admiralty Island, and they, like humans, are sensualists, often making their way to the beach at first light to shake off the chill damp of the forest in the growing warmth of sunrise. The light would soon be perfect for a shot or two if we could find one.

Michio nodded, stroked twice with his paddle to turn the kayak toward the spot at which I was pointing, and blew a stream of vapor into the cool air with his breath. "Getting colder now."

"Yep," I replied. "Trip's almost over, Michio. Summer, too."

He made a humming sound of agreement, then dug in with his paddle. The kayak split the surface of the cove into a widening V behind us, and the light, trickling sound of water under its bow played a gurgling music.

I kicked the rudder to port as we edged up to the rocky beach, turning the kayak sideways. Michio reached out with his paddle, pulled us broadside into shallow water, then braced us as I stepped over the side, crunching a carpet of barnacles and mussels under my boot.

Michio gripped the bow, I lifted the stern. The weight of the kayak staggered us as we made our way across the mudflats and algae-slicked rocks to the edge of the forest. We planned to be ashore for only an hour or so, but in a land of twenty-foot tides it is *always* prudent to tie your kayak to a tree, in case anything delays a return. On

Admiralty, that might be caused by something as simple and common as a brown bear deciding to linger over a patch of grass between us and the kayak, and more than one paddler has stood by watching helplessly as an inflooding tide lifted and stole away his or her boat while a grizzly kept them at bay.

Snubbing off the bowline with a clove hitch around an alder branch, I motioned to Michio to stow the paddles and life jackets inside.

"Light's good," he said, hanging a camera around his neck by a strap. I double-checked a can of pepper spray I carry strapped to the hip belt of my pack. The burning oil of capsicum pepper will usually divert a grizzly from an aggressive or overly curious approach, although the range of the repellent is limited to a nerve-wrackingly close fifteen or twenty feet. But the bears of Admiralty Island are markedly less aggressive than those of the interior or even nearby Chichagof and Baranof Islands, and the small can of pepper spray seemed a reasonable trade-off for the bulk and weight of a rifle, burdened as we were with cameras, tripods, and packs.

We grunted into our packs, hunching our shoulders to settle the straps, and headed down the beach. I patted my breast pocket to check for the small folding binoculars I carry there and pulled at the bill of my cap to shade my eyes from the sun peeking over the trees.

Michio stepped up onto a drift log and teetered its length before hopping back to the ground, then waved a hand across the cove and beach before us. "This was all under glaciers, too, Lynn?"

"Yeah," I replied. "I think everything on this end of the island was covered, except for the peaks." I pointed out the U-shape of the valley stretching back from the head of the cove. "That usually means the watershed was carved by a glacier," I continued, "but I think farther north, up by Angoon, wasn't covered."

Michio stopped and pointed out a bear track pressed into the sand at the base of the drift log. "Not too old," he said. "Maybe since high tide?"

I agreed. The edges of the track were sharp and well defined. Tidewater would have rounded the sandy edges, and since the tides in Southeast are diurnal, rising and falling twice every day, the track couldn't have been more than six hours old. Perhaps, I said, it had been made by the bear I heard foraging on the beach the evening before as it returned in the early hours of the morning.

Michio nodded, then leaned on his folded tripod and was silent. When he spoke again, it was in the even, considered tone of someone who had been pondering a question for a while and finally come to the right time to ask it.

"Lynn, have you ever seen a glacier bear?"

His English was fair—and getting better fast—but it still sounded like a new word when he said *graysha beah.*

I wasn't even sure what a glacier bear was. Rumors of the blue bear's existence had drifted lightly through the atmosphere of my youth in various forms: a passing reference in a tattered back issue of old hunting magazines; a friend of my father's relaying a third- or fourthhand story; a hoary hide, dusty and brittle with age, on the wall of one of the dank café-saloons that gave Anchorage's Fourth Avenue its ratty character in the 1960s and '70s before a flood of oil money brought the city an urban facelift and transformed the pawnshops and dry goods stores into performing arts centers and sky malls. In the decades since, I had never really given the blue bear any thought. I knew they existed, but actually seeing one in the wild seemed about as likely as coming across a snow leopard or yeti.

"Well, it's not really the sort of thing you can expect to see, Michio."

Michio's laugh took me by surprise. His shoulders shook, and an unrestrained jiggling spread to his belly. I started laughing along, too.

"What? What's so funny?" I asked.

Michio resettled his hat on his head, gave one more laugh, then rearranged the tripod in his arms before answering.

"Well, maybe . . . you have to *rook.*"

I WAVED GOOD-BYE to the crew three days later. Michio and the others were flying out soon, bound for more filming locations around the state, and I was in a rush to see them off. The month had passed quickly and enjoyably, but I had a long list of impending charters to organize, paperwork to see to, repairs to be made, and supplies to buy before I could leave port again. I had enjoyed the new experience of film and photography, but it was time to get on to the kayakers, climbers, and research scientists that were waiting for me to return their calls.

The guiding business is one of brief, vigorous relationships intensified by the power of beauty and shared danger, friendships that at the time seem too powerful and intimate to ever dim. But this is an illusion, and one of the first things I learned after becoming a guide was that I would probably never see most of these great friends again. I quickly made a habit of letting go, sometimes even to the point of forgetting names and faces within a few weeks. It came naturally, this habit of rapid disconnection, and looking back, I see that I had unconsciously chosen the ideal profession for someone like myself, someone who preferred to keep much of himself in reserve.

As he walked up the dock, Michio slung his camera pack over one shoulder and turned to give me a final wave.

"Remember, Lynn-san. You have to *rook* for the glacier bear!"

It was late August. The reds and yellows of autumn were beginning to blush the alpine above Juneau, and flocks of red-necked phalaropes were pouring south in synchronized swarms that rose and fell like ribbons in the wind. The season was already changing. Winter was coming.

4 ⟫ Refugia

IN SEPTEMBER the wind rose and disrobed the cottonwood trees. Autumn exhausted itself in a series of southwesterly gales that drove sheets of biting rain headlong and sideways across the harbor. When October came, I doubled up on the *Swift*'s mooring lines in preparation for winter, then watched as November roared by in a wild flurry of snow.

It was December, deep into the darkness of winter, when the sun never glimmers above the southern horizon until nearly 10:00 A.M., falls behind the western mountains before 3:00, and is weak and unconvincing in between. I had the carburetor from an outboard motor dismantled into a mysterious pile of springs and tiny screws on the galley table in an effort to stave off cabin fever when the phone rang. It had taken several tries to get a flashlight propped against a book at just the right angle to peer into the bowl of the carburetor, and I was afraid to reach for the phone lest I knock the arrangement sprawling. But in winter my telephone sits dumb many more days

than it rings, and the mystery of who was calling was more appealing
than that of why a damned outboard motor wouldn't idle.

The phone crackled, emitting a raucous medley of clicks and static
before Michio's unmistakable, slightly breathless voice came over the
line. It was the first we'd spoken since we waved good-bye in August,
and although I certainly hoped to see and work with Michio again, I
didn't expect it. I was genuinely delighted to hear from him, but I was
also surprised and not a little curious. He hadn't mentioned a job,
didn't seem to want to hire me. What could he want? I asked how his
photographs from our trip had turned out.

"Pretty good," he said emphatically. There was a long pause, and I
was waiting for him to ask me if I was free for another charter next summer when he asked me a question that seemed to come from left field.

"Lynn, what is connection between whales and old-growth forest?"

I paused. I was used to being asked about the details of wilderness
travel or the cost of a charter, things I could answer without any consideration, but Michio (as I was beginning to realize was his habit) was
asking a question that required some real thinking. I puffed out my
cheeks, blowing away the mental clutter of needle valves and venturis,
and shifted gears into biochemistry.

"Do you know about isotopes, Michio?"

"Yes?"

I explained as simply as possible (because that's how I understood
it) that certain elements of phosphorus and nitrogen from the ocean
are marked with a signature of marine origin.

"And marine isotopes are distinctly different from those originat-
ing on land and the difference is stable. It lasts for thousands of years."

I was winging it now, feeling my way through an explanation that
I comprehended only poorly and grasped more intuitively than
through any real understanding of the science involved.

"All the little things the herring feed on in the ocean—the plankton and krill and copepods, stuff like that—contain this marine nitrogen and phosphorus, and as the herring feed, they absorb the isotopes

into their bodies. Then salmon eat the herring, absorb the isotopes themselves, and head up the rivers to spawn."

As I talked, I imagined tens of millions of salmon hurling the ripe fruit of their bodies upstream and a horde of bears, eagles, wolves, gulls, mink, ravens, mice, ermine, and voles slipping down to the banks of the rivers to feed on the meat of their carcasses. Even deer have been known to nibble on dead fish, and I had once seen a goose pecking at the remains of a chum salmon a black bear had dragged into the grass and abandoned.

"When a bear stuffs itself until it can't eat another bite, then wanders back into the woods and takes a shit, it's leaving some of the isotopes in the underbrush. Nitrogen and phosphorus are critical to photosynthesis, so when an eagle carries a scrap of fish back to the nest to feed its young and drops part of it, it becomes fertilizer for the forest."

Michio hummed in appreciation as I explained how capillary action then carries the nitrogen and phosphorus into the trees through their roots as nutrients and it becomes part of the cellular structure of the wood. Blueberries and skunk cabbage on the forest floor ingest the isotopes, too, and feed them to deer, who in turn carry the elements farther from the sea before depositing them in a new location.

"It must have taken hundreds or thousands of years for the marine isotopes to work their way through the system and move inland, but they've been found in trees miles and miles from the nearest salmon river." I paused for a minute, mentally tracking the continuing migration of the salmon as minute particles of their bodies traveled inland for centuries, in a sense transforming a fish into a land animal. "Isotopes have even been found in the wood of ancient totem poles, Michio."

Michio quickly brought me back to sea level. "And the whales, Lynn? How does the forest become part of a whale?"

I fiddled for a moment, mentally tripping over windfalls in the forest and wandering through the mountains until I stumbled on an isotope trail back to the coast.

"Someday the tree falls and rots, the isotopes become part of the nutrients washing into the rivers, and"—here I mentally dusted my hands—"eventually the isotopes flow downstream through the watershed and back out to sea, where they help nourish the next generation of plankton." From there it was simple: herring eat the plankton and whales eat the herring, and the isotope cycle is closed.

The telephone hissed, silenced by the complicity of fish, mammals, and forests whirling in a long, slow Möbius strip through the centuries. Was Michio in Japan or his Alaskan home in Fairbanks? I started to ask why he was interested in the forest-whale connection, presuming he was working on another book or magazine article, but he beat me to the punch, distracting me with another seemingly out-of-place question.

"Have you seen any glacier bear yet?"

"No, Michio, no glacier bears yet."

"Keep looking!"

There was a tiny spring left over after I reassembled the carburetor. My mind had wandered, slipping off to follow a glacier bear along a salmon stream through the forest while I worked. I held the slender coil in my hand, trying to imagine its function among the bowls, needles, jets, and floats, wondering where it should go.

And why, I kept asking myself, did Michio call with those questions? What was it he really wanted to know?

TWO WEEKS LATER a package came in the mail, a hard, flat box containing a newly published book of Michio's photos. No note, no letter, just page after page of beautiful photos without captions or explanations, artfully printed from edge to edge of the page. The images captured both delicately and boldly more of the wild beauty of Alaska than any I had ever seen. Turning the pages was like falling into the silence of broad Arctic landscapes, feeling the breeze flowing over steep mountains while a herd of white Dall's sheep grazed nearby, or waking up to a scarlet-torn sunrise over a valley of yellow willows and green alder. He caught the backlit breath of a whale and the ground-eating stride of a grizzly so perfectly that to see the photograph was like being there and hearing the click of his shutter.

When spring arrived I scrubbed the winter's accumulation of grime from the boat, loaded the hold and lockers with supplies for the season, and bought a new secondhand camera. Michio came back to Juneau in the middle of July for another two weeks of whales, bringing with him two more professional photographers.[15] At first it was a struggle to shed my hermit-crab ways and learn to share the *Swift*'s small cabin with others, but I surprised myself by enjoying the company and soon developed an amiable companionship with several of the photographers I met through him.

Everyone had stories to tell about Michio—how he got off a bush plane in the middle of the Arctic without a tent, extra clothing, or sufficient supplies; or the time he went into the forest in the dark, hoping to take flash photographs of rut-crazed bull moose in the full heat of battle—and succeeded; how swollen his hands and face were when he emerged from a blind erected near an owl's nest because he had neglected to bring insect repellent but refused to disturb the bird or her chicks by letting the mosquitoes drive him out into the open.

The general consensus was that Michio's continued survival proved the existence of guardian angels, and it was agreed all around that nobody was more deserving of their protection. I heard stories of how he gave away his coat to a street person in Sitka, got teary eyed watching sentimental movies, and made friends with everyone he met. His consideration and affinity for other people was almost lumi-

15. The business of wildlife photography can be fiercely competitive, with information about great locations, good guides, secret methods, and original ideas for images all being jealously guarded, but I never saw any sign of such possessiveness in Michio. (I once heard him carefully explain to a less talented photographer how a small reflection of light from an animal's eye can create a subtle but powerful emotional connection between a person and a picture, even though earlier in the day that same photographer had refused to tell Michio something as simple as what speed of film had been used for one of his better-known pictures.) Michio willingly shared whatever he had, and as a result, my business picked up rapidly as he referred my services to more and more of his friends in the film and photography world.

nous, they said, whether that person was an ex-governor, the head of a world-class museum, or an old Eskimo woman parting out a salmon on the bank of a muddy river.

Kim Heacox is a lean, bespectacled photographer with a great gift for humor who worked for more than a decade as a ranger in Alaska's national parks. When I called him up a few days ago and asked him to describe his first meeting with Michio—which took place in 1979, when he was stationed in Glacier Bay National Park and Michio was a neophyte photographer who barely spoke English and bowed to everyone he met—I could hear the bemusement in his voice.

"Richard Steele met him first," said Kim, referring to a bluff, square-shouldered ranger who has a heart the size of a pumpkin. "Found him camped on the beach down in Bartlett Cove, near park headquarters."

By carefully deciphering Michio's broken English, Richard learned that Michio had been kayaking "up bay" for so long that he had run out of food and was hungry. *Very* hungry.

"So Richard brought Michio a huge, heaping plate of food." Kim laughed. "And he *inhaled* it. Really got it down in record time."

Richard, being a hospitable fellow, promptly fetched another heaping plate and presented it to the bedraggled photographer.

"Michio had that Japanese sense of courtesy and thought it would be rude to refuse the food or leave any on the plate, so he polished off the second meal as well. 'Course Steele doesn't know anything about Japanese courtesy. He's just amazed at the huge appetite this little fellow has, so he fills up his plate *again,*" said Kim, laughing. "Nearly put the poor guy in the hospital. He was too polite to say no thanks, and just kept eating and eating!"

Throughout that year, at unexpected moments, my phone would ring and Michio would be there asking how old is the ice in glaciers or did eagles use the same nest every year? Sometimes he called just to tell me about something remarkable he had seen—a particularly wild display of the aurora borealis or an unseasonably early snowfall.

And once in a while he would ask me again (half joking or half serious, it was getting hard to tell): "See any glacier bear yet?"

Of course it was obvious to me that the glacier bear—or at least the *idea* if it—fascinated Michio, and his interest was gradually beginning to stoke my own as well. In response to his gentle, persistent broaching of the walls I kept up around me came a sort of half-formed impulse to help in his search, and I began questioning people I thought might know something about the blue bear, only to come away with nothing more than rumors and watery third- and fourth-hand accounts.

But one afternoon in the Triangle Bar—a smoky chili-dog-and-beer kind of joint that sits square in the middle of downtown Juneau like a rock in a river, providing a back eddy of calm amid the flash flood of tourists that washes over the city each year—I asked a new acquaintance, who said she was working on salmon-enhancement projects around Southeast, if she had ever seen a glacier bear in her travels.

"No," she said, taking a sip of her beer. "I'm mostly out on Chichagof or Baranof Island in the summers. Nothing but grizzlies out there." Beth had great cheekbones and the dazzling whiteness of her teeth was accentuated by a field-season tan. "But I hear Yakutat's probably your best shot for glacier bears," she said casually, licking a bead of foam from her upper lip with a flick of her tongue.

Three seats down a bullet-headed fellow in faded red suspenders turned and eyed me. The suspenders held up high-water britches of the kind favored by loggers, cropped several inches above the ankle to stay out of the mud, and rose to a pair of shoulders like the withers of a bull. The stubbled pelt of his scalp faded out before reaching a row of deep ripples up the back of his neck and he was clean shaven except for a tiny patch of hair below his lower lip that twitched as he chewed on some uncharitable thought. He was staring at me in a way that reminded me rather unsettlingly of the last grizzly I'd seen, face-to-face in a dense patch of alder.

"But I might get to work up the Taku River next year." Beth reached for a napkin to wipe a ring of beer from the bar top. A glimpse of a smooth, deeply tanned belly flashed below her T-shirt. "More black bears up there. Wolves, too."

She folded the napkin and dabbed at a spot on her shoulder. I glanced at the bull and looked straight into a pair of little staring eyes that were not distracted by the bounce of my companion's curves as she arched her back to work at some invisible stain near her clavicle.

Shit. I'd seen this sort of thing too many times before, during the fishing-and-fighting years of my twenties, when a long, hard stare in one of the sleazy bars of Seward or Kodiak had meant trouble was brewing. I might be leaving before I finish this beer.

"Have you?" asked Beth.

I missed the question. Caught between Beth's buttery musk and the fight-or-flight buzz starting to bubble in my veins, my brain was going into a spin cycle and had whirled out of whatever conversation we were having. "Have I what?"

She eyed me sideways for a moment, then flicked a tight smile at her own reflection in the mirror behind the bar. She was used to having that effect on men. "Seen a glacier bear."

The logger stared harder. I shook my head as I hunched lower over my drink and fumbled an answer: "Yakutat. Sure, that'd be the place, I guess."

Outside, a tour bus slowed to a crawl and a woman in a brassy hairdo and a cheap plastic raincoat pointed a video camera at the window of the bar. For a long moment I imagined her showing her friends back in Indiana or Florida or wherever she came from a video of the burly logger kicking me up and down the gutter outside the bar—the picture jiggles as the camera zooms in to follow the action, the voice-over shrieking, "He's kicking his *butt!*"

That was enough for me. I straightened up and pushed my drink away. "Let's take off, okay?"

"Hold on." Beth picked up her half-full glass and wagged it. "I'd like to finish this."

The grizzly shifted on his stool, turning sideways to the bar and facing me. Tattoos like old bruises blurred and faded into the skin of his forearms. I could feel trouble coming. He was between me and the door.

"Dammit," I muttered. Beth drew back offended. I tried a smile, but was quivering inside, and the look she gave me was practically audible. *What a jerk.*

I got to my feet. "Look, Beth," I stammered. "I'm sorry. I've really got to go." As I went by the logger, I tried to step wide, but he held out a mitt the size of a butterball turkey to stop me. I froze.

" 'Scuse me." His voice was surprisingly soft.

The courtesy stopped me dead. I tried for an open look on my face, but my voice rang an octave or two higher than usual. "Yes?"

"I heard you talkin' and was wonderin' "—his tongue worked a lump along his jaw—"you seen one of them bears?"

"Bears?" I moved one step toward the door. Little flecks of tobacco snuff browned the corner of his mouth.

"Them glacier bears? A blue bear?"

Trophy hunter. Wants a blue bear hide for his wall. "Nope," I drawled, trying for a folksy-but-distant tone. "Never seen one."

He looked out the window as I edged away. Across the street a wino was harassing a pair of studiously deaf and blind tourists, but the logger's eyes seemed focused a thousand miles beyond.

"Now *that's* a beautiful animal," he finally said.

I was wrong, completely wrong. His stares had not been hostile, or his posture threatening. He was just hitchhiking on my conversation with Beth, who was already swapping smiles with a fisherman moving in to take my place. And I knew, just as surely as I knew I had mistaken his intentions, that he was seeing a glacier bear outside the window, and that the vision was a replay of something he had really seen.

"Did you see one?" I was overeager and stepped in too close. "Where'd you see it?" He jerked back from whatever meadow or beach he was seeing in his head and squinted at me with suspicion.

"Dint say I did."

"But you did, didn't you? You said it was beautiful."

He turned sideways to me and rested his forearms on the bar, then took a slug from a can of beer. "I ain't saying if I did or not. Just said it's a beautiful animal."

I backed up an inch, trying to put him at ease. "You working in the woods around here?" Putting a little good ole boy in it, asking what logging camp he was from.

He looked me up and down, taking in my Patagonia jacket and hundred-dollar running shoes, then sniffed at the dim-witted question. A hardworking wool-jacket man, he saw through my condescension immediately, knew I was just trying to narrow down the range in case he decided not to tell me where he had seen the bear. I decided to come clean.

"Look, I just want to see one, or my friend does. I'm a guide. And I've got a photographer friend who would really like to see one, too." It was tumbling out clumsily, I was trying to condense everything into a burst of short sentences. "You know, get some pictures."

He listened, but he was listening from behind a closed door. He drained his beer and dimpled the can with his thumb, then held up a hand to stop me. "Look, maybe you're okay and maybe your friend is okay. But I tell you and you tell somebody and then they tell somebody else. Next thing you know, the bear's dead.

"No," he said, shaking his head and brushing a hand across his stubbled scalp. "I better just keep it to myself."

Screwed that up. Pegged the guy all wrong, I told myself as I stood outside on the curb a few moments later. If it was Michio, the guy'd be drawing him a map right now, like the drunk in Angoon.

Through the window I could see Beth laughing at something the fisherman was saying. The logger had drifted off deeper into the bar's interior.

My people skills haven't improved much since then; I'm still clumsy when it comes to those types of connections. But I had seen the faraway look in the logger's eye, the gleam when he was talking about the blue bear, and that, combined with Michio's subtle, insistent fascination, was enough. I was hooked.

And if I want to find a blue bear, I told myself, I better start looking in earnest.

I THOUGHT I KNEW a lot about bears. I'd been fascinated by them since 1970, when I was sixteen years old and the first grizzly I ever saw came hulking up over a ridgeline less than a hundred yards away. I had foolishly pitched my tent beside a well-traveled game trail and the bear moved straight toward me at a smooth, rapid pace, gave me a dismissive glance as it passed by a few feet away, then studiously ignored me until disappearing around a bend in the trail. The sudden appearance and disappearance of the extravagantly muscled animal shot a jolt of adrenaline into my veins that branded me with a sense of awe that remains to this day.

I spent the ensuing years vacuuming bear stories and anecdotes from magazines and books. Some were respectable tracts by biologists like Frank Dufresne and Ernest Thompson Seton; others were more hyperbolic, full of "gut-crunching terror" and featured bears as ravening fiends, ready to pounce on any human foolish enough to wander into the woods armed with anything less than a high-powered .375 Holland & Holland rifle.

Before long I could recite reams of statistics and figures—the average weight of a coastal grizzly is five hundred pounds, with rare giants to nine hundred (black bears a quarter to a third of that); a bear's life span might reach fifteen years, but the average is considerably less; sows, or females, are slow reproducers, seldom reaching sexual maturity until six to eight years old, and thereafter producing offspring only every three to five years, after which the cubs stay with their mother until their third year.

I collected apothegms, nuggets of conventional wisdom—*a running bear can reach speeds of up to thirty-five miles per hour, as fast as a galloping horse; sows with cubs are the most dangerous*—that later proved to be inadequate or even untrue. (A better comparison than the speed of a horse might be that of a cat, which can move more quickly, with perfect balance, in a multitude of directions; and it has been my experience that sows with cubs are generally much *less* aggressive than other bears, their primary focus always being the safety and survival of their offspring, which is best insured by removing them from a threat—fleeing—rather than attacking, except under extraordinary circumstances. The threat, however, can be seen as a question of degree: sows do hurt humans while protecting their cubs. One small village near Juneau had two people—one a high school student hiking less than a mile from his school and the other a surveyor working in the timber—mauled on separate occasions in 1998 alone. And my friend Nick Jans asserts that fully 70 percent of all grizzly attacks are by sows protecting cubs.)

But all of the figures and all of the facts did no more to create an accurate portrait of the species than the data found on a driver's license does to define the human who holds it. Height, weight, color of hair—all of this says nothing about personality, quirks, insecurities, or desires. It was by observing the subtle differences between individual bears from widely different habitats (such as bears living amid the abundant food sources of the lush coastal rainforests, where population densities reach ten to fifteen times that of the sparse Arctic plains, being considerably less aggressive than their smaller inland cousins, who must roam hundreds of miles every summer to stay fed) that I began to form my own idea of a species in which each individual seems perfectly adapted to its own time, environment, and place.

When I remember the fluid strength of that first bear's stride as it came down the ridge toward me, it is easy to understand why the Tlingit revered the bear above all other animals and addressed the animal with the same respect used to greet a human elder. "Grandfather," they would say upon meeting a bear on a trail. "We are just going this way on business. We don't mean to bother you." You better believe it.

A hunter was required to show his respect for bears by performing purification rituals such as fasting for four days, bathing in cold water, and smearing red ocher on his skin before setting out in search of his quarry. If a hunt was successful, a special song was sung in the bear's honor, and plumes of eagle down were placed on its head.

The Tlingit revered bears not just because of their tremendous strength, but because in early times people and bears were said to have been closely connected and sometimes intermarried. The bears also shared their knowledge of natural medicine with the People, teaching them how to rub the rotten wood of a spruce tree on a rough stone, mix the powder with a little water or oil, and use the concoction as a poultice for various ailments.

Certain parts of the bear's body were known to have curative powers as well—nothing worked better than bear gall to heal the spear wounds and sword cuts of battle, and a shaman who possessed the spirit of a bear in his *shutch*[16] need have no fear of fire and could walk barefoot over live, glowing coals.

These were all things that I knew in addition to what I had learned about the bears' day-to-day lives by living with them as my neighbors for more than twenty years. It wasn't until I heard what a biologist examining the DNA of Alaska's bears had discovered that I realized how little I—or anyone else, for that matter—really knew about them.

Admiralty, Baranof, and Chichagof Islands are often referred to in land management circles as the "ABC" Islands. They are among the largest islands in North America and have the highest density of brown bears in the world.[17] The three islands lie edge to edge west of Juneau and are separated from each other by narrow channels of salt water. Admiralty, the longest of the three, is snuggled between the other two and the mainland. Glacier Bay lies north of all three.

Twenty thousand years ago the world's climate entered a period of drastic cooling, and the ice that shaped Glacier Bay spread far to the south, blanketing North America under a frozen mantle that spanned the continent from Puget Sound to Long Island. As the glaciers expanded, they were occasionally diverted from their wandering courses

16. A bundle of twigs worn about the neck upon which the blood of a bear's tongue had been dripped.
17. Taxonomic hair-splitting in the early 1900s determined as many as eighty-seven separate species and subspecies of grizzly and arctic brown bear in North America alone. Most scientists today, however, classify *all* brown bears and grizzlies as a single species— *Ursus arctos*.

by the mountainous upthrust of the Coast Range, leaving ice-free pockets called *refugia* at random intervals along the shoreline of Alaska and British Columbia. Geological studies and archaeological excavations have shown that a large portion of the ABC Islands was spared inundation (as were some of the smaller islands to the south) and that these pockets of refuge sheltered the now-extinct short-faced bear and its relative, the giant cave bear.

After a few shivering millennia, the continent began to warm up again and the Ice Age entered remission, peeling its icy blanket back from the mainland and leaving in its wake a lifeless void that was slowly repopulated by animals moving in from the south. Simultaneously, the glaciers quilting the coastal archipelago wasted away, and the inhabitants of the scattered refugia were once again allowed to roam among the islands.

After the Ice Age passed, the ABC Islands and the mainland were left separated only by waterways narrow enough to be an easy swim for a grizzly, but a comparison of genetic material taken from the island bears and the grizzlies of the mainland shows a remarkable distinction between the two populations: according to the bears' DNA blueprints, an ABC bear has more in common with a polar bear living far to the north in the Arctic than it does with one of its cousins on the mainland only a few miles away.

As a layman, I am puzzled by how this happened. After the ice retreated, did some ancient relative of the coastal brown bear wander north from the refugia, traveling up the newly naked coast to evolve into the polar bear? Did the grizzly of the mainland rise from another species coming up from the plains of the American desert or Mexico? How is it that both are the same species? What tool of alopatric speciation, simultaneous coevolution, or other double-barreled mouthful of science was employed? As is so often the case with science and biology, the discovery of the grizzly's diverse genetic history served better to point out how little we really know about the species than it did to broaden our understanding.

The blue bear, like the ABC bears, exists only along the portion of the coast that was once stippled with refugia, and I can't help wondering if there isn't an equally remarkable puzzle twisted into its genes. Unfortunately, research budgets are in serious decline these days and we are left with nothing but unlearned speculation.

I am no scientist. I allow myself the influence of notions and hunches, things I cannot see or prove with raw data. If anyone had asked, I could not have explained why the glacier bear's existence seemed to imply something more profound than simple genetics or why the animal was becoming so important to me. Perhaps it was nothing more than the desire to present a friend with a rare photo opportunity, as a way of saying thanks for worming his way through the fence I had been hiding behind for years. One way or another, I told myself, I was determined to find a blue bear. And when I did, I wanted Michio to take its picture.

When winter came, I dug in at the library, peeling through fragile, crumbling back issues of *The Alaska Sportsman* magazine for an occasional slim reference to a blue bear taken by a hunter. I read through stacks of books on bears in Alaska, then called government wildlife agencies and asked for copies of relevant reports. I talked to biologists, gossiped with hunters, pestered conservationists, telephoned rangers, and bothered other guides. I rolled a map of the glacier coast out on the galley table and drew in what I knew of the bear's history, marking down the rumors with small, penciled circles. Definite sightings got a five-pointed star.

The earliest reference was dated 1877. Charles Erskine Scott Wood was a poet, a writer, a painter, and a lawyer. He was also a military man and came to Alaska with the rank of lieutenant after having served as aide-de-camp to General Howard during the Nez Perce campaign. Lieutenant Wood could rightly be credited with discovering Glacier Bay, being the first white man by several years to explore that part of the country, but he had no interest in glory and never bothered to lay the claim.

Wood's interests lay in climbing mountains and observing the ways of the Tlingit, a number of whom he hired as guides to assist him in his travels. After an expedition to climb Mount Saint Elias stumbled and ground to a halt,[18] Wood joined a band of Hoonah Tlingit on a goat-hunting expedition into what he called the Fairweather Alps. There, he wrote:

> We found a bear that, so far as I know, is peculiar to this country. It is a beautiful bluish under color, with the tips of the long hairs silvery white. The traders call it "Saint Elias' bear" [and] the skins are not common.

It was nearly twenty years before another sighting of the blue bear was recorded. George Thornton Emmons was also a military man detailed to Alaska as a lieutenant in the navy, and he shared Wood's passion for the Tlingit and their culture. Unlike Wood, however, Emmons was dogged throughout his military career by poor health and a captious attitude toward authority. After a number of unproductive years, the navy deemed it best to release Emmons from his commission and reassign him to special duty as a collector and ethnological observer with the American Museum of Natural History.

Emmons proved to be obsessively acquisitive, gleaning shipload after shipload of artifacts and artwork from the Tlingit, Tsimshian, and Haida. He traveled ceaselessly in pursuit of carved cedar hats, Chilkhat blankets, objects of everyday life, and even entire war canoes. During his travels he made copious notes on his observations of Alaska Native hunting and fishing methods and how the various parts of the animals were used.

In his 1896 *Game Diary,* Emmons noted the presence of what was apparently a new subspecies of bear in the area, an animal called *klate-utardy tseek,* or the "snow-like black bear" by the Tlingits, who believed it to be the result of a union between the common black bear

18. Wood's Tlingit guides took him by canoe as far as Cape Spencer, then declined to go any farther, pointing at nearby Mount Fairweather and insisting with exquisite logic that "one mountain is as good as another. There is a very big mountain. Climb that one. . . ."

and a mountain goat. Emmons was so taken by the glacier bear's silvery beauty that he named it after himself, and for decades the glacier bear was catalogued as *Ursus americanus emmonsii*.

After that, the trail grew exceedingly cold. A prospector's letter written in 1898 told how he was saved from starvation along the outer coast by shooting a "snow bear," but for more than sixty years the blue bear left no other sign of its passing. Two adults and a cub were "collected" for exhibit at the Denver Museum of Natural History, but no one seemed to know when, or where, or by whom.

In 1972 a blue bear began appearing regularly near a housing compound at the Coast Guard base in Yakutat. Jim Jensen, Sr., a technician at the base, and his wife, Roxanne, became concerned for the bear's safety because it showed little fear of humans and the autumn hunting season was about to begin. Jim and Roxanne made a series of phone calls that set in motion a massive effort to save the rare bear, and before it was finally captured and sent to a newly built grotto at the San Diego Zoo, Operation Blue Bear had enlisted the services of the navy, the U.S. Coast Guard, the Air National Guard, the Federal Aviation Administration, the Alaska Department of Fish and Game, and numerous Yakutat residents.

Beth had been correct when she sat there in the Triangle Bar and said Yakutat was the epicenter of the glacier bear's world. On my chart, Yakutat was dotted with the circles of rumor, and it was the only place with a cluster of five-pointed stars.

It was a limited picture, however, because the only official effort ever made to enumerate the population of glacier bears across its entire coastal range was centered in Yakutat in the mid-1970s. Department of Fish and Game biologists Bob Wood and Dave Johnson flew a small airplane over the area for several days, tracking slowly back and forth at low altitude, ticking off the number of bears spotted below. When I asked wildlife biologist Bruce Dinneford about the survey, he told me Wood and Johnson "saw a hundred or so bears, something like that, and only one of them was a glacier bear," but he emphasized that the survey was not very scientific because of the glacier bear's coloring. "A black bear can really stand out, but the glacier bear is so well camouflaged in that environment that it could be nearly impossible to see."

Some of the black bears counted by Wood and Johnson in the survey might have been included more than once by appearing on successive days in different locations, and it is possible a glacier bear could easily be missed. Nonetheless, the data the two biologists gathered was all that existed, and by extrapolation, the population of glacier bears across its entire five-hundred-mile range was estimated to be as low as one hundred. And Bruce, who'd worked in the Yakutat area for years, stated matter-of-factly that he'd never seen a glacier bear in the wild, although he had often seen the more common black and grizzly bears while flying mountain-goat surveys.

There it is, I told myself. Even professional wildlife biologists have a hard time finding a glacier bear in the area that is supposed to have the most.

Still, Yakutat was definitely the best hope for finding a blue bear. But the cost of mounting an expedition there would be prohibitively expensive, and the odds of success were atrociously bad. I folded the starred and circled chart, slipped it under the mattress of the upper bunk, and went to work getting ready for spring.

SERENDIPITY RUNS RAMPANT in the world, aligning the unlikely, organizing the impossible, and making pipe dreams come true. It was March the next time I heard from Michio and the ground was naked and thawing. The days were growing rapidly longer, but the slopes above town were still mantled in a thick, heavy blanket of snow.

Michio was again taking part in a film about Alaska, he said, this time for NHK, Japan's public television broadcasting company. The theme of the film translated rather awkwardly into "Ice makes Alaska rich," and Shin-ichi Murata, the producer, intended to follow spring as it swept north across the state.

"Can you go to Yakutat in April?" Michio asked. "We are going to Russell Fjord to film the glacier and want you to come."

I knew which glacier he meant. Hubbard Glacier is one of the world's largest tidewater glaciers and certainly the most active. It spills from the icefields surrounding 15,300-foot Mount Hubbard into the top of Yakutat Bay, where that body of water narrows, turns sharply to the south, and becomes Russell Fjord.

Hubbard Glacier had created a geological sensation in 1986 by surging into a high-speed advance that moved the face of the ice more than a mile forward in the space of a few days, damming Russell Fjord and creating a huge lake. For four months the water level behind the ice dam rose steadily, inundating and drowning the scanty forest that clung to the steep edges of the fjord, and building up enormous pressures. When the water finally breached the ice dam, the violent discharge into Yakutat Bay was probably one of the largest in North America in a thousand years. The roar could be heard for twenty miles, and a photographer on a ridge nearby reported that the ground beneath his feet shook so badly that the vibrations made it nearly impossible to take a clear picture.

I smiled. "That's glacier bear country, Michio," and told him what I had learned.

5 >> Russell Fjord

ALASKA AIRLINES FLIGHT 61 took off from Juneau and climbed west for fifteen minutes until banking slowly to the north above Glacier Bay. From twenty-seven thousand feet the waters of the gulf looked smooth as blue silk and the icefields of the Fairweather Range resembled frozen inland seas. Forty minutes later we descended into Yakutat and as the landing gear hissed and squealed into position, I stared northeast at eighteen-thousand-foot Mount Saint Elias. When I looked away the dazzle of its white shoulders still burned in my eyes. It was clear that the coast might be flirting with spring, but farther inland the world remained firmly in the grip of winter.

I was prepared. In the cargo hold of the jet was my pack, with a heavy goose-down parka, three pairs of polypropylene long underwear, pile pants and a pile jacket, two wool shirts, a nylon and pile cap with earflaps that reached under my chin, an all-weather waterproof paddle jacket with a hood, rain pants, and several pairs of heavy socks. In a separate duffel bag were my heavy boots, a climbing rope, an ice ax, and an assortment of snow anchors and ice screws.

My emergency kit, or "uh-oh" bag, was a waterproof neoprene bag of the sort used by kayakers to keep gear and clothing dry. It contained a battery-powered handheld marine radio, waterproof matches, three plastic film canisters filled with Vaseline and cotton,[19] a plumber's candle, a flashlight, bouillon cubes, half a dozen chocolate bars, a twelve-gauge pistol that fired parachute flares and smoke signals, and a coil of braided steel wire for making small animal snares. There was also an assortment of fishing lures and line, but I have never been a very competent sport fisherman and would be in serious straits if my survival or that of my clients ever depended on my ability to outwit a trout.

The uh-oh bag was wrapped in a large blanket of metallic heat-reflecting foil and stuffed into a watertight canister made from a military surplus .50-caliber ammunition can. A sturdy box of first-aid supplies went in last, and the lid of the can was wired and clamped shut to form an unsinkable, hermetically sealed container. I had shipped a sixteen-foot Zodiac inflatable skiff and fifteen horsepower outboard motor to Yakutat the day before, because where we were going was accessible only by a combination of floatplane and boat. If something happened to overturn the skiff, I wanted to be sure the uh-oh bag and its contents would float to shore.

Stuffed into the bag holding the floorboards of the skiff was a mustang suit, a pair of bright orange full-body coveralls designed to insulate and float a man weighing up to two hundred pounds. The float suit increased the odds of surviving immersion in the frigid waters of a glacial fjord, which can kill a human in twenty minutes with its heart-stopping cold. With the float suit, I might last up to an hour, maybe more.[20]

---

19. Cotton soaked in petroleum jelly makes a good fire starter, effective in wet weather.
20. I only had one mustang suit—no spares for the others—and intended to wear it, not because I considered my own preservation more important than that of others, but because making it out of the water and onshore alive is only half the battle. After that would come the long, hard trial of staying alive in an extremely cold and remote place without shelter, dry clothing, or food. In a place like Russell Fjord in April, it could be a long, long time before help came if there was trouble. I possess some of the knowledge,

Also in the bag of floorboards was a sack of mechanic's tools and a spare pair of oars, in case the outboard went on strike and marooned us a long way from camp. I laminated a topographical map of the area between sheets of clear contact paper before packing my bags, and this, along with a compass, was folded into my backpack beside a tide book and a steel flask of brandy. The last thing I did before leaving for the airport was to clean and oil the Remington 7-millimeter magnum rifle I sometimes carry in bear country and pack it along with a handful of shells in a rigid, weather-tight plastic case.

My carry-on baggage consisted of an aluminum box the size and shape of a briefcase and a plastic bag containing a dozen rolls of film. Nestled into foam padding inside the box was a complete set of camera gear—a body and a complement of lenses—of the same make that Michio favored. The camera was borrowed and several years older than anything my Japanese friend used, but considerably more up-to-date than the ancient camera with screw-mounted lenses I had begun carrying after our first trip together.

Anticipating another of Michio's photography lessons (and perhaps a shot at a glacier bear), I had jumped at a friend's offer to lend me the gear and spent a long evening cleaning the lenses and reading the manual. As I patiently worked my way through the delicate task of replacing a tiny light-meter battery beneath a trap door hidden behind a spring-loaded mirror inside the camera, I had imagined how tickled Michio would be to see me imitating his choice of cameras.

Michio and the others would arrive later, coming south from Anchorage after a stop in Cordova. Michio was in charge of groceries—

---

skills, and experiences that might make survival under adverse conditions possible, but I could not count on anyone else having the same.

It sounds overly dramatic and self-serving to say it, but in the event of an emergency, my own survival would mean the chances for everyone else would be much better, too. After guiding a while, I had come to realize that this was the true task of being a good guide: to think ahead, carefully consider the range of possible conditions and events, expect the unexpected, plan for all hell to break loose, and make the sort of conservative decisions that ensure everyone will come home. Putting people in position for great photos or wildlife experiences was secondary. No photo or film clip is worth anyone's life.

he was still the cook—as well as sleeping bags and camping gear for the others. He was also bringing a tent for the two of us that could withstand a hell storm of rain and hundred-mile-an-hour winds. Yakutat is infamous for foul, windy weather, and we could not count on the days ahead to be pleasant or calm.

At the airport I checked into a lodge that caters to sport fishermen who come to Yakutat every spring for the world-class steelhead fishing offered by a couple of rivers nearby. The first waves of sea-run rainbow trout would be arriving soon, along with hordes of fishermen, but for now the lodge was nearly empty and I had my choice of rooms, all of which featured unpainted plywood floors, three tiers of wooden bunk beds, and a strong odor of cigarettes and old socks. I stacked my rifle, duffel bag, and camera gear on one bunk, laid claim to another by turning back the cover, and went out to find a vehicle to rent before meeting Michio's plane.

The only available vehicle was a rattling, dust-covered van. The engine idled with a distinctly improvisational rhythm, the clutch felt like I was stepping on a water balloon, and it took several good slams to get any of the doors to stay closed, but it was roomy enough for the expedition's massive piles of gear. In any case, I was not concerned with the mechanical condition of the vehicle: Yakutat has a shortage of roads. There is almost nowhere to go, and the small community is so friendly that should a breakdown occur, the next car along would probably stop and offer to help.

It was not hard to spot Michio, Shin-ichi Murata, and Kiyomi Shutto in the small cluster of people disembarking from the jet that afternoon. Michio was smiling, bouncing up on his toes and looking all around as he came through the gate, his trademark Greenland-style knit cap askew on his head.

Michio placed his hand on my shoulder as he introduced me first to Shin-ichi, the producer, then Kiyomi, who kept glancing back at the plane to keep an eye on the baggage handlers unloading the cargo. No traveling cameraman, I've noticed, is comfortable until his equipment is safe in his own hands. The loss or damage of any other equipment—cases, tripods, battery chargers, even sleeping bags or food—can usually be improvised around or otherwise overcome, but if anything takes the camera out of commission, life becomes meaningless. A broad grin broke out on his face when the camera case finally came into view.

It took two trips to move our equipment to the lodge, where Michio and I began organizing the mound of boxes and cases as we swapped gossip about where we had been and what we had seen since we last saw each other in the fall. He had been home to Japan as well as north to the Arctic, where thousands of migrating caribou passed within sight of his camp; I had sailed a small boat from Jamaica to Costa Rica via a sweltering passage through the Panama Canal and was happy to be back in Alaska. After a half hour of trading stories and news, I decided to steer us back to the present.

"Feeling lucky, Michio? Think we'll see a glacier bear?"

He smiled and shrugged. "I'll teach you a new word."

I folded a towel and stuffed it into a box of dishes: "What is it?"

"Tabun," he said. "Japanese for 'maybe.' "

OVER AT THE SMALL OFFICE of Gulf Air flying services, the owner and chief pilot circled a finger around an aeronautical chart of Russell Fjord pinned to the wall. "Nobody has been in there yet this year and the snow is really hanging on. It's several feet deep in most places."

Mike Ivers had the strong, rangy movements of a man used to working with his hands and an air of confidence that said he was used to making important decisions. He was widely acknowledged to be one of the best bush pilots in Southeast Alaska, with an encyclopedic knowledge of the coast's forbidding terrain engraved into his brain by thousands of hours of flying.

He pulled a pen from the pocket of his hickory shirt and used the tip to indicate a small point on the chart. Russell Fjord tends south for roughly thirty-five miles from Hubbard Glacier, averaging two miles in width along its length. Another fjord, the Nunatak, joins in from the east twelve miles from the glacier, and Ivers's pen rested at the junction. "There's a beach here at the mouth of this creek. Depends on the water level, but that's the most likely spot to get you in."

I looked closer at the wall chart, trying to envision the lay of the land from the contour lines under his pen, then marked the spot on my own map. Michio leaned in for a look, then translated for Shin-ichi and Kiyomi. Where Mike was pointing, the lines describing the rise and fall of the land were spaced slightly apart and the wandering blue thread of a creek indicated an area of fairly level ground just large enough to pitch a few tents. Elsewhere around the rim of the fjord, the contour lines clustered so tightly together that they blurred into a promise of glacier-carved cliffs.

"The way the fjords lie," he went on, "this place catches the most sun," meaning the snow should be melted enough by this time of year to allow a small plane to land. It would also mean crossing two miles of open water in a heavily loaded skiff, traveling another twelve miles north to reach the glacier, then doing the opposite to return to camp every night.

And we'd have to keep a sharp eye on the mountains and the weather. When the dense, cold air above an icefield begins to flow downhill, a phenomenon known as a *katabatic* wind can occur. During a katabatic outflow, a moving air mass encountering the natural venturi of a steep-walled valley or fjord can be squeezed and accelerated until it explodes into highly localized, storm-force winds. Microbursts in excess of 180 miles per hour have been recorded along the coast, and the only warning may be a few streamers of snow being blown into the upper atmosphere from the peaks.

Michio translated as Shin-ichi quizzed Mike about the ice and the glacier: Would it be active and calving? Were there seals there, riding the bergs? Would Mike be willing to fly Michio and Kiyomi over the top of the glacier for some aerial shots?

Mike nodded his head. "Shouldn't be any problem, long as the weather's good."

Takeoff was scheduled for seven o'clock the next morning. It would take several flights to shuttle our mountain of gear into the fjord, and by the time we made camp the sun would have been up for hours. I would have preferred an earlier departure, but Ivers had a party of mountain climbers to drop off by ski plane the next day and wanted to get them in early, before the day grew too warm and softened the snow, making it dangerous to land.[21]

The film crew shook hands with the pilot as we left, but I was distracted by mental checklists (Did we have enough gas for the outboard? Were the radio batteries charged? What time was tomorrow's low tide?) and had to jump out of the van and run back to ask Mike the question I most wanted answered: Had he ever seen a glacier bear? Was there a chance we might see one while flying?

Ivers shrugged. "Yeah, I guess they're around. It's hard to say, but I thought I saw one a couple of years ago up in Nunatak Arm."

I would have quizzed him more, but a bush pilot's life is spent at full speed ahead and Mike was in a hurry to get back to his plane. As I walked back to the van and the waiting film crew, the word *Nunatak* kept quivering in my brain: That's where we're going, I told myself. We're camping at the junction of the Nunatak and Russell Fjords.

THE NEXT MORNING the overloaded plane hurtled down the runway, bouncing heavily as it tussled with gravity, then broke free and rose into the sky. Ivers eased the steering yoke away from his chest, fiddled with the throttle, then settled a pair of sunglasses on the bridge of his nose. I was crammed into a seat the size of a first-grader's, clutching a duffel bag and camera on my lap. Behind my head, a solid wall of gear threatened to break free of its restraints and bury me in an avalanche of equipment.

I was going in first with the bulk of the gear. Michio, Shin-ichi, and Kiyomi would follow along behind. It is standard practice in expedition flying to shuttle in as much gear as possible on the first

21. The bush pilot's job is one of frightful risks and danger. One out of five bush pilots who fly for more than twenty years will die on the job. The careful consideration of such things as the effect of sun on the snow determines how long even the great ones like Mike Ivers will live. Tragically, Mike was killed shortly after the NHK expedition to Russell Fjord when his plane slammed into a mountain during inclement weather.

flight. The weather along the glacier coast can change in an instant, and should a sudden storm scream down from the mountains or fog roll in from the sea, it might be days before Mike could fly back in with the others. Marooning one man with enough sleeping bags, tents, food, and gear for four people was imminently more sensible than marooning four with insufficient gear to survive.

But today the sky was cloudless, a dense shade of blue, and the perfectly white wall of the Saint Elias Mountains rose up before me. As the ground fell away, I leaned over to peer out the window and spotted the brown shine of a moose's huge body in a patch of willows at the end of the runway. A bright spark of sunlight flashed off a lake to the south.

The toy buildings of Yakutat came into view, then gave way to a gray-and-green tapestry of muskeg and forest. The mountains rushed toward us at a stately, even speed, and the thick quilt of old-growth forest below us rose until giving onto the slick, white plains of a snow-filled mountain valley.

The altimeter wound steadily higher as the Cessna labored to climb over a granite wall ahead. A spiral of anxiety wormed into my belly and began to tighten at the sight of the onrushing cliff. I distracted myself by looking out—and up—to the side, where a mountain goat clinging to a point of wind-scoured rock above a limitless void paid no heed to our passing.

One second a mountain was rushing pell-mell below and beside us, the shadow of the plane flickering over sharp-edged jumbles of rock, and the next there was nothing, as we hurtled over the verge of a scarp and the mountain fell away, leaving us afloat in an immense space full of nothing but wind.

Ahead, the jaws of Hubbard Glacier spanned the horizon, and Russell Fjord was a mirror at its feet. Mike banked the plane sharply, dipping hard to the left, then pointed at a meandering line of dots across a snow-covered slope beneath the wing. He mouthed something above the roar of the engine—*bear!*—and made a walking motion with two fingers. The marks in the snow were the tracks of a bear, newly emerged from an alpine den.

I craned my head to study the route of the tracks, then twisted in my seat to keep them in sight as Mike leveled the plane. The tracks dipped and ambled across a ridge, circled into a valley, then dropped straight toward Russell Fjord.

Mike tilted the plane up onto one wing tip and banked into a tight circle above the mouth of a stream. Feathering the throttle, he slowed the plane to the verge of a stall as he inspected a sloping, fan-shaped deposit of alluvial material that nosed a few yards out into the waters of the fjord. Flanked left and right by fields of deep snow, the patch of bare gravel looked no bigger than a handkerchief. I wondered where he was planning to land.

Squinting behind his sunglasses, Mike thumbed the bridge of his nose and grunted something I could not hear over the thunder of the engine.

"What's that?" I shouted, nodding at the tiny plot of gravel. Was it the remains of the landing zone? Had winter ice or an avalanche altered the terrain?

Ivers shrugged, tipped the plane back to level, and shouted to make himself heard: "Wish the tide was out a little more. I'd like a little more room to land."

We're turning back, I thought to myself as the plane sped away, then took a deep breath as I felt the world tilt beneath my seat and the horizon spin around.

Ivers lined the plane up along the axis of the "runway," pushed the yoke away from his chest, and nosed toward the ground. "One wheel in the water." He grinned. "It'll help us slow down."

Before I could figure out whether he was joking, there was a hard lurching bounce, then another, as the heavily loaded plane met the ground. Gravel and cobblestones rattled beneath the tires as Mike's hands went into a flurry of motion, pumping furiously at the brake and chopping the throttle while he fought to control our wild, slewing rush toward a snowbank that lay dead ahead. At the last second he revved the engine and spun the plane around, bringing us to a halt facing back the way we had come. The propeller coughed, stuttered, and choked to a stop as he cut off the engine.

Ivers unsnapped his safety belt, piled out of the plane, and began preparing to unload the gear. Putting a small, heavily loaded airplane down on an untested strip was just business as usual to him, but I'd been holding my breath and took a moment to pry my fingers from their grip on the seat.

In a few minutes, a small mountain of packs, boxes, duffels, and bags was piled at the edge of the water. I felt a muscle in my back twinge as we wrestled the unwieldy outboard motor and deflated sixteen-foot skiff from the fuselage, and I hoped I had remembered to put aspirin in my kit.

Ivers tossed a sleeping bag onto the pile and glanced around the inside of the plane. "That looks like the last of it."

I checked for my rifle case, made a quick inventory of food, tent, stove, and other necessities, then looked toward the mountains. "Looks like the weather will hold until you get back with the others."

Weather isn't small talk in Alaska. The pilot pursed his lips, considered the cloudless sky above us, and nodded: "The forecast is good." Then, as if worried the weather gods might find hubris in such optimism, he amended: "I better get back as quick as I can."

Mike settled into his seat, gave me a thumbs-up, and slammed the door. The engine bellowed to life and the plane began to strain forward as he built up power against the brakes, then leaped when he gave it its head. I ducked as the prop wash blew over me, turning sideways and shielding my face with my hands.

The caterwaul of the engine faded to a whine as the plane rose, banked to the west, and disappeared beyond the rim of the mountains. In its place came the immense, humming silence of a vast, unpeopled space. No breeze stirred between the walls of the fjord, and the water was the same intense blue as the sky. Snow-covered mountains rose all around me, glittering and burning with a light so perfectly white that it hurt to look at them in the same way that it sometimes hurts to look at a beautiful woman. Wind-sculpted cornices shaped like breaking waves hung cantilevered from the highest ridges; now and again, the mutter of a distant avalanche whispered through the air as the warmth that felt so good on my face and hands softened the grip of a section and sent it plummeting into the valleys below.

Remembering what Ivers had said about the possibility of a glacier bear in the vicinity, I dug into my pack for binoculars, sat cross-legged on the ground, and began scanning the fjord. The rise and fall of the tide had etched a thin, snow-free band of shoreline around the rim of the inlet, but everything above this was snowbound. The mountain-sides were marked here and there with meandering lines of tracks that could have been made by bears pushing through the snow, but they were all too far away to tell.

An hour later, after glassing until my eyes blurred and swam, I had seen only a single ragged moose—all hollow-hipped and rib-boned by winter—and a few ravens that scolded me harshly. I gave up, returned the binoculars to their case, and was starting to move the camping gear to a suitable tent site when the buzz of the returning airplane inter-rupted the silence.

Michio and Shin-ichi were smiling when they climbed out of the plane. Kiyomi, too, looked pleased as he emerged clutching his cam-era to his chest. Calm, clear weather is ideal for aerial photography, and Ivers had flown them close to the face of Hubbard Glacier for an intimate view of the ice, then risen soaring above it and pressed deep into the mountains beyond.

"He gave us the *whole movie*." Michio grinned.

I laughed at his enthusiastic mangling of the slang. "I think you mean the 'whole show,' Michio," I said, and pointed at the camera around his neck. "Did you get some good photos?"

With characteristic modesty, he dissembled: "I hope so."

"Look what I've got," I said, digging out my borrowed camera from the stack of equipment. Snapping the aluminum case open, I turned it to Michio for his inspection, expecting to see a look of plea-sure on his face.

Instead, he glanced briefly at the camera, then looked puzzled.

"It's the same kind as *your* cameras," I explained rather foolishly. "I ought to get some good photos on this trip."

Michio shook his head emphatically and pointed: "The camera won't take the good pictures."

I was dumbfounded. The manufacturer was known worldwide for the quality of its cameras; the lenses were reputed to be razor sharp. Had I borrowed the only lemon the company ever made?

As if reading my thoughts, Michio held up an imaginary camera to explain: "A camera is just . . . ," he groped for a word. "Just a *box*."

It took me a moment to understand what he meant. The camera was just a tool, like a chisel; it was up to the photographer to carve something worthwhile. He was saying that no amount of fancy gear or expensive optical glass would make me a better photographer. There would always be a newer line of cameras with longer lenses and faster motor drives, but if I did not learn to take good photographs with a simple, basic camera, the rest was just junk that would simply allow me to take lousy pictures faster and from farther away.

The tents blossomed easily into yellow and gray domes with the help of all hands. Michio and Kiyomi busied themselves setting up the stove, scattering out sleeping bags, and arranging cooking equipment while Shin-ichi and I pieced together the skiff. It took all four of us to hoist the assembled boat to the water; I went in too deep and filled my rubber boots with cold water.

Securing our supply of food from scavenging bears proved impossible.[22] The few trees that had once grown along the edge of the fjord had been drowned by the flood that built up behind Hubbard Glacier when it surged and closed off the arm a few years before. Although still standing, the trunks had shed all their bark, turning silver and too slick to climb, and the few branches within tossing distance of a rope were too brittle to bear the weight of a bag. We'd just have to cache everything a hundred meters from camp and hope that if a wandering bear

---

22. My normal procedure is to place everything edible or odorous—including toothpaste, scented soap, hand lotions, even beer—into a waterproof duffel bag and hoist it into a tree, either by climbing or by rigging a line over an upper limb. Black bears and young grizzlies are capable climbers, but it seems they seldom look up. I have never lost my food to a bear.

did get into our food while we were away at the glacier, it would leave us enough to get by until the plane returned.

Next I dug out the map and a compass, oriented myself to the land, and started plotting a route to the glacier. It was twelve miles from our camp to the face, and I wanted as little exposure to katabatic winds (or *williwaws,* as many Alaskans call them) as possible. A small point of land a mile or two south of the glacier's face would provide a safe place to leave the skiff within hiking distance of the glacier. Any closer and we risked having the skiff damaged or destroyed should the glacier undergo a full-face collapse.

All tidewater glaciers drop large columns and blocks of ice into the water in a more or less continuous fashion, generating surge waves that spread out from the face. Ice falls from one part of the face, then another, as the down-flowing glacier muscles its way unevenly into the sea. Although rare, a full collapse occurs when the pressure creates sufficient instability to cause the disintegration of the entire face at once. The collapse of even a relatively small portion of a glacier as massive as the Hubbard could drop several million tons of ice into the water, sending a series of catastrophic waves pulsing deep into the fjord.[23] Stashing the skiff a mile or more short of the face—and carrying it up well above the high-tide mark—would give us some chance of being able to return to camp should such a thing occur.

With four people, cameras, tools, supplies, extra gas, and safety equipment aboard, the boat would be heavily loaded and slow. Commuting to the glacier and back would be a long, uncomfortable journey if it began to rain, snow, or blow, but it would provide Michio and me with an opportunity to search nearly two dozen miles of coastline for a glacier bear every day.

---

23. I have witnessed the collapse of an entire face only once in my life, but the surge that resulted was enough to put the fear of God in me as it roared, frothing and tumbling full of shattered bits of ice, straight toward the *Wilderness Swift.* I survived that one by speeding toward an ice-free area a hundred yards away and turning the bow of the boat into the wave just as it swept beneath my keel. That face was only a half mile wide; Hubbard Glacier spans more than *five.*

I folded the map lengthwise, creased it flat with the blade of my hand, and looked around for my friend. Since our last trip, he had begun to affect a yellow-stemmed pipe and was strolling slowly along the beach a hundred yards away, fiddling with a pouch, a pocket knife, and some matches in a complicated effort to keep the smoke going. As I approached he surrendered, bent to knock the bowl against a stone, and tucked the apparatus in his pocket.

"You're too young to smoke a pipe, Michio," I gibed. He had commented earlier about feeling middle-aged, joking that his back-pack always seemed to be getting heavier even though technological advances were supposed to be making things lighter.

Looking sheepish, he covered his pocket with his hand. "It's very useful in the Arctic. It helps keep mosquitoes away." I knew he had been working for several years on a book about caribou in the Arctic, where it is estimated that the weight and volume of mosquitoes may exceed that of all other forms of animal life combined. During the peak of the mosquito season, moose and caribou lose up to a quart of blood every day and sometimes go mad, running themselves to death in desperate attempts to escape. The image that popped into my head of my friend bounding across the tundra puffing frantically on a pipe in an effort to keep the swarming, blood-sucking horde at bay was more humorous than realistic, and I shuddered, waving away a non-existent mosquito. "We're lucky."

Michio nodded. The early season here would spare us that misery. "Very lucky," he agreed. "Lucky many ways."

He shoved his hands into his back pockets and stared at the mountains. A goldeneye paddling in the mouth of the creek suddenly uttered a soft cry and dove, plunging headfirst into the water with a motion so perfectly fluid and arching that it left scarcely a ripple behind.

Michio spoke softly, as if sharing a secret: "This place is *spectacular*."

I waited for the goldeneye to reappear before responding.

Then, slowly and without really intending to, I began telling him about a dream I had once had of building a home in a place as beautiful and distant as this.

6 ❯ Johnstone Bay

ALASKA WAS the last place in the United States to offer up wild lands to the public for settlement. Until well into the twentieth century, the now-defunct Federal Homestead Act had offered settlers 160 acres with the requirement that the land be cleared, plowed, and farmed before a clear title would be granted—a daunting, often impossible task, given Alaska's poor climate and soils. The state of Alaska supplanted the unwieldy federal act with a variety of claims programs that offered title to smaller pieces of land in exchange for the effort of staking out, surveying, and making certain mandatory "improvements." Under state control the available land was often remote, inaccessible, and inhospitable, and "improving" generally meant building a cabin or stripping away the ground and pouring it through a sluice box in search of gold.

Impose a drawing of Alaska over a similarly scaled map of the forty-eight contiguous states and it will reach coast to coast. The southernmost part of the state will almost reach the beaches of Florida; the outer islands of the Aleutian chain dangle to the left of Los Angeles. The Arctic Slope on either side of Point Barrow covers everything from North Dakota to Wisconsin, while Anchorage and the Kenai Peninsula below it land somewhere in Oklahoma or Arkansas. Parcels of land were available for claiming across the length and breadth of this immense chunk of the globe.

The first time I entered the state land office in Anchorage I was eighteen years old. The crowd jostling the counter and questioning the clerks consisted largely of callused and bearded men in flannel shirts who, like myself, probably envisioned themselves as pioneers. Overpriced surveyors hustled the crowd, handing out business cards, and a few ragged souls who appeared to have fled to Alaska with this, a chance at a free bit of land, as their only remaining hope for a place in the world puzzled over fistfuls of forms.

A surly clerk gave out information piecemeal and grudgingly, doling out answers only to direct questions that could be answered with an abrupt yes or no. The program had been scandalized for months by quick-buck artists running a variety of scams virtually subdividing public lands for their own quick enrichment; persistent rumors circulated that the state planned to end the program.

Fearing I might lose my chance at a slice of the pie, I stayed in the city for weeks, fingering my way through drawers of survey plats and endless files of microfilm records. My simple technique for identifying the most desirable piece of land was to find the parcel farthest from any human settlement; I had the idea that the farther I landed from people, the closer I would be to contentment.

I found what I was looking for on the Gulf of Alaska, where the maps showed a broad indentation of coastline east of the Kenai Peninsula and west of Prince William Sound. Johnstone Bay offered no shelter from the storms that enrage the gulf into forty-foot seas. The bay—an ambitious word for what was only a slight curving inward of the coast—lay between mountains so vertical the altitude lines of a topographic map ran inseparably together. The northern boundary of the valley was a glacier that bled from a dangerously crevassed icefield into a lake.

No one had cared to claim any part of this inaccessible place. The nearest human habitation (the homesite of a couple with one small child) was twenty miles away, the closest road or telephone almost forty—impossible distances over such broken, ice-burdened ground and unlikely by water due to the hazards of the sea.

I paid two dollars for a plat of Johnstone Bay and tacked it to the wall of my room, confident it was a map to Nirvana.

Three days before I turned nineteen (the age at which I would become eligible to participate in the truncated homesteading program) I paid the cigar-puffing pilot of a floatplane an exorbitant sum to land among the icebergs on a glacier lake at the northern edge of the valley. Dodging and weaving through floating bits of ice, the pilot idled the plane into the beach and put me ashore with a small tent, a cardboard box of canned and dried food, and enough naïveté to fill a duffel bag.

With me was Niles G., a recently transplanted Californian excited by the possibility of claiming his own patch of ground. Splitting the cost of the air charter made sense, and in spite of my commitment to becoming a hermit, there was an unavoidable comfort in the idea that I might not be the only human being within a hundred square miles.

We had three days before the pilot planned to return. I walked the riverbanks, beaches, and creeks of the valley all of the first day and the next, measuring the suitability of tree trunks for cabin logs and the distance to drinking water while the sun looked on from a hard blue sky and Niles did the same. Offshore I could see the salty exhalations of whales marking exclamation points against the horizon. Gulls and terns checkmarked onto the sky keened high-piping counterpoints to the rhythm of surf. A half dozen sea otters resting on the strand scattered and charged into the sea at my approach, except for one—larger and more bold than the rest—that hissed, rolled over in the wet sand to face me, and stared unafraid.

On the morning of my birthday I felled a small tree, limbed and axed it square, and chopped it into four rude posts. Using a rope and a compass I laid out a rectangle four hundred feet north and south by five hundred feet east and west. With the flat of the ax I drove the sharpened posts into the ground at the corners. I wrote my name and the date on a piece of paper, wrapped it in plastic, and placed it in a can nailed to the first post.

If I returned to the state office and recorded the location of the posts in the language of meridians and angles, I would have earned the right to pay a certified surveyor to measure the plot and label it as mine. Where a clear running stream curved around a meadow studded with shooting stars and western columbines, a short walk from a broad, surf-pummeled strand of south-facing beach, four and a half level acres of broad-bellied spruce trees and green mossy swales would be mine.

It was the only day of my life I would turn nineteen and I felt contentment as firm as the thump of my ax as I pounded the posts into the ground. I could not imagine a better life than the hermitage Johnstone Bay offered. I would build a warm, strong cabin of carefully chosen trees and hunt deer, bear, and goats in the mountains that ringed the valley. I would put in a garden of potatoes and learn to read the tracks of marten, otter, and weasels along the beach.

The furrowed brow of a weather front rose over the horizon to the southwest while I walked back to my camp. Raindrops began to fall as I folded the tent and scattered the stones Niles and I had arranged for a fire ring. An eagle perched on an iceberg in the middle of the lake ignored the activity as I moved gear to the shore to wait for the return of the floatplane.

The raindrops increased until a steady downpour blocked out the mountains and glacier. The plane did not come, and wind began to shake fat drops from the branches of the hemlock tree under which I sheltered. Only the sound of wind dancing with the trees and an occasional grumble from the floating ice came to me as I strained my ears for the approach of an airplane engine.

By nightfall the plane still had not come, and the tent billowed and thrashed in the storm as we set it up again in the darkness. I slept fitfully, twisting my body around the puddles of water seeping through the floor of the cheap tent.

Throughout the next day and night a hard, unbroken rain poured down. The storm shouldered the sea into ragged black swells that broke on the beach with the weight of falling mountains.

We ate the last of our food—cold pork and beans straight from the can—then I wandered through the rain with my rifle under my coat, imagining deer on the edge of the dripping forest. I startled when an otter broke from the underbrush ahead of me, bolted into the grass along a creek bed, and disappeared, whistling *chirk-chirk-chirk* in alarm; in its wake came a silence that wrapped solitude around me like a fog. I felt marooned, abandoned in the wilderness, and I liked it.

The storm broke apart during the night. Daybreak came clear and the surf calmed to a mutter. Escadrilles of dark-eyed juncos churred in the upper branches of young spruce trees as I spread my sleeping bag and tent to dry. Seals swam from the sea up the river to lie sunbathing on ice in the middle of the lake, where I eyed them hungrily, considering them meat.

The plane came around the headlands west of the beach without warning. One moment it was silent but for the pop and crackle of the icebergs moving about in the lake and the next the intrusive whine of an engine announced the Cessna's return. The plane skimmed low over the sea and banked up the river, flying at the height of the tree-tops, then pulled up and circled, banking steeply as the pilot slowed the plane into a tight reconnaissance of the lake.

The days and nights of storm winds had pushed the icebergs away from the shore, leaving a clear landing path. The seals panicked and stampeded into the water as the plane roared in and skimmed to a stop by our camp.

After loading our packs and clambering aboard, the plane pushed the earth away beneath its wings, and we rose into the last red eye of sunset. The pilot handed me a candy bar, tossed another to Niles in the back, turned northwest, and pulled the plane into a steep climb. Below us the broken teeth of the mountains and the icefield between them turned pink in the lingering light.

I pressed my forehead against the window to watch the earth peel away beneath the wings. The pungent smell of woodsmoke lingered on my clothes and I ached with a desire to turn back. I hungered for the satisfaction of stacking logs head to toe in the shape of my own cabin, filling a smokehouse with the ruby-colored meat of fresh salmon, and washing the soil of a garden from my hands.

I felt lucky for the first time in my life.

"SOUNDS LIKE a wonderful place, Lynn." Michio pried gently into my reverie, bringing me back to Russell Fjord. The sun had moved west while I rambled, drawing shadows on the walls of the fjord. Shin-ichi and Kiyomi had built an evening fire of driftwood and a plume of pale smoke curled its scent through the air.

A cooking pot rattled. Shin-ichi raised a hand in our direction and Michio nodded. I realized I had been talking for at least an hour, probably more.

I picked up a wrist-sized piece of driftwood and cracked it over my knee, then picked up another. Michio followed suit, tugging at a dead branch to free it from the sand, and we worked until we each had an armload.

"And your cabin, Lynn. Did you build it?"

I shrugged. "Yeah, I built it. But it was a waste of time." This wasn't exactly true, but I turned my back and took a few steps toward camp to make it clear that the subject was forbidden territory and said, "We better check the tide book, make a plan for tomorrow." (At the time, I guess I just wasn't ready to discuss it; now I wish I'd come clean.)

Michio followed, squinting to show how perplexed he was by my abrupt change of subject; I busied myself with the wood in my arms, shifting and balancing it to avoid the question in his eyes. Too polite to penetrate my sudden evasiveness, he fell in beside me and was silent for the walk back to camp.

By the time supper was eaten and the dishes packed away, we had fed all the firewood to the flames. As the first crisp stars began to appear above the rim of the mountains, I secured the skiff for the night, double-checked the food cache, and threw a tarp over the rest of the gear.

Inside our tent Michio wrapped himself in a heavy down parka, pulled his sleeping bag up to his waist, and closed his eyes. I pulled on a pair of dry socks before slipping into my bag, snugged a wool hat down over my ears, and settled into the silence of the night.

Michio shifted, rolled onto his back, and whispered my name: "Lynn?"

He paused, then spoke softly. "That camera you borrowed? It's a good one. I used to have one just like it."

I grunted in response.

7 » Malaspina and Disenchantment Bay

WE ROSE THE NEXT MORNING to a fjord still draped in blue shadows. Overhead, a clear sky promised a day as fine as any ever offered by spring, but on the ground it was still winter and our breath steamed as we hurried into our clothes.

Michio pulled on a purple jacket, blew on his hands to warm them, and knelt before the stove to make breakfast. Kiyomi and Shinichi built a fire of small sticks; I loaded the skiff with our gear. We ate standing, clustered about the fire and sipping mugs of coffee until a blazing crescent of sun peeked over the mountains and threw our shadows out long and slender on the ground.

The outboard started after a few determined pulls, growled as I backed the heavily loaded skiff from the shore, then settled into a steady hum. Behind us our wake shattered the calm water into rippling blue shards and left a pattern of foam like white lace on its surface.

The producer and cameraman sat across from me, bulky as weight lifters in the life jackets I insisted everyone wear. Michio cinched the zipper of his coat to his chin, thrust out his jaw, and pointed straight ahead as if mocking some long-lost, determined explorer: "*Ngan ngan iko! Let's go for it!*"

I smiled to myself, considering how this gentle, kindly-eyed man would have fared among the early European and Russian explorers who first mapped this coast.

The Russian *promyshlenniki* who swarmed east in the 1700s to ravage it for furs were brutes, greedy savages who introduced Alaska's Natives to genocide. Concerned only with reaping the phenomenal wealth to be had by harvesting sea otter pelts for trade with China, one of the czar's expeditions forced three hundred Aleut men to paddle *bidarkas* (small two-man boats similar to kayaks) more than a thousand miles across the gulf from their homes in the windswept Aleutian Islands to Southeast Alaska, where the otter population was much larger. When the entire crew of enslaved hunters died from eating poisonous blue mussels,[24] the Russians simply loaded the bidarkas onto their ships, sailed back to the Aleutian Islands, and kidnapped some more.

Compared to the Russians, the Englishmen who sailed into Yakutat Bay under the command of George Dixon in 1787 were the vanguard of the Enlightenment. Dispensing gifts and indulging in trade, the British did nothing more outrageous than plaster English toponyms all over the landscape like graffiti.

Four years after Dixon came Alesandro Malaspina, commanding two Spanish corvettes designed and built specifically for carrying out detailed scientific inspections. Armed with only enough firepower for self-defense, the *Descubierta* and *Atrevida* were staffed with young volunteer officers handpicked for their interest in various scientific fields from among the elite of the Cadiz Naval Academy. The ordinary seamen, also volunteers, were enlisted from Spain's northern provinces because it was thought they would be less troubled by the cold.

It was Malaspina himself who commanded a mapping party that

---

24. Mussels and other bivalves that feed on a dinoflagellate often associated with the "red tide" may contain deadly concentrations of a neurotoxin that paralyzes the respiratory system and causes death by asphyxiation.

penetrated deep into Yakutat Bay in search of the fabled Strait of Ainan.[25] Victualed with supplies sufficient for fifteen days, Malaspina's men poled and prodded two small launches through fields of floating icebergs until being frustrated by an impenetrable ice pack several miles short of an island they named for a civilian naturalist in their party, Tadeo Haenke. After spying a solid wall of ice several hundred feet high in the mists beyond the island, Malaspina called the exploration to a halt and named the ice-choked bay *Desengaño*—an antonym for deceit, or a sudden, disappointing revelation. English cartographers subsequently softened Malaspina's apparent bitterness, translating the name into the milder *Disenchantment Bay*.

On the early-June day in 1791 that Malaspina decided to end his search for an easy route to the Atlantic, the face of Hubbard Glacier was much farther advanced than it is today; Russell Fjord was an isolated arm, cut off from the sea just as it was in 1986, a few years before I visited it with Michio and the others. There is no record of how many times the glacier opened and closed the door to Russell Fjord during the intervening centuries.

At the junction of Nunatak and Russell Fjords the water was still glassy and calm, marked here and there with brush strokes of blue by a light breeze feathering the surface. Craning my neck to scan the ridges for telltale plumes of blowing snow, I decided the calm would hold and steered for the other side.

A mile from shore the outboard coughed, slowed to a rough idle, and threatened to stall entirely—then just as suddenly began to run smoothly again. I worked the throttle, revving the engine, then checked the filter for obstructions; made certain the tank vent was open; fiddled with the sediment bowl; and found nothing to blame for the sudden epilepsy other than the random, infernal demons that seem to possess *all* outboard motors from time to time.

---

25. Also called the Strait of Lorenzo Ferrer Maldonado, the Strait of Admiral Bartolome Fonte, and the Strait of Juan de Fuca, the mythical waterway was known by other European nations as the Northwest Passage.

Crossing a few miles of reasonably protected water by skiff is normally nothing to fret about; but inflatable skiffs do not row well under the best of circumstances. If the outboard quit working and the wind began to blow, I would be doing well to maintain *any* control of the heavily loaded skiff. If we could not fight our way to shore, we would be blown either twenty miles south to the snow-covered end of the channel or ten miles north into the icebergs and wild currents at the foot of the glacier. Some choice.

I "knocked wood" on an oar and cranked open the throttle. The rest of the way across I concentrated on memorizing the skyline; if fog rolled in, being able to recognize the dim outline of a peak or other distinctive feature of the landscape might help me set a course back to camp.

The outboard hummed contentedly until we made Cape Enchantment, sputtered a moment, then began to run smoothly again. I turned northwest, relieved to be running close to shore. I broke out my camera, imagining how the sun would glisten on a blue-gray bear against a background of snow, and nodded at Michio to do the same.

An hour later the cameras still sat unused on our laps when we pulled ashore to stretch our legs at Marble Point. Arching my back to ease a cramp along my spine, I pointed out to Michio a finger of white marble peeking from a patch of snow-free ground. Ralph Stockman Tarr, a member of the U.S. Geological Survey expedition that mapped the area in 1906, had named the point for a distinctive mile-long band of marble that runs along the shore.

We beached the skiff and heaved it to the top of the tide zone. The sun was beginning to bear down, and rivulets of meltwater trickled and sang among the stones of the beach; we unzipped our jackets and pulled off our gloves as we worked. I looped the bowline around a boulder the size of an engine block, measured out enough slack to allow the skiff to float on a wave, and made it fast.

The combined action of the sun and the tide had carved the winter pack of snow along the beach into a vertical four-foot wall, revealing a banded and layered record of the past winter's storms that resembled the stratified sandstone bed of some pale, ancient sea. Along

The author. (PHOTO: JON POND)

The author with Michio Hoshino. (PHOTO: LYNN SCHOOLER)

Michio Hoshino. (PHOTO: NAOKO HOSHINO/MINDEN PICTURES)

The Wilderness Swift. (PHOTO: LEE SCHOOLER)

A humpback whale explodes to the surface while bubblenet feeding.
(PHOTO: LYNN SCHOOLER)

The face of a tidewater glacier, approximately three hundred feet high.
(PHOTO: LYNN SCHOOLER)

A tidewater glacier calving icebergs into the sea.
(PHOTO: LYNN SCHOOLER)

A large grizzly eyes the author. (PHOTO: LYNN SCHOOLER)

Skunk cabbage meadow in dense rainforest. (PHOTO: LYNN SCHOOLER)

Professional hunter Vladimir Ovsyannikov and a Russian Special Forces officer eye the bear that killed Michio Hoshino, which they tracked and shot from the helicopter behind them. (PHOTO: CURTIS HIGHT/**flora**and**fauna**.com)

A humpback whale breaching on the evening I learned of Michio's death.
(PHOTO: LYNN SCHOOLER)

The author's photo of a glacier bear. (PHOTO: LYNN SCHOOLER)

Photographer John Hyde's picture of a glacier bear.

(PHOTO © JOHN HYDE)

a narrow pathway between the snow and the rim of the tide, shoots of new-green grass were being hurried to the surface by the sun.

A high, thin skein of clouds was moving slowly in from the south, but as we walked we grew warmer and peeled down to our shirts. The awkward lump of the aluminum camera case shifted inside my pack, and the familiar ache of carrying a heavy backpack began to gnaw at my spine.

Topping out on a small rise, I held up a hand to halt the others. Fifty yards ahead was an avalanche chute packed with muddy, jumbled snow. A patch of dark, plowed-looking ground fifteen hundred feet above our heads showed where the slides had started, and I could see a scrawl of pale blue fracture lines on either side of the release zone, where the snowpack was sagging.

During summer, the chute was probably a clear running stream kept alive by rain falling on the steep slopes of the mountain; today it was more like the barrel of a gun, cocked and loaded with a charge of wet, heavy snow, and the sun had its finger on the trigger.

In my pack I carried a bundle of avalanche cords, bright red nylon lines a hundred feet long. The normal procedure for traversing a potentially active zone would be for each client to tie one end of a cord around his or her waist and hurry across one at a time, trailing the cord behind. If a slide pounced, the theory goes, some part of the red line would rise to the surface and provide a beacon for survivors to follow in an attempt to locate and dig up a victim.[26] In this case, however, using the cords would be pointless. We were traveling at water's edge, and anyone caught by a slide would instantly be blasted out into the fjord. The unseen snow mass above our heads was a Kushtaka trap, capable of making someone disappear in an instant.

There was nothing to do but cross quickly, one at a time.

"Unbuckle your pack, Michio." I motioned for Kiyomi and Shin-ichi to do the same. "Ditch it if you have to run."

26. Small radio transponders, or "avalanche beacons," have generally replaced the use of avalanche cords by back-country travelers since our trip to Russell Fjord.

I went first, scurrying across the uneven surface of the solidified flow as best I could with one eye turned uphill and the other on my feet, my ears cocked for an oncoming roar. The others crossed without hurrying, skeptical of the need for such haste. After all, it was a beautiful day. The air was sensuously warm, without a hint of a breeze, and the landscape around us was stunning—but I was thinking about a time twenty years before on a day much like this when a companion and I had crossed a similar chute without incident only to have a waist-high wall of shattered tree trunks, ice, and boulders burst without warning from the top of the slide and explode into the sea right behind us. I motioned for the others not to tarry, and when Michio stumbled on a slick patch of ice, I fought off the urge to shout "Hurry!"

Beyond the slide the trail was unobstructed, other than the odd scramble over a snowbank or two. Icebergs the size of automobiles littered the beach, left high and dry by the tide, and where the path skirted the stranded ice, shoots of new grass worked a needlepoint of green up through last year's dun-colored straw. While Michio stopped to snap a picture or two, I scoured the ground for some sign of bears.

Michio looked up from his camera, asking me with his eyes what I'd found. "Nothing," I said, a bit disappointed. "I don't think there's anyone around."

It didn't surprise me to find the tender young grass undisturbed. The scattered patches of new growth were hardly sufficient to support a field mouse. Beyond that, nothing but snow. Any wandering, hungry bear would surely be driven toward the coast, where the moderating influence of the sea offered a relative abundance of green.

The glacier muttered and rumbled at our approach, booming and popping in a slow cacophony of rifle shots, kettle drums, and thunder. Belts of crumbling brash ice sweeping by on the tide hissed and popped at our passing. After climbing to a knob of bald granite, we shed our packs and dropped to our knees, instinctively assuming a posture of supplication before the spectacle of a hundred square miles of ice sliding down the flank of a fifteen-thousand-foot mountain and hurling itself into the sea.

The wildly fissured wall of the glacier spanned the horizon, and as we watched, a tower of ice the size of an apartment building began to tilt, then crumbled and rolled into the bay, exploding into a geyser of spray. A rolling hump of water surged out of the chaos and swept across the narrows, tumbling icebergs and clusters of brash ice down its face until flinging itself ashore in a wild dash that carried it to the foot of our perch.

I measured the terrain above our position, estimating the time it would take for a wave generated by a large collapse to reach us. From our knob, the best route to high ground would be a spine of stone like a rusty knife blade that rose at an angle toward a ridge. Dry and firm, the rock would provide an easy evacuation route, *if* we had enough time.

I waited until another block of ice leaped from the glacier, using the second hand of my watch to time the wave's rush to the shore. "A little over a minute," I told Michio, holding out my watch for him to see. "Should be plenty of time. And we'll run faster if we're scared!"

We were situated on the eastern side of Gilbert Point, a broad wedge of bedrock that seperates Russell Fjord from Yakutat Bay. Our vantage point from the shoulder of the hill gave us a view north along the face of Hubbard Glacier into Malaspina's Disenchantment Bay. The island the Spanish explorer had named for the naturalist Tadeo Haenke was too far west around the point to be visible, but it was possible one of the *Atrevida*'s seamen may have come as far as our position.

During a ceremony designed to claim the new territory for the king of Spain, a gunner named Manuel Fernandez had wandered away and was nearly given up for lost. Malaspina, however, was a consci-entious commander and ordered a search for the missing gunner. The search party scrambled and rowed their way deep into the ice pack beyond Haenke Island before sighting a figure stumbling toward them along the shore.

When Fernandez was recovered, he was completely exhausted. He told a story of having penetrated so far into the icebound terrain that he had come to open water again, which "ran between [the] moun-tains and was lost to view, winding like a snake." He had done this, he claimed, to prove beyond a doubt that the ice-locked bay was not the strait for which they were searching,[27] and from his description of the large waterway beyond the glacier, it seems likely that he had penetrated as far as Russell Fjord, perhaps turning around somewhere near the spot where we were now sitting.

Kiyomi and Michio set up their heavy tripods, working them firmly into the ground. Michio selected a telephoto lens, mounted it to his camera, and sat down. I imitated Michio's choice of a long lens and began snapping pictures, shooting left and right until I had burned through an entire roll of film. Then I noticed that Michio was doing nothing, simply leaning back against his pack and watching as the glacier sent trainload after trainload of ice and rubble sliding into the bay.

"Something wrong, Michio?" I asked.

He shook his head and pointed: "I'm waiting for that one," he said, indicating a column of ice two hundred feet high.

All up and down the glacier pillars of broken ice were moving inexorably toward the sea, pressing forward like lemmings to the precipice until it was their turn to tilt slowly into an explosive collapse. The column Michio had chosen was larger than the rest but stood perfectly square and plumb; it showed no sign of conceding to gravity any time soon.

Nonetheless, he explained, he had chosen it for the way the mountains arrayed beyond it showed "how *big* everything is."

I said it didn't look ready to fall; he said, "I'll wait."

He had envisioned a photo that said something about the size of the land, and it didn't matter if it took ten minutes, an hour, or all day; he wouldn't settle for anything less—certainly not a bunch of random, shoot-from-the-hip pictures like those I had just taken. Once in a while he would glance at a band of thin clouds that came and went across the face of the sun. As the light changed, he adjusted the camera's exposure, constantly preparing for the inevitable moment when the column would fall.

27. For his arduous effort, Fernandez was promoted to mainmast lookout.

During a lull in the calving I used my binoculars to scan the open water. The tide was in full flood and it appeared as if the entire contents of the Pacific Ocean were attempting to squeeze through the narrow opening between Gilbert Point and Hubbard Glacier. The current boiled, spinning in slow whirls, and swept the drifting ice into sinuous windrows. Heaving and crackling, the ice pushed past the point with a noise like some large carnivore gnawing its way through a loose stack of bones.

Michio nudged me and pointed past my feet. A pair of small yellow birds were running along the beach, darting in and out between waves to peck at the sand. Sidestepping like miniature toreadors, the tiny birds dodged a block of ice the size of a refrigerator that surged in on a swell, then fluttered in to snatch up some tiny bit of food from its base and retreated with a faint, triumphant *teet!*

Then he motioned with his chin toward a seal swimming through the maelstrom of the current. With a great deal of wriggling and heaving, the well-upholstered animal hauled itself up onto a flat pan of ice and then lay there head up, wide-eyed and staring, as it plunged into the carnival ride. It struck me how comfortable the animal was in its chaotic environment and how, like the birds, it seemed almost to be playing with the onrushing ice.

Michio returned to his vigil, staring at the column. Shin-ichi and Kiyomi changed the lens on the video camera to shoot a panning shot of the glacier. I lost myself in the seals and the birds, marveling at how easily they moved through the turbulence of their lives.

I worry too much, I told myself. Always bracing for some avalanche or windstorm or tidal wave that might sweep us away.

I watched Michio for a while, wondering at his total absorption and the focus with which he attended to his work in spite of the mudslides, rockfalls, and avalanches all around us. There was no doubt that everything in this wide, wintry landscape seemed to be falling or waiting to fall, as if gravity were somehow more potent here than in tamer regions, but it seemed to have no effect on his single-minded determination to get the best picture.

A sharp *crack* interrupted my ruminations, followed by a cannon shot that swelled to a roar. Michio's tower began to lean slowly outward, then paused for a moment at an untenable angle while it shed a litter of blue-and-white debris from its shoulders.

Beside me, I could hear the *chi-chi-chi* of Michio's motordrive as his camera consumed film; I rushed to frame the scene in my own viewfinder, winding and snapping as fast as I could while the fractured wall collapsed. The falling column hurled a barrage of boulders into the water, then erupted into an explosion of white spray that blossomed and rose until it covered the face of the glacier. A sonorous thunder swelled from the icefield, grew into something palpable and restless, then rolled across the water and marched into the mountains, leaving a series of receding echoes in its tracks.

THE LONG SKIFF RIDE back from the glacier was smooth and uneventful, with the outboard humming contentedly and everyone in good spirits. Shadows rose up from the base of the mountains as we traveled, then spilled into the high valleys and gathered there like pools of dark water. By the time we made camp I was steering by the silhouette of the peaks and our tents looked like gray boulders in the gloom.

After getting supper on the stove, Michio dug into a knapsack, pulled out a folder stuffed with loose scraps of paper, and began shuffling through the contents by the light of a lantern. Receipts, letters, and—oddly—a fistful of cheap Christmas cards spilled to the ground.

"Have you seen this, Lynn?" Michio asked, handing me a page torn from a magazine.

I unfolded the sheet and angled it toward the lantern. It was an advertisement for a travel company or something similar (I no longer remember). Michio's interest was obviously not in the company or its services, but in the photograph that provided a background for the ad. A broad field of wildflowers filled the foreground; the middle ground was a lake of blue icebergs; beyond the lake was a mountain range, slightly out of focus, from which a glacier reached down to the lake. It was a pedestrian composition—I could easily imagine an art director saying something about "capturing the *essence* of Alaska" for a cruise ship company's advertising campaign—but it was equally as easy to imagine what a photographer like Michio could make of its bold elements and colors.

Michio's cap slipped as he bent to pick up the litter of papers at his feet. He stuffed the Christmas cards back in the folder, glanced at a letter and fed it to the fire, then reached up to straighten his hat. "Do you know where it is?"

"It's Harlequin Lake, I think." I waved a vague hand. "Over there. On the coast south of Yakutat."

As the crow flies, the lake was probably less than forty miles away. It was possible to drive there from Yakutat on logging roads, but it wasn't someplace I thought Michio would really want to go; the area around the lake itself was undeniably beautiful, but industrial-scale logging had been chewing at the Yakutat forelands for years. Not too far from the pristine Alaska promised by the photo, huge tracts of the forest had been reduced to muddy fields of stumps.

"I want to take a picture like this," Michio said. "The flowers, the ice. They . . . *expire* me."

"*Inspire,* Michio," I said, correcting him. He accepted my pedantry with grace. "If you say the flowers 'expire' you, it means something like they *kill* you."

"Well," Michio's eyes sparkled with the effort to repress a grin, "they are *wild* flowers! Very *dangerous!*"

He burst into a full-bodied laugh and I went along, feeling his unfettered delight and innocent pride in the wordplay ease the last of the day's worries from my shoulders. Still chortling, I folded the picture and explained about the logging.

"There's got to be other places," I said, and began counting off glacier-fed lakes on my fingers. "There's Alsek, farther south, and a lake at Cape Fairweather. Bering Lake, up on the Copper River." I continued until I had used up a handful of fingers; Michio listened carefully, then reminded me of one more: "How about the lake by your cabin?"

I folded the lakes I held in my hand, kicked a loose ember into the fire and dissembled, "You'd have to fly in." Trying to make it sound unreasonable, even though every lake I had just mentioned was the same. "It'd be pretty expensive for just one picture."

Michio peered sideways, sensing an emotional fault line.

"Besides, I don't really remember what it looked like there. That was a long time ago."

"Ah," he said, giving me a way out, "maybe someday we can go see the other lakes." The lantern light threw his features into relief and his face was round with concern. In his eyes was an empathy—for what, he did not know, but nonetheless freely given—and I felt the knots in my shoulders tighten up again. I hadn't been back to Johnstone Bay in nearly twenty years.

And I wasn't going back any time soon.

EVERY DAY THEREAFTER was much like the first. Each morning a flood of dazzling white light announced the rising of the sun, lit the water with a brilliant reflection of the mountains, and poured its warmth across our faces and hands. Luck—and the weather—stayed on our side, and the long trip to and from the glacier was easy. At the glacier the light was unceasingly perfect, either crisp and dramatic or softened by a layer of high, thin clouds that brought out the blues in the ice, and Michio worked steadily, metering and framing his way through roll after roll of film. When he noticed I had shot up all of my own, he tossed me a half dozen canisters from his own dwindling supply, then waved aside my thanks and showed me how to protect my exposed rolls by double-bagging them in resealable plastic bags.

Once we had to cross a small slide of fresh snow that had come down the avalanche chute while we were filming the glacier, but nothing came near us, and after a few days it began to feel commonplace and sane to live under the ax of the tenuous snowpack.

On a day with less calving activity than the others, I steadied my binoculars on my pack and watched the tiny speck of a faraway creature move slowly across the slope of a distant mountain. The size and measure of the land was so vast, so completely lacking in reference or scale, that it was difficult to estimate the animal's size.

It was too dark to be a goat and plowed ahead with a solidity unlike the leggy, high-stepping gait of a moose; if it was a wolf or a lynx, I told myself, the relatively large paws and lighter weight of those animals would allow it to run on top of the wind-crusted snow and travel at a faster pace.

Maybe it's a glacier bear.

I took a deep breath and held it, letting the glasses float lightly against the tips of my fingers to keep my heartbeat from shaking them. The fly speck seemed to labor, meandering first uphill, then down, and its tracks sketched an irregular line against the clean-paper color of the snow.

"Could be a wolverine." I grunted, pushing back my desire to see a silver bear. The bullish persistence of the far-off animal matched what I knew of the surliest member of the weasel clan, but the odds of seeing either animal were exceedingly slim: after a quarter of a century in Alaska, I could count the number of wolverines I had seen on the fingers of one hand (and still have one left over for a glacier bear). In either case, my hopes fell as the animal paused, seeming to consider the folly of its exertions, then turned and moved steadily away along its own backtrack until it disappeared behind a ridge.

Day after day Michio and I continued to watch the beaches and snowfields for some flicker of silver or blue, but by the time the last can of fuel had been tipped into the outboard motor and all but one of the food-storage bags emptied and folded away, finding a glacier bear had begun to seem unlikely. When the plane dropped out of a windless midday sky to begin ferrying us back to civilization, we had to admit our chances were gone.

At the Yakutat airport I shook hands with Shin-ichi and Kiyomi, then tried out my bow as we said good-bye. Michio and the camera crew were catching a northbound jet to Anchorage, and from there it was just a few air hops to the Arctic; I was heading south, back to

Juneau, where I had work to do to prepare for the upcoming charter season. Since telling Michio about Johnstone Bay, I had been having bouts of feeling vaguely out of sorts and now was suffering the disorientation that comes of being transported abruptly from an unconfined space full of wind and clean light into a world of noise and walls; the dozen or so people milling around the terminal seemed an intolerable crowd, and the smell of cigarettes and floor polish made me want to run screaming for the door.

When a crackling speaker announced boarding for his flight, Michio hoisted a small pack to his shoulder and held out his hand: "Next time, Lynn-san." His grip was easy, and he had a way of holding a person's hand and eye for a long moment that made me feel like he was listening—really *listening*—for some unspoken reply.

I nodded. "Next time, Michio."

Anyone listening would probably have heard an all-purpose *sayonara*, a sort of "until we meet again," but to me, it was obvious he meant that next time, we'd find the blue bear.

8 ⨠ Tsunami

I STEPPED CAREFULLY around a gill net spread along the dock and brushed aside the greetings of the fishermen mending it. I didn't mean to be rude, but the plastic sack I held in my hand contained pressing business, and I was in a hurry to get to my boat. After checking my signature on the charge slip and handing me the bag of film, the clerk at the photo lab said, "Better have your camera checked. You've got some kind of problem."

I dug into a jumble of gear piled on the *Wilderness Swift*'s top bunk, tossing aside a spare bedroll and a duffel bag of clothes to get at a small, portable light table I kept there. The balanced-spectrum bulb flickered to life as I held down the switch with one hand and slid open the first carton of slides with the other. Shaking a cheap editor's loupe out of its imitation leather bag, I scattered a handful of slides across the opaque surface of the slide table and groaned when I put the magnifier to my eye.

The first slide looked as if something had obscured the bottom half of the frame when I snapped the shutter. The second and third slides were the same. Each was cut neatly in half by a dark, unexplained blur. I chose two boxes at random, pulled a few slides from each one, and put them on the table. I repeated the process with boxes four, five, and six; then tore through the rest with shaking fingers. Every photograph I had taken in Russell Fjord was ruined, leaving me with nothing but useless pictures of icebergs and mountains cut in half by a fogbank of black, unexposed film.

A quick examination of the borrowed camera identified the problem. Cameras capture photographs by exposing light to a film plane behind the lens. Most old-style cameras and many modern point-and-shoot models have a separate viewing aperture above or beside the lens to allow the user to see and frame a subject. This offset occasionally results in a photograph that is framed a bit differently from what the photographer sees with his eye. Modern SLR, or single-lens reflex, cameras overcome this by placing an angled mirror between the lens and film plane to reflect the true image up through a prism into a viewfinder. The mirror is synchronized to flip up as the shutter is tripped, then drops into place again after the film is exposed, leaving the camera ready for the next photo.

When I replaced the internal battery beneath the camera's mirror, I had failed to secure its tiny spring-loaded cover. Every time the mirror flipped up, the battery cover sprang into its place and blocked half the film.

I slumped against the bulkhead, feeling a doomed thin-ice sensation seeping into my blood that for years had come upon me at odd moments and left me feeling bone bruised and sour. I usually managed to keep the feeling at bay by staying busy, hurling myself into work, reading, or hiking through the woods, but that day I sat for a long, long time with the detritus of my photography scattered across the table in front of me.

For reasons I cannot name, I kept thinking of Michio and how badly I had wanted to impress him—perhaps as a way of paying him back for the gentle, consistent efforts he made to help me understand photography. I also thought about the breathless way I had described the beauty of Johnstone Bay to him, then dodged his questions when he wanted to know more.

And I thought about how, like the ruined, partially exposed slides, I had told him only half of the story.

⌃

I'LL CALL HER KELLY. She had a head of unruly copper hair she tamed by twisting into an inexplicably stable knot at the base of her neck—a mysterious twist-and-tuck that defied everything I knew about gravity by staying in place without the benefit of a band whether she was splitting kindling with an ax or wrestling with one of the five dogs she kept around her cabin. On occasion she wore large pink-rimmed oval glasses, and when there was something to ponder, she would tuck her lower lip under her front teeth and look at the ground. She was beautiful, with the right bones and skin, but those things are common. What was unusual about Kelly was her complete indifference to her own appearance and an ability to consider everyone she ever met her good friend.

That's probably what cost her her life.

Writing this isn't easy. When I first started trying, I didn't sleep for two days and then I threw up. Here is the first sentence I wrote:

Sometimes I wake up hoping with all of my heart that there is a fundamentalist hell where the souls of the evil blister and pucker in the flames like so much eternally frying bacon.

She was strong for her size, which was slender without being petite, and a full head shorter than my six feet two. The first time we met, she was packing an old-fashioned circular grindstone in her arms. Counterbalancing the weight of the thick, heavy stone pitched her torso back at an angle and she waddled, face shining with effort as she walked.

I noticed a hint of an overbite when she leaned the grindstone against the fender of my pickup and smiled. She was living, she said, in a cabin alongside a creek south of town.

"Squatting, really," she said, laughing and flushing a bit at the same time. It was a shack, a tiny plank-and-frame bunkhouse abandoned by the loggers who had worked in the forest near an estuary a mile and a half beyond the end of the road in the mid-'50s and '60s. Technically it was trespassing to occupy the cabin because it was on government land, but, as she said, "they never minded the *loggers* living there."

There was a bit of defiance, sweetly spoken, in the words, and I had a feeling that this hippie-looking woman was the sort who would offer a passing lumberjack a cup of tea and a smile, then plant herself in front of his chainsaw to save a tree.

I had few such sentiments in those days, beyond knowing I felt more comfortable when I was in the forest or by the sea. Timber—and fish—was where many coastal Alaskans got their money. I was working in a salmon cannery to scrape together the grubstake for my next trip to Johnstone Bay, but I knew lots of people who made their living pulling green-chain at the local sawmill, driving skidders, or felling trees. The cannery was the antithesis of my dreams, a factory full of yellow-clad figures bent to loud, repetitive tasks in a moist field of steam, but that blue metal building perched at the head of Resurrection Bay was literally as close to my homesite as I could get and still earn a whopping five bucks an hour. And if I shared nothing else with the trimmers and choker-setters of the timber industry, we had the proud misery of aching backs and lean wallets in common.

It was the 1970s, women's lib was in full bloom, and I was mistaken enough about the intent of that movement to think that I shouldn't offer Kelly help with her burden—but a week later I found myself at the lip of her valley, sweating a bit from the rise and fall of the trail. While I paused to cool down, I stripped a handful of blueberries from a bush, popped the tart, acerbic fruit into my mouth, then licked at the purple stains the berries left on my fingers as I inspected the scene below.

Her cabin lay at the foot of a steep hill. A riot of shrubs and tall grasses tried desperately to cover the leavings of an old clear-cut scattered across the muddy, sloping ground, but the level floor of the valley was steepled in green timber and carpeted with moss. Spruce and hemlock crowded the banks of Tonsina Creek, which ran rippling and clear over a bed of clean stones. Where the mouth of the creek bent itself into a winding S-curve before pouring into the bay, a falling tide had revealed an arrangement of gravel bars and sandbanks that embraced a pool of spawning salmon.

A square-headed Alsatian tethered to the porch blew out his cheeks and *hoofed* at my approach, then leaped up and spun in circles when Kelly opened the door.

"He's deaf." Kelly smiled, knuckling the dog's forehead. A smaller shepherd appeared in the doorway behind her, grinned at me, and began nuzzling Kelly's hand for affection.

"This one," she said, straddling the second dog's back and gripping an ear in each hand, "is blind in one eye from a porcupine quill."

She spoke as if greeting someone she had known for years, and in less time than it takes for a kettle to boil, she made it clear that there was no place in her world for the formalities or social jockeying of mere acquaintances. At a rough plank table placed squarely before a window giving out onto a meadowland of lush grass, she led the conversation deftly from light gossip about the neighbors (the nearest a mile away, and all of whom she believed to be uniformly good and worthy of trust) to our personal histories and lives. Through one cup, then another of some spicy, fragrant tea, her faith in the world and its people curled lightly but persistently around the cynicism entrenched in my own views and plucked it out. Freed of that weight, my heavy hiking boots felt somehow lighter and more buoyant when I took my leave; and as I wound back along the curves and ridges of the trail, I thought of the best bumper sticker I've ever seen, which read, God, Please Help Me Be the Person My Dog Thinks I Am—and of how rapidly the sentiments of Kelly's hounds had become my own.

"SHE GLOWS," someone told me later, "when you've been by to visit." It had never occured to me before that anyone could be truly happy just to see me. I'd gone from the cannery to working the deck of a halibut boat, and whenever we steamed back into port after a trip to the fishing grounds, I'd begin thumbing through my excuses to make the long hike out to see her.

Winter came, she moved into a cabin closer to town, and as we sat by the light of a lantern I learned how easily a circle can be made of two people if one of them has a quiet and listening heart. As we talked, she sometimes worked at a hobby, which was to make necklaces and earrings of beads and found objects. When I brought her the quills of a porcupine, she showed me how to clip the ends from the delicate ivory-colored thorns and flatten them into slender, hollow reeds that could be strung in fine patterns.

One night after a period of thoughtful silence, I realized whenever I was with her I felt something new: comfort and friendship of a complete and intimate sort, with no need for the posturing of words or the tiny rustlings we humans often use to remind each other of our presence. Simply sharing a silence accentuated by the tiny click of beads against her needles and the hiss of the lantern was enough. Contentment rose up, fitting itself around me like the arms of a favorite chair or a sleeping bag on a cold, frosty night. I didn't say anything. I just relaxed and took a slow sip of my tea.

SPRING CAME AGAIN and then summer, and on a day with more heat and dust than is common in that part of Alaska, we climbed halfway up the mountain behind her cabin, following a shale-filled ravine to timberline, and from there, a winding ledge up a brush-covered slope. The youngest of her platoon of dogs sprinted ahead of us, pausing now and then to stare, tongue lolling over its shoulder, while it waited for us to catch up so it could lick at her hand. While we climbed, we talked of a hundred nothings—the weather, the taste of blueberry jam—and where incline fell back to level and brush gave way to open, stony ground, we chose a low, narrow boulder to sit on while we took turns sipping at a bottle of water pulled from a bag on her hip and the sun lit a copper-colored fire in her hair.

"Can you pour?" she asked, bending down to cup her hands as a dish for the dog.

I poured, the pup slobbered up the water, and she dried her palms on the leg of her pants before turning to straddle the boulder like a saddle and shade her eyes with one hand. Below us, the wake of a fishing boat steaming slowly south toward the gulf split the length of the bay. I mounted the boulder likewise, facing the opposite direction, and we chatted back and forth over our shoulders for a while before stopping to listen to the call of a distant raven.

In the silence that followed, she leaned her back into mine, and slowly and tentatively, I did the same, moving together until touch became pressure and pressure equilibrium, and we relaxed into an apex of rapport. A minute later, I felt the heave of her breath become slow and even, and her head nod as she slipped into a doze.

For five minutes, or ten—I have no true idea—I remained as motionless as possible, unwilling to give in to the need to scratch or ease my bones as the stone beneath my buttocks grew too hard, for fear of disturbing her, or worse, disrupting the feeling that was beginning to germinate within me.

We are drawn to people not so much for who *they* are, but for the way they make us feel about ourselves, and now, more than a quarter of a century later, when there are times when I can no longer remember Kelly's face or the exact shape of her features, and almost never can I remember the precise contents of conversations or events, I do remember with great clarity the presumption of trustworthiness that seemed implicit in that back-to-back touch, and the elevating sensation it gave me of being someone who could be counted on and leaned upon for support—and how it was enough to make me think I was in love.

BETWEEN THE CANNERY AND FISHING, my cash reserves grew, but not fast enough to stack up supplies for Johnstone Bay at the rate I desired. When the halibut season ended I returned to Anchorage, threw in my lot with an international freight airlines that was making a fortune shipping war materials to Vietnam, and traded what freedom I had for a regular paycheck. By the time the United States began winding down its involvement in that messy war, I had a blue-and-white Volkswagen van loaded down with enough cabin-building supplies and cases of canned food to see me through several months in the wilds.

Saltier hands—that is, anyone experienced with small boats in the gulf—must have shaken their heads as Niles G. and I carted a mountain of equipment and supplies down the dock and hefted it aboard the thirty-foot sailboat I had arranged to shuttle us to Johnstone Bay. The *Flying Squirrel* was a sloop-rigged trimaran, homebuilt of plywood, and I had to duck as I entered the cabin. Once inside, I could not stand without stooping or move without knocking something down. Every available space was covered with our provisions, and the floor was a precarious litter of tools.

"This is bonkers," Kelly said as she stood, arms akimbo, on the dock and watched Niles and me pile an overflow of gear into a small inflatable raft we had decided to tow astern. She hated to see us go, and I was having pangs about leaving, but at the same time we were giddy with the sense that something vital was unfolding.

It was the fifth of July and hot under a clear, blue sky. Fireworks left over from the previous day's celebrations rattled like gunfire in the distance. Alan, the *Squirrel*'s swarthy, bearded owner, waved a cigarette at the small motor bolted to the stern of the trimaran and said, "It's gonna hafta work." Trimarans are meant to be hot rods, light-footed darters that skim across the water. With this load, he meant, the boat would handle like a waterlogged plank, and the two-cylinder engine would be laboring like a draft horse just to move us. Sweat worked its way down my forehead and dripped onto my glasses as I hefted another load on the pile.

When the last item was stowed and all the knots double-checked, Alan stood back to inspect the waterline, then clambered aboard and yanked the outboard's starter. "If we go now," he said, "we can still catch the ebb." It was fifteen miles to our anchorage for the night, and there was just enough outgoing tide to boost us on our way.

I handed Kelly the key to my van. She stuffed the key in a pocket, sniffing and feigning an enormous red-eyed interest in something on the horizon, then clutched me and tucked her head to my shoulder. A half hour later, a blue-and-white Volkswagen van pulled off the road and coasted to the water's edge as the *Flying Squirrel* made its way down the bay. The headlights flashed once; a hand reached out the window and waved. I caught a glimpse of red hair and clasped both hands above my head in reply.

If I had looked a bit harder or watched a little longer, I might have seen the shadow of the Kushtaka flitting along the road behind her or taking shape in one of the cumulus clouds boiling slowly up over the horizon. Instead, I simply watched as the van reversed and drove away; then I went aft to take my turn at the helm.

ALAN PUSHED THE TILLER OVER and held it there until the compass settled on a course that would allow us to clear Cape Resurrection. A low swell running in from the south broke in languorous slow motion against the base of the cliff, and the boat began to roll to its tempo. A torrent of seabirds spilled from the face of the cape at our approach and rose into a screaming gyre that showered us with bits of broken feathers. The noise was deafening, like a horde of hysterical teenage pop fans against a background of thunder, and I snugged down my hat to protect myself from the outrage of kittiwakes armed "to the bill" with fresh guano.

When Nathaniel Portlock carried the British flag to the Alaska coast in 1787, he named the bay we were leaving Port Andrews. Five years later a storm in the gulf battered a ship of Alexander Baranof's Russian-American Fur Company so badly that the crew began praying for their lives, and when by divine agency or some freak of the wind their ship was thrust through the slender opening of the bay into shelter, the Russians expressed their wonderment by naming it *Voskresenskaya Gavan*—Resurrection (or Sunday) Harbor—and the name stuck, perhaps because sailors who have experienced the tantrums of the gulf know more about the virtue of miraculous salvation than they know (or care) about who Andrews was.[28]

28. Baranof's sailors set up a sawmill on the shores of Resurrection Bay and and hammered together a replacement ship seventy-three feet long and twenty-five feet wide. The *Phoenix* was a crudely planked vessel, roughly built and caulked with a mixture of whale oil and ocher, but it was the first ship ever built on the Pacific coast of North America.

Between the end of September and the early part of April, a semi-permanent weather trough called the Aleutian Low moves into the gulf and squats there in intense cyclogenesis, spawning more low-pressure weather systems than any other place on the globe: during winter, the gulf averages a storm every five days and waves that can reach heights in excess of a hundred feet.[29]

In May, however, the North Pacific High moves up from its winter home near Hawaii, displaces the Aleutian Low, and grants the gulf a radical personality shift that renders June, July, and August relatively benign.

Today the gulf was tranquil. As the *Flying Squirrel* breasted Cape Resurrection and the next bay to the east hove into sight, I watched for the homestead of a couple I had come to think of as my nearest neighbors.

The stout cabins and barns John and Ginger Davidson built in Driftwood Bay lay halfway between Seward and Johnstone Bay. John was the person that every homesteader wanna-be in Alaska aspired to become: he made his own tools, pounding scrap steel into shape over a forge of his own devising, then used them to turn logs into buildings. He and Ginger raised a few chickens and kept goats to make cheese, but most of their meat came from his gun; sea lions, mountain goats, and deer all made regular appearances on the Davidson table. Ginger mulched barrowloads of kelp into the soil of a huge garden, put away enough vegetables to get them through winter, and tended to their only child, who was precocious and knew the proper names of the seabirds at an age when many children still have difficulty differentiating a dog from a cow.

The sea moved slowly beneath our keel, heaving like the belly of something breathing. I shaded my eyes, uncertain if a pale haze hang-

29. A study of giant waves cited in *Smithsonian* magazine indicates the maximum theoretical wave height in the Gulf of Alaska is a horrifying 198 feet. This, of course, is completely *nuts,* and can never be verified; no one could ever witness such a thing and survive.

ing along the coast was smoke from their homestead or the mist that rises from breaking waves.

(Two years later the Davidsons would disappear after making an emergency trip into town occasioned by their son's falling off the barn and breaking his collarbone. It was a foul day when I spoke to them on the dock after their visit to the doctor, and the forecast was for increasing winds. They were in a hurry to leave, they said, because they had left a houseguest on her own in Driftwood Bay and wanted to return before the deteriorating weather trapped them. They never made it home. We searched, but no trace of the Davidson family or their boat was ever found.)

A storm petrel flitted by, dipping on curved wings, and a sooty shearwater peeled away from our bow. My eyes ached from the glare of sunlight reflecting off my glasses; I wanted to remove them, but without them I see the world as a blur. There was nothing I could do but squint a bit harder and try not to stare directly into the sunlight that burned on the water.

When the white mass of Johnstone Bay's glacier rose into view, Alan nosed the bow in toward the shore until the surf sounded like someone sighing and pitched the anchor over the side. "Sixty feet," he mumbled, checking a marker woven into the line, then paid out a few fathoms to swing on. I took a deep breath, drawing in the resinous smell of the forest beyond the beach fringe and listened to the clatter of cobblestones in the waves.

Niles pulled the inflatable raft alongside and snubbed it to a stanchion. "We better go in empty the first time," he said, and began clearing it of gear. He grew up surfing in California and knew the power of waves. "They can *eat* you," he said, glancing toward the beach as a swell larger than the rest crashed ashore. He pointed out how the steep offshore bottom created a "fast break," stacking up the low, innocuous swells into a wall of water that broke suddenly into a surge that charged up the beach and pulled back as a powerful, sucking undertow.

Alan dug two coils of line from a hold. "Pay one out between the skiff and the boat," he said, bending down to sketch a plan on the deck with his finger. "And tie the other to the stern of the skiff when you're ashore." Once we were ashore, he explained, he could use the first line to haul the empty skiff back to the boat and load it with supplies, then Niles and I could use the second line to pull it back through the surf—a much faster and easier way to shuttle our supplies ashore than rowing repeatedly through the waves.

Niles rowed us to the edge of the shore break, backed one oar and spun us around. We drifted, feeling small and vulnerable in the raft, and watched the backs of the waves rise up and hurl themselves onto the sand. The swells that had appeared so minor from the deck of the boat looked like a series of small, rolling hills when viewed from down low.

Niles crossed the oars on his lap, then stared toward the horizon and timed the intervals between the waves, waiting for the right set.

"Got it," he said, chopping with one oar to turn the stern to the swell. He grimaced, bending his back to the oars, and pulled hard to catch the next wave.

The raft was no surfboard and responded poorly to the oars; we both knew immediately we had misjudged the speed of the waves. I looked over my shoulder into the smoothly concave mouth of a swell just as it crested above my head and engulfed us.

The raft flipped up to the vertical, dumping Niles and launching me into the maelstrom. Salt burned in my nose and the upside-down raft slammed the top of my head. I was hurled against the bottom, then felt myself tumbling in deep water. There was a momentary sensation of weightlessness, then falling again, as the next wave lifted me up and threw me onto the shore.

Suddenly I was on all fours in shallow water, with a slurry of sand washing over my fingers. Niles grabbed me by one arm, then dragged me upright and hustled me up the shore away from the undertow before sprinting back to grab at the skiff.

I was shivering, cold and stunned. Sand and tiny bits of seashell grated against my scalp as I ran my fingers through my hair. I bent over and rubbed my eyes. "Oh my God," I moaned. I wasn't just wet and disheveled—I was blind!

The wave that tore away my glasses and threw me into a world of amorphous shadows changed everything, bringing with it the cold, wet lesson that *there are no small oversights* in a wilderness setting, only mistakes that can suddenly develop enough weight and mass to knock everything down. In my preparations, I had studied pamphlets on how to deal with hypothermia and broken bones, assembled a first-aid kit, and put together a bag of splints and dressings. After listening to John Davidson describe how he had stitched up a gaping chainsaw wound in his own thigh, I pinched a bottle of antibiotics from my mother's cupboard and bought a suture kit to put in my supplies. I never once considered how vulnerable I was to the loss of my glasses—and the only spares I had were in my van.

Once aboard the *Flying Squirrel* again, Niles and I agreed it was impossible to continue. I huddled in a corner, feeling useless and blind while Alan hoisted the anchor aboard. I sat with my eyes closed for the long run back to the anchorage.

No one had much to say that night after the anchor went over the side; the cove was like a mirror, unruffled by the slightest breeze, and as we polished off a late-night dinner of lukewarm canned stew, it was difficult to believe that such a calm sea had pitched us ass-over-tea-kettle and scattered our plans.

The waves just weren't that big, I told myself as I rolled out my sleeping bag and wormed my way in. Next time, I promised myself, I'll be better prepared.

I didn't know then that there are sometimes waves so monstrous and violent about to sweep through our lives that it is impossible— truly impossible—to be prepared.

⌃

SOMETHING IS WRONG.

The first warning whispered in my belly as I pulled up to Kelly's cabin and climbed out of the van. There was too much alarm in the barking of the dogs, and their howls carried a feverish, hungry tone that rose a full octave beyond the frantic yapping that normally greeted visitors.

I rapped a knuckle against the door. "Kelly?"

Silence emanated from the cabin. Alf, the deaf headmaster of the pack, began a low moaning that climbed to an anguished wail. Buff, the half-blind shepherd, leaped in circles at the end of his tether and knocked his water dish spinning. I did a quick head count of the dogs—*three, four, five*—and my stomach dropped when I saw that all of the food dishes and water bowls were empty.

I knocked again and called out in a voice that quavered like the dogs. "Kelly? Where *are* you?"

I hesitated, then opened the door and poked my head inside. The cabin smelled of cold ashes; the sound of my own breathing filled the room.

There was a note from a passing friend on the table, a three-day-old invitation to go berry picking dated the day I left for Johnstone Bay. On a second note I recognized the cryptic handwriting of a neighbor who had stopped by to visit the next day, then returned later and added a plaintive postscript across the bottom of the page: "Where are you? I'm worried!"

When I try to remember what happened next, in the following hours and days, the memories elude me, darting away like the shadows of fish up a stream. I remember Kelly's boots leaning against each other at a drunken angle beside the door; I remember a wooden matchstick she used to mark her place in a book before placing it carefully beside her bed on the floor and how seeing it made the entire cabin resonate with her absence; I remember how cold the surface of the woodstove was against the palm of my hand and the smell of food that was starting to rot.

I also remember the look on a policeman's face as he brushed aside my terror with the casual reassurance that someone "like her" was "probably somewhere partying" and his hostility when I tried to convince him that five starving, thirsty dogs made that callous presumption a lie. ("Is she your wife?" No. "Your girlfriend?" I shook my head at the grilling. He was skeptical, suspicious that any man would be so concerned about a woman who wasn't his wife.)

Of course, Kelly's friends formed search parties and combed the woods around the cabin, pushing through incongruously beautiful fields of fireweed blossoms and thickets of alder aflame with birdsong. They tore their clothes clambering over shattered deadfalls and filled their hands with thorns worming their way into dense patches of devil's club on trails blazed by bears; others skiffed for miles along the beach, imagining her lost somewhere within the profoundly vast forest, wandering to the end of one of the rugged fingers of land that stretched out into the sea and waiting there for a rescue.

Every ravine, overhang, and cliff base within walking distance of the cabin was searched and searched again. The riverbeds were scoured, and her favorite berry patches probed. All the while, the dogs howled and whined as if trying to convince us: *She would never go anywhere without us.*

THE NIGHTS WERE BAD, but the mornings were worse. After squirming with worry until two or three in the morning, I would look for sleep in a tumbler of whiskey, then flinch during the rise to consciousness an hour or two later as I struggled to remain asleep in the face of the onrushing certainty that something dreadful was waiting at the surface. Sitting bolt upright, I would fight the bedclothes from around my body, then rush outside to probe the litter-filled ditches by the road: What if she was hit by a car?

I was willing to believe anything. Maybe she really did leave town for a family emergency or was a closet alcoholic, off on a binge. What if there was a side to her character that nobody knew and she really *did* forsake the dogs by taking off in search of adventure?

These were desperate fantasies, of course, and I knew it. Having the posters printed was an admission that the truth was much worse.

There was a description—red hair, pink glasses, gray sweater, and jeans—and a headline that promised a reward. Bold lettering above a yearbook-style portrait asked, Have you seen Kelly? and carried an unwritten subtext that said, *One of you has taken her.*

And that's where it stayed. Kelly was gone. She had completely vanished from the face of the earth, disappearing shortly after waving to me from the beach as I left for Johnstone Bay and then dropping off my van with a friend. Day in and day out, while the posters I placed in the window of every store and restaurant that would accept one turned yellow and faded, I looked into the face of everyone I met and silently asked, *Are you the one?*

People I had known for years became suspect; affable strangers, I was certain, were someone else inside. The man idling in the aisle of the grocery store over a display of canned peas was a monster, capable of tucking his child into bed that night and snatching a woman off the street the next day. Women, too, were suspect, for reasons of envy or one of the other squirming emotions that live deep within the dark cracks of a mind.

The horror of it was not that the one responsible for her disappearance was so inhuman, but that he would prove to *be* human, just like the rest of us, only morally vacant behind a papery facade of decency. Absolutely no one was to be trusted, I learned, because even I was a criminal inside.

A COLT .357 MAGNUM REVOLVER weighs about three pounds. This was enough to dampen the tremor in my hand as I thumbed the last of six 150-grain hollow-point bullets into the cylinder and slipped the gun in my pants. Ten minutes later I was parked outside a neglected frame house on the outskirts of town, listening to the Volkswagen's engine tick as it cooled down.

The house belonged to a local weirdo, a tall bad-eyed fellow with an aura like barbed wire, the sort of person you turn a shoulder to when he sits next to you in a bar and avoid making eye contact with on the street. He did not, as best I could learn, hold down a job and was given to wandering for hours along the railroad tracks north of town.

A few weeks after Kelly disappeared I was sitting in a café when I caught him staring at me over a cup of coffee with what seemed a look of smugness unsupportable in one so dirty and strange; a week later I heard he had exposed himself to a woman; on another occasion he was seen masturbating in a parking lot. I pondered and expanded on this information, filled in the gaps, and made up the answers to questions I did not know until finally I twisted that single protracted glance in the café into an unsupportable conviction, *He was the one.*

I watched the house long enough to be sure it was empty, then climbed out and walked to the rear. My hand was shaking as I knocked at the back door. Go to the police, I told myself, then argued, Why? They had acted largely unconcerned and offered no help with the searches; after sufficient pressure was brought to bear, there were a few desultory interviews of Kelly's friends, but then even that minimal effort was set aside.

I knocked again. When there was no answer, I tried the knob. The door was stuck, swollen in its jamb, and made a horrendous noise when I stiff-armed it open.

I held my breath, listening to the silence that engulfed the room. I was in a kitchen that stank of garbage, with patches of bare flooring showing through a layer of cracked linoleum tiles. Dirty dishes and empty food tins covered the surface of a greasy stove to the left and overflowed a sink to the right. I eased the gun in my waistband; I was scared, and there was comfort in its bulk.

I was breathing rapidly, ready to jump out of my skin as I walked quickly through the house to make sure I was alone. I don't really know what I was looking for—her sweater? The small army-surplus pack she used as a purse? I started opening cupboard doors at random, kicking aside piles of unwashed clothes, and flipped over a stained mattress to see what was underneath. There was a shotgun in a bedroom closet (which meant nothing; half the closets in Alaska hold a gun), and beneath a loose stack of magazines beside the weapon was a trapdoor.

It fought me at first, then yielded to a solid yank; my pulse hammered wildly as I bent to peer into a crawl space beneath the floor. I hesitated, wishing I had thought to bring a flashlight, then took the gun in my hand to keep it from falling from my pants, and dropped through the opening into a crouch.

I waited for my eyes to adjust to the gloom, then started crawling through a loose web of water pipes, old wiring, and ducting, probing into the darkness for freshly dug ground and waiting for the terrible smell of decay.

There was nothing. Just the odor of mildew and dirt.

Gravel crunched under a footstep on the driveway. When a Steller's jay squawked in alarm outside the house, I froze until a second rusty, piercing call jerked me upright. My heart hammered, threatening to break out of my rib cage, and adrenaline fizzed in my veins. I bolted for the opening, suffused with fear, and all thoughts of Kelly were driven from my mind, replaced with the fearful knowledge that inside that house, *I* was the criminal, a burglar with a gun, and had absolutely no evidence to justify what I was doing.

I panicked, knocking my head against a floor joist as I scrambled out of the crawl space and dashed from the room. The front door crashed behind me and I didn't stop running until I was in the van; my hands shook so badly it was difficult to fit the key in the ignition.

I sped down the road, barely missing the large dog whose footsteps I had heard, and as I fled, I banged my fist on the dashboard and screamed in frustration.

That flight was the start of a running away that lasted nearly fifteen years, a removal from any meaningful connection with other people driven not just by the unsettled, personal horror of Kelly's disappearance, but by the greater realization that such terrible things could—and did—happen; that no matter how cruel and uneven the world had at times seemed before she disappeared, it was now unavoidably clear that there was nothing so abominable or wrong that it couldn't happen, and that life, even at its most dreadful, could always hold something worse, and was therefore undeserving of any form of trust.

9 》 The Butcher,
the Baker

TWO HUNDRED MILLION years ago, Alaska as we know it did not exist. The land (like most of its human inhabitants) drifted in from elsewhere, thrust along by forces beyond its control. In 1972 a graduate student named Duane Packer and Professor David Stone of the University of Alaska discovered that the orientation of magnetic particles fossilized within the stones of southern Alaska suggested the land had been formed somewhere between the tropic of Capricorn and the equator, then moved north to become part of Alaska 50 million years ago during the Eocene.

By the mid-'80s, scientists with the U.S. Geological Survey were suggesting an alternative history—that a series of undersea volcanic eruptions during the Carboniferous period (between 250 million and a half billion years ago) had lumped together a large chunk of land named Wrangellia, which stuck to the edge of the Pacific plate and drifted north over the next 100 million years or so.[30] When North

30. The Pacific plate is one of thirty rigid pieces of the earth's lithosphere—the thin, rocky crust that makes up the surface of the earth and consists of all dry land and the floors

America broke away from the supercontinent Pangaea and hurled itself into the path of the Pacific plate 150 million years ago, Wrangellia crashed ashore somewhere around Washington or southern British Columbia and went skidding north along the coast, peeling off parts like a Hollywood stunt driver. It didn't stop until it smashed full bore into the sedimentary Yukon-Tanana terrane and crumpled into the great, jumbled arc of stones we now call the Wrangell–Saint Elias Mountains.

"Does that make sense?" I asked Michio, after sketching out my disjointed interpretation of creation on a piece of paper with a pen. It was September, the weather was lousy, and an autumn gale had already kept us penned in the Juneau harbor for three days. With fresh rumors circulating of a glacier bear being spotted in a fjord fifty miles south of town, waiting was frustrating—but not quite as frustrating as trying to clarify the riot of subducting plates, drifting terranes, and crumbling plutonic belts that make up the incomprehensible puzzle of Alaska's birth.

Michio placed his hand over the drawing and furrowed his brow at the math: "Then Alaska is . . . how old?"

I hesitated, reluctant to give a definitive answer, then backpedaled by explaining that a paleobotanist working for the U.S. Geological Survey up near Malaspina Glacier had found fossilized broad-leafed plants that were 50 million years old. The palm fronds Jack Wolfe discovered were of a type that grows not only where it is warm (as Alaska may have been at various times during its history) but also where there is the same amount of daylight year-round—in other words, the fossils could only have been formed near the equator, then drifted north to their current location in Alaska.

This fit in with Packer and Stone's proposal that the southern portions of Alaska finished migrating here 50 million years before Michio

---

of all the oceans. The lithosphere floats atop the mantle, or asthenosphere, a thick plastic layer of molten rock that in places reaches temperatures of thirty-six hundred degrees Fahrenheit, which in turn rests on the dense core of the earth. The Pacific plate spans almost the entire Pacific Ocean, from Alaska to the Philippines and south into the Antarctic Ocean, spinning slowly in a counterclockwise direction at a rate of about ten centimeters a year.

and I did, but it didn't gibe with the Geological Survey's theory that Wrangellia had crawled up on the shores of North America between 100 and 150 million years ago.

Science (including geology) is a Kushtaka thing, no more static than the land: it shifts, moving left and right with the currents of inquiry and knowledge, and takes advantage of whatever new evidence comes along to disguise itself as certainty—and has done so throughout history.

Pliny the Elder was born in A.D. 23, and by the time he died fifty-six years later, he had written at least seventy-five books, including the thirty-seven-volume *Historia Naturalis,* which put him at the forefront of scientific thought for hundreds of years. In it, he said, he had attempted to "set forth in detail all the contents of the entire world," which is a remarkably ambitious claim from someone who also set forth a great many details that *weren't* of this world: people with no heads, their eyes in their shoulders; others with the heads of dogs who communicated by barking; serpents that snatched birds out of flight; and others so venomous that when one was killed by a man on horse-back, "the infection rising through the spear killed not only the rider but also the horse." There is probably no truth to the rumor that Pliny marketed his epic work under the slogan *Satis veritatis superque,* or All of the facts and then some!

Pliny's perception of the natural world finally killed him when he went ashore at Pompeii in A.D. 79 to reassure the frightened populace of that city that the flames and thunder belching from nearby Mount Vesuvius were no cause for alarm; he died with the rest in the eruption. Nonetheless, his boundless curiosity, energy, and imagination carried his influence well into the future, until his theories were supplanted by the works of thinkers like the eighteenth-century Swedish naturalist Linnaeus, who elevated the Aristotelian concept of genus, species, pro-pria, and accidens into the modern system of taxonomy—a system for sorting out the ingredients of the world that is still in use today.

This was the same Linnaeus, however, who wrote in his *Systema Naturae* (1758) that *Homo sapiens afer* (the black African) was "ruled by caprice," while *Homo sapiens europeanis* (the white European) was supposedly "ruled by customs"—an observation that, with its implication of a racial hierarchy, entrenched the racist sentiments of eighteenth-century Europe as a scientific paradigm that, unfortunately, the occasional pseudoscientific buffoon among us will still attempt to argue today.

It was the Linnaean system that George Thornton Emmons used to attach his own name to the glacier bear by identifying it as *Ursus americanus emmonsii* during the wild rush of discovery and naming that took place throughout the nineteenth century and into the twentieth (see footnote 17, page 81). If Emmons's fascination with the elusive animal was as acute as my own, the ego implicit in that naming was forgivable, as was his mistaken certainty that the silver-and-roan animal constituted its own species.

Michio watched as I dug out a map and spread it on the table. "This is Endicott Arm," I said, tapping the outline of a fjord with my finger. "It cuts thirty-five miles into the mainland and passes through several of the terranes that floated in to make up the Coast Range."

"And that's where we find a glacier bear?" Michio's optimism was tentative. We had made nearly a dozen trips together, and while we had always had resounding success photographing the grizzlies, whales, and other species of wildlife that abound around Southeast Alaska, we had never found any sign of a blue bear.

Heading for the airport to pick up Michio and his ever present mountain of gear had become a regular part of my season over the last half dozen years, one that I looked forward to more and more every year. As time went by, I noticed that the slight bow with which we had so awkwardly greeted each other at our first meeting had become more natural, deeper and easier in response to the pleasure I always felt at seeing this friend. I'm not sure why I found him different from the other clients I was guiding; I don't have the vocabulary to describe his appeal. Unfailingly kind; courteous above all; gentle, generous, and considerate? Unflinchingly honest; apparently without ego? He was a sum greater than his parts. Perhaps Celia Hunter, one of Alaska's foremost conservationists, said it best when she said, "He had sensitivity for the 'other,' which came across as a sincere interest in each person he met, and an instinctive awareness of their sense of values. He was truly shy, but never allowed that diffidence to keep him from making the first move when [you first met]."

In any case, when we did not speak with or see each other for long periods of time (as frequently happened; Michio was often away on some remarkable adventure, traveling in Africa with Jane Goodall or off to Siberia with a band of nomadic reindeer herders), I missed him, and now I was glad to have the rumor of a glacier bear to lure him back.

This year he had arrived with even more equipment than usual, including a folding kayak, a twelve-foot inflatable raft we planned to use if the ice pack in the fjord was too thick for the *Swift* to penetrate, and a copy of his latest book.

The book was a gift, he said, and it contained several photos from our trips. After I admired the photos and the quality of the printing, I lamented that I could not read it because the text was in Japanese. Michio looked smug for a moment, then pulled out a second, more crudely wrapped, package and placed it on the table in front of me.

"This is *real* present, Lynn." He squirmed in his seat, grinning with anticipation.

Inside was a set of flash cards. The face of each square of white pasteboard had been laboriously hand printed with a figure from the Japanese *hiragana* alphabet, and on the reverse with the figure's pronunciation in English. Also in the package was a children's book in Japanese and a sheaf of loose papers onto which Michio had translated the simple text into English.

"Now you are five years old again." Michio giggled. "And you must teach yourself how to read."

I cleared my throat once or twice, then mumbled, "Thanks . . . arigato," and watched a seagull blow sideways past the window.

To change the subject, I moved the books and flash cards aside, then sketched a circle on the chart with my finger. "What I heard," I said, pointing to a small bight on the chart, "was that a naturalist on a tour boat saw a glacier bear in Endicott Arm. And from the way she described it, I think it was somewhere around here."

We both leaned in to stare at the spot as if a conjuring were possible. The mooring lines groaned, fighting the wind, and a burst of
heavy rain rattled against the windows. The map was outdated and
inaccurate in places; the survey was dated 1961. A land as dynamic as
the Coast Range can change significantly in three decades, and I
pointed out to Michio how far inland Dawes Glacier had receded in
that time.

"It's current position is nearly three miles from what the map
shows," I said, measuring the distance with my fingers.

"Three miles?" Michio leaned back and frowned. A pensive look
flitted across his face, and he reached out to draw a finger through a
film of condensation on the window: "That's just in our lifetime."

"That's right. A block of ice three miles long, a mile wide, and
over a thousand feet high has disappeared since you and I were born."

Michio groaned, then patted his face with both hands. "Lynn, do
you think I look fat?"

It was unkind of me to laugh, but I knew the source of his anxiety and the question wasn't the nonsequitur it seemed. Talking about
the passage of time always aroused one of his deepest concerns: that
middle age was upon him, he had never gotten married, and his
prospects of having a family were rapidly diminishing. "I want to do
something *important* with my life," he had told me several times. "Not
just photography all the time."

"You're a hunk, Michio," I reassured him. "Women would throw
themselves at you if you ever stayed home."[31]

I rolled up the charts and put them away, then switched on the radio
to catch the weather. Another low-pressure system was heading our
way, the droning voice promised, but it would take a few days to arrive.

THE GALE DIMINISHED during the early hours of the morning,
and a north wind eased into its place. Fresh snow on the mountaintops

31. Many wildlife photographers spend two hundred or more days a year in the field—a
poor recipe for achieving domestic bliss.

turned the sky powder blue, and as I steered the *Swift* into the channel I zippered my jacket to my chin against the chill, then glanced aft to make sure Michio's inflatable skiff was towing well. It felt good to be under way again, with Michio humming in the galley, fuel and food for a week or two onboard, and the hurly-burly rush of summer behind me.

Twelve miles south of Juneau a black, fist-sized fin sliced through the water, and a pod of Dall's porpoises announced their arrival with a staccato of flying spray.

Michio sprinted to the foredeck and leaned over the bow as one of the black-and-white porpoises *chuffed!* alongside and carved a slick arc through the water. "Should I get camera?" he asked, eager to get a photo but reluctant to go inside and risk missing anything. The porpoise cut sharply under the bow, water hissing from its small dorsal fin.

"Better be quick," I said, nodding toward the speeding creature. "They may not hang around long."

A Dall's porpoise is a compact, muscular animal that looks like a miniature killer whale; it has the largest heart-to-body-mass ratio of any mammal, and all of that powerful pumping gives the animal a tremendous, frenzied energy that seems to embody joie de vivre.

This group was no exception. First a bull (judging from its size and the boldness in its eye), then a slightly smaller pair conjured up from the depths and waltzed in, taking turns riding the bow wave for a few thrilling seconds before rippling away with a flick of a muscular tail.

It puzzles me that porpoises make no appearance in the Native legends of the Pacific Northwest; killer whales, bears, ravens, goats, seals, eagles, sea lions, otters—even sharks and toads—populate the stories of the Tlingit and Haida, but the members of the *phocoenidae* family have been largely scorned, even as food for anyone but slaves. In her epic compilation of George Thornton Emmons's work on the Tlingit Indians, Frederica de Laguna notes that the meat of porpoises was reviled as a cause of nosebleeds and foul body odor.

The pod playing tag with the *Swift* suddenly veered, as if insulted by my thoughts, wheeled east, and began a series of slow, smooth-as-silk rolls, curtsying to the surface for quick snatches of breath. After a

few relaxed, directionless circles, the pod broke into a sprint and disappeared as quickly as they had come.

Michio lowered his camera and smiled at the empty horizon.
"*Iruka* always having a good time," he said, making a diving motion
with his hand. He faced me, pointing over his shoulder in the direction of the porpoises, and said, "That was a nice family."

I nodded, unsure. The importance of kinship varies widely among
mammals, with little long-term bonding between animals like caribou
or moose, while others, like the killer whale, are rigidly organized into
matriarchal clans. I knew relatively little about the smaller dolphins
and porpoises, other than that at least one Atlantic species gathers into
pods that engage in recreational, multipartner sex whereas others, like
the spinner dolphins around Hawaii, form feeding groups that can be
several hundred strong. I could not say one way or the other whether
the Dall's porpoise cared about family ties.

Michio shook his head at my dithering. "That was a *family*, Lynn."
The felicity of the group was all the proof that he needed. Anyone so
apparently happy (he was emphatic about this) *must* be part of a family.

I unfolded a chart on the table and flattened it with my hands, then
plotted a rough fix of the *Swift*'s position. Many of my charts have
been with me for years, and the smooth, worn feel of this one aroused
something akin to affection within me. It was dog-eared and torn, its
margins penciled with memories: *"Gilbert Bay, sow with 4 cubs, June
'87; Pt. Coke, goshawk nest April '91."*

Beneath a layer of accumulated coffee stains and smudges, chart
number 17300 (Stephens Passage to Cross Sound) was marked with a
warning that a nearby zone of "extreme magnetic disturbance" might
render a ship's compass unreliable. On other charts tucked into the
rack beside the helm, the letters PA or PD next to a submerged rock
or sunken wreck warned mariners that the position of the hazard was
approximate or *doubtful*. After Kelly disappeared and I could no longer
look into another human's face without seeing deceit and corruption,
this willingness to confess their own fallability became a sort of proof
to me that charts were more honest and reliable than people, and after

I learned to harness the wind in the belly of a sail and translate its strength into motion, they became passports to a world where movement filled the hole left by the loss of all trust, a world where life was reduced to the simplest elements of survival. Warm food, dry boots, a deck that didn't leak over my bunk were important; connecting with other human beings was not.

I was angry, I suppose, full of a quietly furious grief that was like tar on my hands, smearing everything I touched, and never went back to Johnstone Bay. I drifted instead, wandering without purpose or intention from one boat to another, from saloon to saloon, and from day into night, waiting (without realizing I was doing so) for some resolution to Kelly's disappearance. When after ten years of such wandering the resolution came, it sprang like the trap of a gallows, leaving me dangling over a pit much worse than anything I had ever imagined—a horrible place, where for all their warnings of hazards and dangers, even charts became unworthy of trust.[32]

❮❮

ON JUNE 13, 1983, a seventeen-year-old prostitute working the streets of Anchorage under the name "Kitty Larsen" was abducted and chained to a post in the basement of a home belonging to a baker named Robert Christian Hansen. Hansen was a trophy hunter, and the glass eyes of the caribou and mountain goats mounted on the walls of his den had witnessed this part of what Hansen later referred to as his "summer project" many times. After raping and abusing his teenage captive in the most frightful manner, Hansen handcuffed her, forced her onto the floor of his car, and threw a blanket over her, telling her, "I like you so much I'm going to fly you to my cabin and keep you for a while."

Hansen is a small, ugly man with a complexion heavily marked

---

32. Kelly's name has been changed and certain facts omitted throughout this narrative. This was done out of respect for those who suffered through the horror of her disappearance and would not wish to revisit it in such a public forum. If those people should ever read this, please know I have never forgotten you and hold you in the highest regard for the strength and courage you showed in rebuilding your shattered lives.

with the scars of adolescent acne and greasy black hair. He stutters and spits when he talks; his eyes swim behind horn-rimmed glasses; and while he was never a particularly bright man, he was sufficiently devious to maintain the facade of a modestly successful businessman with a wife and two kids.

He lived in a suburban-style home, owned his own airplane, and kept a small boat down in Seward. An "avid outdoorsman," several of his hunting trophies were impressive enough to make the Pope and Young record book for animals killed with a bow and arrow. He is, where his hunting skills and most other things are concerned, a chest-thumping braggart. Nonetheless, a snarling bear-skin rug on the floor of his basement was not the result of any prowess, but rather of baiting the animal into the open with a pile of meat scraps and killing it from the safety of a tree. When he unlocked the handcuffs to shove Kitty into his plane, he was practically strutting; after all, he figured, he had been doing this for a long time and none of the others had ever gotten away.

Despite her fear and the terrible abuse, Kitty had retained the presence of mind to carry her fashionable platform shoes in her hand. "I knew I couldn't run in them," she said later. And run she did, screaming out into the middle of a road near the runway, where she forced an oncoming truck to a halt and threw herself into the cab.

No charges were filed. The police let him go. They took no photos of Hansen's basement, seized no evidence (including a roll of speaker wire identical to that binding the wrists of a woman found frozen to death at the base of a waterfall south of town or a blanket like the one Kitty said had been used to cover her). In spite of her precise description of Hansen, his basement, its contents, and the post, the police demanded that Kitty submit to a polygraph. When she refused, they said there would be no arrest, because Hansen's alibi was better than her story. An executive with one of Anchorage's most prosperous insurance firms and another businessman respected in the local community for his contracting work and boatbuilding said they were with Hansen during the time the hysterical girl claimed to have been kidnapped and raped.

"Repairing an airplane seat," they said. "Watching some television and drinking a few beers." The investigating officers apparently did not think it very strange for men responsible for running large, complex companies to be piddling around with a buddy until nearly five o'clock in the morning.[33]

In September of the previous year a hunter had found a shallow grave on the banks of a glacial river that flows from the Chugach Mountains onto a floodplain at the head of Cook Inlet. Tufted in thick clumps of willow, birch, and alder, the area provides prime riparian habitat for moose and good cover for snowshoe hares. As a teenager, I skipped school more than once to hunt along its brushy banks, and during one fruitless but memorable search for Dall's sheep, I climbed to the nearby summit of six-thousand-foot Pioneer Peak to look down on the shifting braid of sandbars along the river. Thirty years later I cannot remember the exact thoughts I had from that vantage, except a bit of fear (I'm not good with heights) and a stomach knot of worry surrounding the descent, which involved a lot of crumbling shale, overhangs, and tapering ledges. I'm certain it never occurred to me that the sandbars below me would someday be a mass grave.

A few months after the first body was found, another floated up from the sands. Then a third corpse was found, and the police finally had to admit that someone was making a hobby out of killing Alaska's women. After a police investigator more astute and conscientious than the rest put the bodies washing out of the Knik River together with Kitty Larsen's story, it was just a matter of time before Hansen's "summer project" was finally brought to an end.

I WAS IN HAWAII when the telegram came:

> Serial killer Robert Hansen responsible for Kelly's death STOP Confesses seventeen STOP More expected STOP

---

33. Months later, when the investigation finally turned from one of abduction and rape into murder, John Sumrall and John Henning recanted their stories.

In that brevity of language, more than a dozen years of terror were described. As investigators dug and sifted through the layers of Hansen's work, the numbers quickly grew into a logarithm of cruelty beyond anything I had imagined. He had thrown one woman off a bridge into a river; was charged with four counts of murder; revealed the location of a dozen graves; confessed to seventeen killings; and spoke of at least thirty random rapes in which his victims had survived.

Before it was over, Hansen's wanderings were tied to nearly forty disappearances, and investigators were certain there were many more bodies to be found: a flight chart recovered during a search of his house was marked with twenty-three crosses, seventeen of which matched the gravesites of those victims he had already confessed to killing.[34]

"There were posters and stuff all over town," he said, referring to Seward while being questioned about Kelly. "But that one, um, I didn't . . . that one wasn't mine."

Mine. The demented possessiveness sickens me, revealing as it does the twisted workings of his mind: *Mine*—my toys, to do with as I please; *mine*—to play with and break if I want to; *mine*—to throw away when I'm done. The only good number that came from the litany of his perversions was 461—the number of years, plus life, Judge Ralph Moody handed down when he sentenced the butchering baker for his crimes.[35] The judge also threw in an order that Hansen be forced to undergo psychiatric treatment for no other reason than that with it, "he might someday realize how evil he is."

There is no doubt Hansen was lying about Kelly, even though her body was never found. He was in Seward the day she disappeared, and his demented record-keeping condemned him as her killer. On the pilot's chart marked with the locations of his victims' graves, a small, penciled cross marked the cold blue waters of Resurrection Bay.

---

34. Hansen would admit only to the torture and murder of women involved in prostitution or topless dancing; all the rest, including Kelly's, he denied.
35. Alaska has no capital punishment.

IT TOOK another five years of purposeless, saltwater wandering before charts held any magic for me again, but eventually the passage of years and the layering over of those terrible revelations with experiences like the one I was embarking on with Michio gave charts back their allure, and as we motored south toward Endicott Arm, I pointed out to Michio the history of various landmarks along the way: Grand Island, where Vancouver's survey team was trapped by a storm in August of 1794; Stockade Point, where the Hudson's Bay Company built a fort in the 1800s; Limestone Inlet, home to a trapper who froze to death in his cabin during a bad winter in the 1930s.

A half hour after leaving the porpoises, the glistening back of a humpback whale rolled to the surface, blew once or twice, and disappeared again. Beyond the whale I could see an iceberg snuggled up to the shore, and beyond that one, several more. The moon was gibbous, growing closer to full, and under its increasing influence the level of the tide had risen high enough to float icebergs over the bar at Tracy Arm. In the brilliant autumn light the ice glittered topaz and silver; the closest berg was covered with resting gulls.

Michio pointed at the shoreline and crinkled his brow. "What is it?" he asked.

I started to say something flip like "Haven't you ever seen an iceberg before?" then did a double-take in the direction he was pointing; an animal was snuffling through the tidal debris along the shore.

Michio reached for a pair of binoculars and raised them to his eyes. *"Ku-ma!"* he whispered: *bear!*

Judging from the size of its head and the narrow width of its shoulders, the animal was a young one, and like most bears, it was busy looking around with its nose.

I eased back on the throttle and took the engine out of gear. We were a half mile or more offshore, but if I estimated the set of the tide correctly and positioned the boat in the right spot, we might intercept the ambling bear by drifting along the beach and put

Michio in position for a photograph composed of the blue ice, the green forest, and the black bear—all a photographer with Michio's abilities needed to "tell a whole story" in one frame.

The bear had other plans. As soon as I shortened up the towline to the skiff and idled the *Swift* into position, the animal dabbed a final time at the kelp with one paw, then turned its rump toward us and meandered into the trees.

Michio laughed when I screwed up my face to show my disappointment, then raised his camera and snapped a shot of the shore. "Beautiful iceberg! Lucky the bear got out of the way!"

The shoreline of Stephens Passage bends east at Point Coke to form Holkham Bay, from which two long, winding fjords branch north and east in the shape of a twisted Y. Tracy Arm reaches inland for twenty-one miles before terminating at Sawyer Glacier; Endicott Arm, which is blocked at its eastern end by Dawes Glacier, pierces the coast for thirty-five miles. Both fjords reach depths in excess of a thousand feet but are restricted at their mouths by a pile of rubble and boulders bulldozed into place during the last ice age by the advance of the glaciers. The shoal created by this glacial morraine covers and uncovers with the rise and fall of the tides, and by the time we reached Point Coke more than sixty square miles of water was flowing out of the fjords, forming immense whirlpools and swirls of current as it poured across the bar and fought to wrestle control of the boat from my hands.

As the *Swift* plowed ahead, Michio's skiff jerked and pulled at its towline. Thousands of Bonaparte's gulls and marbled murrelets dove and swam all around, gorging on a dense cloud of marine invertebrates being flushed to the surface by the upwelling tide. Murrelets are alcids—a family of small, heavy-bodied birds that waddle like penguins on land but swim and dive extraordinarily well. Unlike its puffin, murre, aukelet, and guillemot cousins who breed in raucous colonies on seaside cliffs, the murrelet is a secretive nester that raises its chicks on heavily mossed branches deep in the shadowy canopy of a virgin rainforest.[36] More than 95 percent of the murrelets' habitat in the Lower 48 has been destroyed by clear-cut logging, with the result that fewer than five hundred breeding pairs survive along the coast of northern California, Washington, and Oregon.

"There are probably ten times that many around us right now," I pointed out to Michio, raising my voice to be heard above the birds' cries. "During the winter, I've seen flocks of old-squaws and white-winged scoters in here that were twenty thousand strong."[37]

Once the *Swift* was across the bar and into the calm waters beyond, we slowed to a stop. I switched off the engine. "Just listen," I said in reply to Michio's questioning look; he appeared perplexed for a moment, then realized what I was trying to give him.

There was not a breath of wind and the waters were as placid as glass. To the north, wreaths of vapor twisted slowly into the air above a forested gorge at the base of a deeply crevassed glacier. The water reflected the blue of the sky, and a few rags of cloud clung to the peaks without moving. Without the sound of the engine or the rush of water along the hull, the world seemed utterly silent.

"So calm," Michio whispered.

"The Tlingit called that area Soun-doun," I said, pointing toward the shoreline below the glacier: "The Sit'kweidi clan had a village over there." (Sit'kweidi translates as "People of Sit'ku," the clan's name for the bay.)

Soun-doun, I explained, meant either "place without storms" or "the sound the glacier makes when it falls into the sea." Taken together, the seemingly disparate interpretations reveal an intimate sense of place that is almost poetic in its simplicity and accuracy. The waters of the bay are often calm when nearby Stephens Passage boils with breaking seas, and to hear a gravel-voiced elder pronounce Soun-doun deep in his throat is like hearing the glacier mumble its name.

36. Fewer than a half dozen marbled murrelet nests have ever been found.
37. Sadly, the population of old-squaws has declined by more than 85 percent in the last decade, and the numbers of other marine duck and seabird species have diminished drastically as well.

Tlingit speech is full of subtle accents and tones difficult for Westerners to grasp. After prospectors corrupted Soun-doun to Sum Dum in the late 1800s, cartographers condemned the Place Without Storms to a future of inevitable, slow-witted jokes by inscribing the mispronunciation on their maps.

A succession of Westerners eliminated all other Tlingit names outright, beginning with George Vancouver, who tossed aside Sit'ku in 1794 and replaced it with Holkham Bay to honor a small town in Norfolk, England. A century later, Lieutenant Commander H. B. Mansfield of the U.S. Navy named Endicott Arm after President Cleveland's secretary of war and Tracy Arm for the secretary of the navy. Two years later, the U.S. Geological Survey honored Henry Lauren Dawes (a Massachusetts lawyer and statesman) by applying his name to the glacier at the east end of Endicott Arm.[38] The Tlingit villagers fared little better than their language; the last member of the Sit'kweidi clan to live at Soun-doun was an elderly man nicknamed "Sumdum Charlie," who lived there alone until he died in 1931.

Michio sat on the hatch cover and closed his eyes; I followed suit, taking a deep breath to absorb the silence and still my mind, then listened carefully as the music of the fjord began to play.

First the faint roar of a distant waterfall; behind us, a cloud of seabirds shrieked and squabbled; icebergs scattered here and there popped and hissed at their own reflections; and an eagle shrieked at a flock of passing crows, who in turn began hurling obscenities at a

38. In 1880 John Muir paddled a canoe through Endicott and Tracy Arms (which he called Yosemite Bay for the landscape's resemblance to that valley) and named the glacier after the Reverend S. Hall Young. In his autobiography, the "mushing parson" lamented: "For ten years the maps printed my name on this glacier; then some aspiring surveyor, doubtless for patronage's sake, changed the name to Dawes—stole *my* glacier! I mourned the loss silently and not until the visit of President Harding in 1923, when one of the officials of the Department of Topography learned of my loss, and took the matter up with the Department, did I get my glacier back." (One gets the impression the Reverend Young's mourning was somewhat tongue-in-cheek, but nonetheless, he was wrong: USGS charts still call it Dawes Glacier.)

raven. The raven fled into the shadows of a small island to brood and gave a series of liquid, burbling cries.

I have no idea how long we remained engulfed in that peaceful symphony, but when I returned, I was sprawled on the deck and the sun had moved well across the sky. Michio smiled: "Totemo ki-re." *Very beautiful.*

"This is one of my favorite places," I agreed. "It always seems so *alive.*"

Michio looked toward the head of the fjord, where a series of pastel blue-and-white ridges came together at the horizon.

"You've been here a lot?" he questioned.

"I've lost count." I shrugged, then ticked off a calculation on my fingers. Between charters with photographers and film crews, I often filled in my schedule by taking tourists on day trips to Tracy Arm or guiding kayakers and wildlife enthusiasts on excursions that could last several days. No matter how often I came or how long I stayed, I always felt drawn back by the stark beauty of the area.

"Then you should make a book," said Michio. "Your photos are getting pretty good."

Pretty good was a catchall in Michio's glossary of English phrases; it could mean anything from "marginally acceptable, with plenty of room for improvement," to something quite a bit better than simply "good." I had learned to interpret the careful nuances of his judgments by his inflection (whether rising or falling), its placement (on the first or last word), and by the degree to which he furrowed his brow.

When I asked him to look over some of my slides after one of our earlier trips, he had squinted, then cocked his head to the side and said they were "*pretty* good"—a subtle indictment that was the diplomatic equivalent of "lousy . . . but keep trying." Now, after several years of intermittent tutelage under his gentle, insistent eye, a few of my photos qualified for a slight emphasis on *both* words.

"It's a small area," I said, objecting to the idea. Most photography books on Alaska covered vast portions of the state. Besides, after witnessing the tremendous effort expended by my clients on their own books, undertaking such an enterprise by myself seemed too daunting.

Michio shook his head. "If a place is very important to you . . . ," he fumbled, breaking *im-por-tant* into distinct syllables, then holding up one finger to emphasize his next words, "it is . . . it becomes your *responsibility* to make a book."

I just nodded and said I would think about it; Michio's use of words was often creative (like the time early in our friendship, before his English improved, when he had remarked on the "fruitility" of the forest and its abundance of edible plants); at the moment, I wasn't sure what he meant by *responsibility*.

As if reading my mind, he continued. "A lot of people can never see something like this," he said, waving a palm across the mountains and water. "And maybe something will change."

"What do you mean?"

He crossed his ankles and squeezed his hands between his thighs. "Everything is always changing. Forests getting cut down or maybe a big hotel gets built and too many people are coming." He hunched his shoulders to demonstrate the uncertainty of the future. "Maybe even the glaciers come back!"

"And if I don't make a book?"

"Then this whole . . . *story* can get lost," he said, shaking his head at the thought. "It is like *at-ow*."

I squinted to show how befuddled I was. He pointed toward the site of the extinct Tlingit village. "*At-ow*, like the Native stories."

With that, I knew what he was getting at. For his last birthday I had given him a book of Tlingit legends prefaced with a description of the Native system of property rights known as *at.oow*. Roughly put, at.oow acts as a sort of copyright law that assigns the rights to certain songs, stories, and legends to the clan whose ancestors originated them. Translated literally, at.oow means "owned thing" and can be applied to material objects, such as masks, rattles, helmets, and carved wooden screens used in the telling of stories, as well as to resources such as salmon streams or berry patches. But where the concept gets a bit fuzzy to anyone steeped in the Western concept of modern private property rights is in its failure to differentiate between the rights

of ownership (with the implied power to deny the resource to others
or dispose of as one pleases) and the obligations of stewardship,
because while an individual may claim at.oow of a place or thing, that
ownership is understood to be for the benefit of the clan and not nec-
essarily the person who claims it. The underpinnings of the culture,
such as food sources and songs, are not harbored as personal assets but
are nonetheless considered private property.

It is a complicated concept that has bewildered legal scholars, and
while I wasn't sure if Michio's use of the term was appropriate I
thought I understood what he meant.

*If you love a place for the things that it gives you (in this case the peace I
always found in Holkham Bay), you have a responsibility to share its beauty
with others, and in doing so, perhaps bring others to love it and lend something to its care.*

This also explained why Michio had been willing to work for
more than ten years on a book about caribou in the Arctic, even
though there was little possibility the revenues from such a book
would ever repay his expenses. There had been awe in Michio's voice
when he described the sight of a hundred thousand caribou migrating
across the tundra—and pain when he talked about how the glory of
that sight may be lost.[39]

"We better get moving," I said, glancing at my watch. The tide had
turned, a phalanx of icebergs was drifting our way, and I wanted to be
in a safe anchorage before dark.

---

39. There is oil beneath the Arctic coastal plain. Despite the protestations of the Gwi'chin
Indian people, whose way of life depends on the health of the caribou herd, critical calving grounds within the Arctic National Wildlife Refuge may be sacrificed to supply
America's refineries with a meager nine months' worth of oil. When members of the
Gwi'chin nation met with the Bush administration's secretary of the interior, Gale Nor-
ton, to plead for their way of life, her response was to tell the representatives of the
ancient culture that they should "broaden their worldview."

10 » The Place Without Storms

I ROLLED MY SHOULDERS to ease the tension from my neck. Picking our way through the ice-studded darkness into the safety of a cove had taken a long time, but just as we were getting under way Michio noticed that the setting sun was rimming the icebergs in gold, and so we lingered, trying to capture the iridescent light. Now the fathometer said the bottom was rising, and as I followed the shoreline into the harbor, the knotted muscles between my shoulder blades began to work loose.

When I went on deck to lower the anchor the air was sharp with the chill of autumn and the green smell of the forest filled my nose. Michio was busy in the galley, sizzling something in a skillet and poking at the stove. When I went back inside he looked up from a steaming pot and asked: "*Graysha* bear tomorrow, Lynn?"

I nodded, then moved aside a stack of plates to unfold a chart. "We're here," I said, fingering our cove, "and we'll start looking on the other side."

Michio dried his hands on a dish towel and leaned in for a closer look. The fjord was three miles across, an easy run in the skiff, but we had little to go on beyond the sketchy description of a naturalist on a tour boat who had glimpsed a silver-blue animal disappearing up a creek with a fish in its mouth. That had been several weeks past, back in August, and Michio raised his eyebrows as if to ask, "Why there?"

"There are salmon streams on both sides of the fjord," I said, "but the tour boats favor that side." To save fuel, I reasoned, the tour boat would have been following the shortest route between points of interest within the fjord; in Endicott, that meant following the northern shore.

Michio's lips worked as he puzzled at something, then he traced a hesitant finger across the map. "So late in Sep-*tem*-bah?" he asked, putting a lot of question in the word. "The salmon will still be spawning?"

He was right to be concerned. The season was well advanced and the bulk of the pink salmon in the creeks had already spawned and died.[40]

"The bear might still be around," I said, rapping a pencil against the chart with more confidence than I felt. "At least this way we know we're on its home range."[41]

Michio was too polite to question my flimsy reasoning. Without a readily available food source to keep the bear in the area, it could have wandered a dozen miles away—or might even be nothing more than the product of an overeager naturalist's imagination. Still, I said, the streams seemed like the place to start. "And if that doesn't work," I said, "we'll try something else."

Michio spooned equal heaps of rice and fried vegetables onto two plates and slid open the window beside the table. We ate without speaking, preferring instead to listen to the small flutterings and

40. There are five species of salmon in the North Pacific: pink, red, silver, chum, and king (also known as humpies, sockeye, coho, dog, and spring, respectively). In general (but varying significantly by area) the order in which the different species return to their natal streams to spawn is king (in early spring), sockeye (early summer), pink and chum (midsummer), and silvers (which run well into fall). There are, of course, exceptions to this pattern, such as the chum salmon that spawn in the Chilkhat River until late November and a return of sockeye to certain lakes and rivers on Russia's Kamchatka Peninsula as late as December.

41. A "home range" is the area contained within a bear's regular wanderings and often overlaps with that of other bears, whereas "territories" are areas from which an animal or group of animals bars intruders of its own kind.

whistles of seabirds disturbed in their dreams, the rustle of something moving beneath the trees. After an iceberg outside the cove gave a baritone mumble and rolled over in its sleep, Michio scraped the leftovers into a bowl.

I washed, he dried, in a routine that was silent and familiar. After turning the stove down, I rolled out my sleeping bag while Michio leafed through the pages of a book, sipping at its words with a cup of tea. He was still reading when I fell asleep.

AT SIX-THIRTY the next morning the sky was still dark, but rimmed with a faint shade of gray. I put a kettle on to boil, nudged Michio awake when the coffee was ready, and watched quietly as dawn unfolded the details of the day. By the time breakfast was on the stove, daylight had turned the dark forest into a patchwork of greens.

I dropped an uh-oh bag into the skiff, double-checked the charge on a handheld radio, and puttered with the outboard while Michio gathered food for our lunch. The skiff was covered with moisture; a light rain had passed in the night, and my hands grew stiff in the chill.

Michio grunted *"omoi"*—heavy—as he bent over the side of the *Swift* to pass down our packs. As an afterthought, I stuffed a spare sleeping bag, a heat-reflecting tarp, and a two-man tent into a river bag of heavy vinyl material and crammed it into the bow alongside a patch kit and an air pump for the skiff. We would only be a few miles from the warmth and security of the *Swift,* but more than one unattended skiff or kayak has been lost to the tide or destroyed by a wandering bear, and if that happened we might be marooned for a few days before we could hail a passing boat for a ride.

When we left the cove Soun-doun was living up to its name and the widening V of the skiff's wake rippled out behind us, tumbling the glassy water into splinters of gray and green. More ice had appeared during the night, pulled down from Dawes Glacier by the tide, and I watched over my shoulder with a bit of trepidation as the cove diminished, then disappeared behind us. The *Swift* was reasonably secure, but it was my home and my livelihood, the center of my world, and

I had heard stories of boats left at anchor in Endicott Arm being sunk by drifting ice.

The movement of ice is unpredictable. As it pours from the glaciers, it gathers into dense pastures and undulating plains that drift up and down the fjord at the whim of the tides, winding into bands that twist and coil the length and breadth of the fjord. It seems to appear and disappear, spinning into mile-wide gyres that blow apart and scatter like dandelion seeds on the first puff of wind, then coalesce on the next change of tide. In the morning the waterway may be impenetrably choked but by noon be as clear as a tropical sea. After fifteen years of picking my way through ice-packed fjords, I am still reluctant to make any predictions about its movement.

I steered through a line of boulder-sized chunks, being careful to keep well clear of a towering berg the shape and size of a cottage; the stability of floating ice is always in question, and the larger pieces may crumble and break apart without warning.

Michio pointed at an intensely blue berg and reached for his camera. The ice glistened like wet cobalt, and its gleaming surface had been licked into a pattern of scallops and whorls by the smooth tongue of the sea. After I shut down the outboard, trickling meltwater filled the silence with a liquid, silver sound.

Michio whispered, *"Hijo ni utsu kushii."*

"It's so . . . delicate," he murmured, as if speaking louder might upset some fragile poise of the berg. "How is it so *blue?*"

The question was rhetorical. Michio knew as well as I did that the convex surfaces of thousands of tiny air bubbles trapped during the slow transformation of snow into ice will reflect the full spectrum of light, making most icebergs look white, while ice formed in the deeper parts of a glacier may be subjected to such intense pressures that the gas is squeezed out, leaving ice so pure and gas free that it reflects only the blue wavelengths of light.[42]

42. Cloudy days also make ice appear bluer by filtering out the warmer wavelengths of light.

Michio raised his camera, clicked off a few frames, then motioned for me to reposition the skiff for another perspective. The mass of the berg gave it the unmoving presence of a somnolent, living thing, a sleeping animal that might suddenly rumble and rise to its feet.

Long, long ago, perhaps in Charlemagne's time, a single tiny snowflake had fluttered to the ground in a distant mountain valley, like a seed entering a womb, and been buried under the weight of billions of its fellows. Over the course of a century or two the combined weight of a thousand winter storms compressed the snow into ice that gained mass and density until gravity compelled it into a long, slow slide through the mountains and dropped it into the waiting hands of the sea.

Now the water was slowly licking and fondling the ice to death, absorbing it drop by drop into the circulatory system of the planet. Some of the water molecules crystallized into the original feather of snow might sweep south on an oceanic current, cross the Pacific, drift below the equator, be carried west around Cape Horn into the Atlantic, and wander into the Baltic or Mediterranean; others would evaporate into clouds, surf into the mountains on the pressure wave of a wild winter storm, and fall again as snow, only to be transformed into ice and begin the long journey again.

Now Michio's camera was snatching at the iceberg's fleeting blue life as fast as he could swap lenses and adjust for various exposures. I stroked lightly with the oars, holding the skiff stationary in the slow-moving current, and watched the small wrinkles at the corner of his eye tighten into lines. I knew from past experience that this meant he was totally absorbed, consumed by the pursuit of a certain image, and when he gave a small, tight smile before snapping a final frame, I took it to mean he had succeeded. Only after we were well away from the berg did I realize that I had been so absorbed in the migratory incarnations of the ice that I neglected to take any photos of my own.

AT THE FIRST CREEK there were no salmon. The heavy, rotting smell of their passing still lingered in the grass along its banks, and a few carcasses in an advanced stage of decomposition clung to the shallow stream's glistening stones.

"Strong smell," said Michio, sniffing loudly through his nose.

"Smells good if you're a bear." I nodded, prodding with my toe at a hooked jawbone that was all that remained of a scavenger's dinner.

All summer long, eagles, bears, gulls, wolves, otters, and mink had been feasting on fresh salmon, but now all that remained was detritus. The ground was littered with gill plates, thin and translucent as butterfly wings, and scattered vertebrae. The banks of the creek were dotted with rags of skin and bone.

Michio kicked into the grass at the edge of the tree line and pointed out a number of decomposing carcasses, each oddly complete but for a single bite wound to the top of the head, and for the females, a torn and missing belly. After a summer of consuming up to eighty pounds of meat a day, a protein-gorged bear had begun dragging fish after fish from the water and consuming nothing but the eggs and the brains.

At first glance, killing dozens or hundreds of heavy-bodied salmon for the sake of a mouthful of pearly orange eggs or a single walnut-sized bite of brains seems frightfully wasteful (unless one takes the time to count the number of gulls, eagles, Steller's jays, ravens, crows, and smaller mammals that make their living cleaning up the master's leavings), but it may be a bear's only way to satisfy a raging hunger for the carbohydrates and fats it needs to get through winter. Scattering so much good meat around and letting it rot is actually a smart investment on the bear's part, since nutrients from the bodies of the fish come back the following spring in the form of protein-rich grass just as the bear arises hungry and lean from its long winter's sleep.

We located a rise of land that afforded a view upstream and down, then set up our tripods and waited. The grass was dun colored and olive and had been combed into springy cowlicks by the wind. We sat quietly, listening to the creek laugh as it ran away around the bend. A mink loping along the edge of the water jerked to a stop and pushed its nose into our scent, then sniffed with the disdain that only a weasel can muster before plunging on its way. A few minutes later a tiny shrew rustled through the grass, wandered to the creek, and threw itself into the water, where it paddled like mad to make it to the other side before being swept away.

For hours we watched a parade of forest characters enter stage left or right to twitter, croak, or mime a few lines, then step out of sight again. Chestnut-backed chickadees, deer mice, and a short-tailed weasel made minor appearances, a porcupine waddled bucktoothed and squinting across the stage. After a particularly long intermission a flurry of warblers, pipits, and wrens broke the silence, followed by the squawk of a jay. All the tiny comings and goings made it easy to feel that we might at any moment hear the sound of something large moving softly through the brush or catch a glimmer of blue fur, but by the end of the day, we had yet to see any sign of a bear.

The next day was the same, with coffee, eggs, and potatoes at sunrise and a light shower of rain. Creeks number two and three were alive with small animals, and on four a fresh wolf track marked the mud beside the hoofprints of a deer. At low tide we skiffed along the beach, hoping to spot bears foraging among the rocks, but saw only a single heron, standing one-legged and wooden at the edge of a tide pool, and a pair of curious seals that shadowed us as we puttered along.

"Let's go ashore here," I said, pointing to a small bight. "I've got something to show you."

The small cabin was in an advanced stage of decay. The galvanized metal roofing was a patchwork of rust and muted grays; fireweed and bristly black currant poked up through gaps in the porch, and the remaining planks sagged under my weight; on the northern side of the cabin, where the sun never reached, the wall was moldering with rot. Inside, the floor of the cabin was a litter of spruce needles and mouse droppings that crunched underfoot.

Henry "Tiger" Olsen came to Alaska in 1918 after a stint of sheepherding in the Bitterroots of Montana. He described his voyage north from Seattle in a leaky rowboat with two other pilgrims as nine hundred miles of "one fella rowing, another fella bailing, and the third one hollerin' for help!"

One of the others was Doc Foche, who froze to death in his own cabin twenty-five miles away in Limestone Inlet during a particularly harsh winter in the 1930s. It was Tiger who found Doc and buried him.

"We was friends," explained Tiger, speaking of the man he had prospected with for years, "But if we'd ever found a good strike of gold, we'd have both gone for our rifles and then we'd have seen who got the gold."

Tiger settled twenty miles south of Juneau in Taku Harbor, working as a watchman at a salmon cannery during the summer and prospecting the high reaches of the Coast Range in his spare time. Sometime during the 1920s or '30s he had carefully notched and squared each log of the tiny cabin in Endicott Arm and stacked them into the shape of this shelter for winter trapping. He must have felt much as I do about Soundoun, because a short biograpical pamphlet penned for the local library by a Juneau writer quotes Tiger as saying "[Holkham Bay] is where I should have stayed . . . it's such a rich place."

Even though he lived alone for more than fifty years, Tiger was no reclusive hermit. He enjoyed human company, especially that of children, and boaters anchoring near his cabin knew to put the coffeepot on because Tiger was bound to row out for a visit.

Despite having received only three months of education during his childhood ("Them were the good old Republican days"), Tiger was an avid reader and thinker. Like many who spend a lot of time alone, he avoided idle chitchat, preferring instead to dive right into the philosophical and metaphysical subjects that crowded his mind.

Where do we go when we leave this world? That's some question, that is. It's beyond the human mind.

Tiger's best shot at explaining his view of the infinite was to translate it through what he saw in the physical world: "If there's a blueberry bush . . . and the raindrops come on it . . . and the water from the rain drops into Taku Harbor, it's immediately the Pacific Ocean, it's immediately on all the shores of this world. And that's the way with the human soul. When it drops into the eternal spirit, it's in all the places of the world, and all the places of eternity."

Tiger believed in reincarnation, too, but thought it wasn't for him. "No," he said, "I think I'm one wolf that's trap shy by this time. I'll never make the mistake of coming here again."

Michio listened carefully as I prattled about Tiger, then asked when he died.

"The late seventies, I think. He was at least eighty years old."

He fingered a strip of rotting canvas tacked to one of the walls; the wood underneath was soft. "I don't think this cabin lasts much longer."

"Nothing does," I replied, meaning the rainforest eventually consumes everything. At the turn of the last century the cove where the *Swift* lay at anchor had sheltered a mining town of 137 people, including a store, a post office, a school, and a saloon. Now there was nothing left of it except a row of stubbed-off pilings in the mouth of a creek and a few moss-covered timbers on the forest floor. Hell, I wanted to say, back in Juneau, where it rained even more than Holkham Bay, even my *car* had moss growing on it—and it was only fifteen years old.

Michio set up his tripod in front of the cabin and selected a lens. Frowning, he went to work with an intensity I had seldom seen. *Compose, focus, wind the shutter. Click.* "He never marry." *Click.* "No children." *Click.*

He spoke without question, in a voice that was somewhere between sad and angry, then paused a moment to stare wide-eyed into the viewfinder. After making a minute adjustment, he tripped the shutter and stood upright to face me. "Now this is what he . . . *is.*"

He repositioned the tripod, nestling the legs firmly into the ground. After swapping lenses again, he framed a shot, then stood aside and turned up his palm in a gesture that invited me to come see.

The result was poignant, a single stalk of russet-and-brown fireweed pushing up through a pattern of weathered planks. Topped with a head of feathery, foaming white seeds, the aging flower spoke volumes about the process of creation and procreation and how time erodes the efforts of man. There was hope and promise in the seeds, fading beauty in the leaves, and a sense of inevitability in a small patch of moss that was slowly eclipsing the rusty head of a nail.

Michio photographed the window, organizing the peeling wooden frame and log wall into a composition that made it easy to imagine Tiger's weathered face looking out through its cracked and missing panes. Bending to peer into the viewfinder, I marveled at how the cabin no longer seemed quite so empty and marveled again when Michio moved in close to capture the marks left by the teeth of Tiger's saw across the ends of the logs.

Stepping back, he mounted a wide-angle lens on the camera and took a few shots, blending the mottled gray walls and rusty tin roof of the cabin into the autumn pastels of the forest.

"It's time to go home," he said, dropping the film in his pack. We were halfway to the skiff when he turned around and went back. Stepping carefully across the sagging porch, he placed both hands against the swollen door and pushed it closed.

"WE SHOULD GO UP," I said, peering out the window. A cold gray mist had moved in during the night, obscuring the mountains and the trees. "We're not having any luck on the streams."

Michio looked up from the camera he was cleaning and agreed. We had been watching the salmon streams for several days without seeing a single bear. Once a pair of ravens had squawked and whooped from tree to tree on the other side of a stream as if following something on the ground, but after watching for a few minutes and seeing no telltale shaking of branches or glimpse of dark fur, I began to suspect that the ravens' raucous alarum was the prank-loving birds' way of crying wolf to the pitiful, flightless bipeds on the ground. The weather was becoming increasingly thick and unpleasant, but if we were going to find a glacier bear, we had to keep looking.

"They're after berries now," I mused, envisioning an army of sugar-hungry bears browsing slowly through the undergrowth beneath the trees. It would be difficult to find an animal in that dense chaos, where the only sign of a bear might be the crackle of breaking branches, and I reasoned we would be better off climbing fifteen hundred feet or more up the mountain, up to the alpine where an unimpeded view would allow us to scan a vast area of open ground. There were crow-berries there, as well as dwarf blueberries and other succulent low-lying treats. From the higher vantage, we would also be able to look down on a belt of lush subalpine meadows carpeted with cow parsnip, deer cabbage, and a variety of other herbs bears consider decent fodder.

Our packs were heavier than ever. In addition to my own camera gear I carried a tent, dry clothes, food, dishes and a stove, a bottle of fuel, two flashlights, a head lamp, and extra batteries. The days were getting too short to make it up the mountain and back in a single day, and we planned to spend at least two nights away from the boat. There was no room in our packs for sleeping bags, so I crammed them into a vinyl dry bag that made an awkward lump on top of my load. I also carried a waterproof ground cloth, a grommeted tarp, a tube of fire-starting gel, the handheld radio, a full set of rain gear, a map, a compass and binoculars, an ice ax, three carabiners, a smattering of ice screws, two snow anchors, and a rope. Last but not least, I hung a small bag of first-aid supplies to the outside of my pack, looped a knife to my belt, and shouldered my tripod and rifle.

Michio grunted as he struggled to his feet. The weight of two full sets of camera gear (35 millimeter and medium format) dug his pack-straps into his shoulders, and when he staggered under the load, he mut-tered something I presumed was the Japanese equivalent of "holy shit."

I glanced back at the skiff as we headed up the stream. The only color in the foggy gray scene was a bright yellow bag hanging from a tree—what a friend who has spent a great deal of time camping in grizzly country calls a "bear piñata." Inside was a supply of chocolate bars and canned fruit that would make being marooned a little more enjoyable if the skiff was damaged by a bear.

At the first bend in the creek a dozen geese lifted off a narrow sandbar, crying out in nasal alarm. Michio stopped to imitate the *lonk, lonk, lonk* of their call as they passed overhead, then followed me up a cut-bank into the woods. Once inside the tree line he stopped to peer at the base of a peculiarly formed tree and shot me a questioning look.

The base of the tree was open, as if the tree were tiptoeing on its roots, and beyond it stood two more saplings of identical size and form. Together, their freestanding roots formed a tunnel that would have been irresistable if I had had a bowling ball.

"Nurse log," I explained, pointing toward a downed tree lying farther off the path. "See how that one has seedlings sprouting along its top?"

The log I was pointing at lay flat on the ground and was upholstered in a thick blanket of moss. Its surface was littered with thumbnail-sized flakes of spruce cones and supported a row of tiny seedlings.

"If the seedlings survive long enough, their roots reach the ground." I held out one hand with the fingers pointing down and drew a circle beneath it with the other. "Then the log rots away and leaves a line of saplings."

Comprehension beamed from Michio's face. *"Uba,"* he said, crooking his arm as if feeding a baby, *"this* kind of nurse!"

He was right. With more than 90 percent of the organic material in a rainforest organized into living plants or rotting vegetation, the soil is notoriously poor, and nutrients milked from the decomposing log could give the seedlings a headstart over those trying to make it on the ground. The tiptoe posture of the young trees might make them more vulnerable to strong winds later in life, but that was just the scattershot luck of survival.

Every plant has to scramble for light and nutrients as best it can while fending off a host of enemies that want to nibble, chew, choke, suck, or shade out its life, and a hundred yards past the nurse logs the trail faded into a stand of plants that go through life armed to the teeth. Devil's club is the only member of the ginseng family that grows in Alaska, and every part of it, including the stalk (which can grow to ten feet) and the underside of the shiny green leaves, is studded with brittle half-inch spines that break off and fester beneath the skin of anyone careless or unlucky enough to brush up against it. Thorns are a good idea for any plant as nutritious as this; in the spring I like to steam a potful of the tightly wound buds for their clean, tangy taste. If it was not for the spines that develop soon after the leaves unfold, devil's club would probably be a favorite of every browser in the forest.

Like most plants, however, devil's club knows when to fight and when to seduce, and at the top of each threatening stalk is a cluster of brilliant red berries that grow without thorns. The berries have no thorns because it is the purpose of *all* berries to be eaten, and they are red because that is the color of attraction; what the devil's club wants more than anything is for its seeds to attract the attention of a bear, pass through the animal's digestive tract, and be deposited along with its own source of fertilizer in an ideal location for propagation. For devil's club that means the well-drained soil of streambeds and flood-plains such as the one we were traversing, and I solaced myself that my efforts to slither, twist, and limbo through the thorny patch with-out getting stabbed was the result of the berries' success at attracting the very bears for which we were searching. As such, I told myself, the snagging, pricking, and stinging was something to be appreciated, so I should *stop my goddamn cursing!*

Sweat dribbled into my eyes; I used the barrel of my rifle to move a thorny stalk aside and hunched my pack to ease the weight from my back. "We'll be through this soon," I said over my shoulder.

"Good!" was all Michio said. He was using his tripod as a shield and made a slashing motion with one hand. "I wish for a machete."

Luckily I was right about the extent of the thicket, and before I had time to give in completely to my thorny misery we had worked our way to the edge of a marshy meadow, where the ground under-foot squished like a sponge. Before stepping out into the open I stopped to scan the tree line and listen. There was little chance our crackling, swearing progress through the devil's club had gone unno-ticed by any wildlife in the area, but it never hurts to look.

The meadow was small, the size of a large vacant lot. A swatch of cot-ton grass edged a pool of black water in the middle. On a clear, dry day the white seed ball atop a stalk of freshly bloomed cotton grass is silky and beautiful, but these were yellowing and bedraggled from the rain.

Along the edge of the meadow the thick, heavy leaves of skunk cabbage were beginning to lay down under their own size and the weight of autumn. Skunk cabbage is a distant relative of cotton grass, with dark Pleistocene-looking leaves that can grow to five feet. It is a vigorous plant, so eager to live that its tightly rolled spath is the first thing to burst from the ground in the spring, and it grows so rapidly and wildly that the heat generated by its cellular respiration will melt snow. The butter-yellow spath and the clublike spadex it shields are a favorite spring treat for deer and bear, but in spite of its crisp, succulent appearance, skunk cabbage is not meant for human consumption—crystals of calcium oxalate embedded in its tissues make nibbling on a bit of the leaf the equivalent of licking splintered glass. The crystals can be removed from the roots by roasting and the resulting product pulverized as a starchy substitute for flour, but in general skunk cabbage isn't something you want near your mouth.

We cut across the meadow at an angle, skirting the pond toward a low ridge that would lead us to the shoulder of the mountain. Out in the open the rain was falling harder and I turned up the collar of my coat. Pace is critical when hiking in rain gear—go too fast and you'll sweat, which means being cold when you stop; go too slow or unbutton too far and you wind up just as wet. Baggy pants make it awkward to step over logs; hoods make it difficult to hear; falling into a head-down beast-of-burden trudge in the rain means missing everything that is happening around you, or maybe stumbling into a bear.

I fell into the trudge, anyway, as we made our way across the meadow, hypnotized by the sucking sound my boots made in marsh. I was thinking about horsetail—a strangely spare, segmented plant that resembles a wire brush, grows well in saturated ground, and has changed little in millions of years—when I noticed we had walked right into a colony of carnivores.

"Sundew," I said, pointing out the tiny plants to Michio. The soil of wet meadows is highly acidic, which is believed to limit the amount of nitrogen and phosphorous available to plants; sundew makes up for this shortage by trapping insects in a sticky fluid secreted by a row of glistening red glands along the rim of its leaves. The leaves then roll up around the hapless bugs, and the sundew uses digestive enzymes to absorb the nitrogen and phosphorus from their bodies.

Sundew seems to have taken this highly specialized strategy even further, putting out different-shaped leaves for different environments. The leaves of the sundew here on the edge of this blackwater pond are long, rather ovoid in shape, while those on drier ground are usually round. In addition, sundew near open water holds its leaves up in the air; the round-leaf variety keeps them flat on the ground. Why this should be so I cannot imagine, unless it has something to do with the different species of insects the plant "hunts." Does the long-leafed marsh variety eat more mosquitoes and the dryland version catch more ants? I probed the glistening jaws of a leaf with a twig of bog laurel, hoping to imitate the tiny tread of an insect, and was disappointed when it failed to respond. Musing out loud, I wondered if a botanist would consider the different varieties of sundew as separate species of plant.[43]

This question of what constitutes a species is a puzzling one: the trees around the rim of the meadow are garlanded in streamers of old-man's beard and usnea—long, olive-gray strands of lichen that lift and flutter like prayer flags in the wind. There are three forms of lichen—crustose, which looks like dry, peeling paint; foliose, which more closely resembles leaves; and fruiticose, which includes lichens with protruding stems and those like usnea and old-man's beard, which hang from trees.

Each comes in numerous varieties that are catalogued as separate species, but the kicker comes when one considers what a lichen really *is*. Lichen is a cooperative relationship between an algae and a fungus, which are unrelated organisms, separate species in their own right. (The fungus makes up the body of the lichen, and the algae uses its chlorophyll to manufacture the lichen's food.) Throw in a third

43. I have since learned that there are indeed two separate species of *drosera* in Alaska: the long-leaf sundew and round-leaf sundew. For a wonderfully readable and informative look at the region, I commend to the reader *The Nature of Southeast Alaska*, by Rita O'Clair, Robert Armstrong, and Richard Carstensen.

species—the blue-green bacteria that is a component of several lichens—and this mysterious life-form becomes a small community that begs the definition of a species.

Michio's response is typically single-tracked. "Like a family," he says. "All for one and one for all." The homily is so obviously studied that it takes on new meaning, and for a moment I imagine him sitting alone in his cabin, carefully forming the rs and ls on his tongue.

We started up the hillside, panting and huffing across the uneven ground as we followed a faint game trail that sidestepped a patch of blueberries, rose sharply to a narrow shoulder, then coursed along a shallow ravine. A gurgling stream muffled our footsteps with its mutterings, running brown as tea from tannins leached from the soil.

Biologists, lacking a place to put fungi in the plant or animal kingdoms, have assigned them their own taxonomic group, which includes everything that reproduces by scattering spores that bloom into hypha—tiny threadlike fibers that cluster together to form the familiar shapes of mushrooms, bracket fungi, and coral fungi.[44]

"Look at this one, Michio." I held up a stick studded with tiny nodules. The branch was light and fragile with rot, and I had to hold it carefully to avoid damaging it. A single bird's nest fungus protruded from the surface, complete with tiny egg-shaped seeds. I held it close to Michio's face so he could study it.

"The 'nest' is a splash cup," I explained. "When a drop of rain hits it dead center, the sloping sides are designed to create a hydraulic force that splashes the 'eggs' out in all directions."

Michio shook his head in wonder. The miniature nest would have fit neatly on the tip of a baby's finger. "If I could do only one more book in my life," he said, "it would be details like this."

Even fungus is beautiful if you see it the right way.

A half hour later I paused to sling my rifle upside down from my shoulder; it was raining harder and I didn't want water in the barrel.

---

44. Not all spore-bearing life-forms are fungi. Several terrestrial plants, such as ferns, reproduce with spores instead of seeds.

Michio extended the legs of his tripod for a climbing staff and I did the same. My knees hurt and my heart was thudding in my chest. Michio and I were both panting from the exertion of hoisting our overloaded, forty-year-old bodies over deadfalls and pushing through thick brush. It was quiet—birds don't sing in heavy rain—and we felt quite alone.

This was wrong, of course. Every moss-muffled footfall of our progress was rocking someone's world. While we were climbing straight up in hopes of finding a silver-blue bear, a microscopic animal less than a millimeter long called a water bear was using its sharp claws to cling to strands of the moss beneath our feet. Moss is too high in cellulose to be edible for most animals, but the water bear is armed with sharp styles that allow it to penetrate individual cells of a plant and suck out the contents, leaving the indigestible wall of the cell behind. The world swarms with life-forms beneath our notice.

I kicked a purchase into the slope with the side of my boot and clutched at an eye-level root. This must be what it's like for the water bear, I thought. Spending your life climbing and scrambling through wet, knotted moss.

The most bizarre form of life in the forest isn't the water bear, however. That title has to go to a thing called a slime mold. For lack of a better definition, slime mold has been tentatively categorized as a fungus, but in truth seems to wander a twilight zone on the margins of the animal kingdom. The first part of the slime mold's life is spent as thousands of individual amoebalike cells that crawl independently around the forest. For reasons no one quite understands, the individual cells occasionally come together and aggregate into a single large mass, forming a blob of protoplasm that resembles scrambled eggs. This thing oozes slowly around the countryside, creeping along the ground and over trees until it fruits into millions of microscopic spores that dissipate out into the world at large and become individual cells, thus completing the strange life cycle of the creature.

There is another fungus, called a mycorrhizal fungus, whose purpose is better understood. In a relationship reminiscent of the algae-fungus intermarriage that gives the world its lichens, mycorrhizae fungi infect the roots of trees and plants and use them as a source of nutrients such as sugars and amino acids. The relationship, however, is not as parasitic as it seems at first glance. Because the mycorrhizal relationship involves an equal transfer of phosphorus, potassium, calcium, and nitrogen from the soil into the roots of the infected tree via minute hypha the fungus extends throughout the soil around its host. Most forest trees simply won't survive the sapling stage unless properly infected with a mycorrhizal fungus, and a decade or so ago it was discovered that trees linked together by this mycorrhizal "internet" can send each other gifts of water and nutrients via the permeating hypha, with healthy trees passing some of their own reserves along to those more in need.

I pulled back my sleeve to look at my watch. Two o'clock. We had been climbing for several hours, and as we rose higher into the clouds the rain had evolved into a curtain of heavy mist that formed pearls of cold water on every surface. Wind was starting to tug at the trees.

Grunting, I heaved myself up another step and tried to distract myself by imagining the immense network of delicate, hollow hypha and hairlike roots at my feet moving an endless stream of nutrients through the forest, sucking and pumping like those pneumatic tubes mercantile stores once used to connect cashiers and clerks. Among the nutrients siphoned through the web are the stable marine isotopes of nitrogen that enter the forest in the carcasses of salmon (see page 70). I was already so tired that laying my own carcass down on the moss and letting my nitrogen dissipate into the stream of nutrients flowing through the forest had a certain appeal. Michio was wearing out, too; when we stopped for a brief rest, he sprawled on the ground and fell asleep faceup in the rain.

A SHOWER woke me up. Hard pellets stinging my face. I wiped water from my eyes and peered at the tops of the trees. I was shivering, damp with sweat beneath my rain gear, and I ached from my neck to my knees. I watched a gust of wind whip a lacy hemlock into a hula dance and pushed myself to my feet.

"Weather breaking?" asked Michio, rubbing at his eyes.

"Gettin' worse," I replied unnecessarily. "If this keeps up, it'll be nasty above timberline. We'll have to make camp in the trees."

Two hundred yards later we broke out into the subalpine meadows. Waist-high vegetation wound through belts of alder and windstunted trees. Everything was dressed in the muted colors of autumn, and when the rain pulled back for a moment the pale blue glacier peeked through the clouds. A knob of bald stone at the edge of the alpine beckoned as a vantage point from which to scan the slope, but as Michio pointed out, even if we were lucky enough to spot a glacier bear, the weather was too foul to break out the cameras.

It took an hour to reach the base of the knob. We moved slowly and carefully, watching for bears. Here and there, stands of aging parsnip and clusters of monkshood had been flattened by foraging bruins, but I saw no sign I could be certain was fresh.

At the base of the knob I jerked to a stop. Nestled into the heather at my feet was a slender, ivory-colored bone tipped with black hooves. A tassel of white hairs clustered around the ankle joint identified it as the remains of a goat.

"A young one," I said, hoisting the bone in my hand. It felt polished and fragile, like a delicate shell. Except for the white hairs, it had been licked slick and clean.

"Got a little too far out into the meadow." It was easy to imagine a wolf bursting from the trees and the brief scramble that followed. It was sad, I thought, that the kid had been overtaken so close to the vertical safety of the knob.

Michio gave a fatalistic shrug. "Nature," he said. "Everything has to die. This is why we love nature so much." It was a covenant, he said, that "makes me want to get the most from my life. To really *live*."

"Like the kingfisher?" I asked. "Remember, on our first trip up in Glacier Bay?"

Michio thought for a moment, then grinned as he remembered how I had wanted to throw a stone at a flock of crows tormenting an injured kingfisher, only to have a young eagle swoop in and snatch up the wounded bird before I could interfere.

"Wolf, crow, eagle, bear," he said; the words came out like some kind of poem. "Everything lives the best it can, until it, too, has its own time to die."

"*Ngan ngan Iko!*" I replied, dredging up one of my few Japanese phrases. It was a poor interpretation of what he was trying to say, but the sight of an autumn leaf tugs at our hearts precisely because it *is* in the process of dying—and the leg bone was beautiful in the same way.

Michio rubbed a hand across his face and blinked the rain from his eyes. He was soaking wet and muddy, there were twigs in his hair. He grinned, holding out one hand and squinting into the rain in a gesture that said, *Look at us! We're shivering, tired, and muddy, traipsing around a mountain in the rain to look for an animal we have almost no hope of finding! Go for it, indeed!*

As if to get in on the joke, a gust of wind snatched my hat from my head and threw it at my feet. Whatever sheltering arrangement of peaks and ridges made Holkham Bay the "place without storms," we had climbed above it, and the gale the weather service had predicted before we left Juneau was moving in.

11 » South to Cape Fanshaw

THE GUST THAT BLEW our tent apart also knocked several trees to the ground. In the dark, the monstrous hemlock that splintered and fell a hundred yards away sounded like it was just outside the tent, and Michio yelped as he curled into a ball—whether in fear that the falling tree was about to crush us or to protect himself from my mad thrashing and kicking as I clawed the wet nylon from my face, I cannot say, but somewhere in the melee the tent was torn, and by daybreak our sleeping bags were soaked.

We stuffed our sodden gear into our packs and retreated from the mountain, hurrying for fear that the gale might have driven ice into the cove with the *Swift*. The rain was still coming down hard as we picked our way through a barricade of splintered limbs and upturned earth left behind by the storm, but the wind had started to abate. By the time we stumbled out at sea level, Soun-doun was living up to its name. The fjord was calm, the color of green glass, and there were no icebergs in sight. Nonetheless, when we skiffed into the cove and found the *Swift* safe on its anchor, I breathed a sigh of relief.

By sunset the weather was breaking. Sunlight spilling through a rupture in the clouds drew the shape of the window on the table, and Michio hummed to himself as he padded around the galley in dry socks.

"Should we keep looking?" I asked. Neither of us was feeling particularly defeated by the days of fruitless searching, but neither had we seen anything that made me think we were going to meet with success.

Michio answered with a noncommittal sound, then leaned against the table and cupped his hands in the light.

"I've been thinking," he said, rotating one wrist as if to pour the warm red tint of the sunset across the table. "I don't have any photo of whale in this light."

Over the years, Michio and I had photographed a lot of whales, but always during the burning days of summer, and now the rapid declension of the October sun was creating a soft, diffuse light that would add a new dimension to his portfolio.

"It isn't easy," I told him, "to find whales this late in autumn." Storms and gales roar in from the gulf every four or five days. Throw in another three or four days a week of winds blowing twenty to thirty knots, divide that by the one day in nine when the sky is free of rain or heavy clouds, and the odds against being able to find and photograph whales in calm, clear weather begin to look like the kind of numbers only a fool would buck in a casino.

We had had a single lucky glimpse of a humpback on the run from Juneau to Endicott, "but besides that," I said, "I'm not sure where to look."

Humpbacks disperse when the weather system changes, drifting away from their summer grounds, looking for better feed or even leaving Alaskan waters entirely. I once stumbled upon a pod of a hundred or so animals feeding near the mouth of a canal in early November, but during most of my autumn and winter rambles, whales were as elusive as butterflies.

"No whales in Frederick Sound?" Michio asked. (We had had several successful trips there since our first.)

"Maybe," I answered. "But I can't say for sure."

I reminded him that the weather would be no better in Frederick Sound and that the farther south we went the more exposed we would be. I suppose I was still feeling buffaloed by the gale on the mountain, but I didn't say that after that experience the idea of running a gauntlet of autumn storms in Frederick Sound made the harbor in Juneau seem like the place to be.

"No," I said. "The odds are too slim. We'd be better off heading for home."

WHEN I ROLLED out of my bunk the next morning, an acrylic blue sky changed my mind. The clear sky meant the barometer was rising, and clear, cold air would be flowing down from Canada as a north wind.[45] Heading for Juneau would mean bucking forty miles of chop, but running to Frederick Sound would be an easy sleigh ride downwind.

"It might work," I told Michio. Ride the northerly down to Frederick Sound while it was sunny and hope for a day or two of calm. The next weather system would almost surely be a low, and we could count on a southerly to push us home.

I checked the fuel, Michio inventoried the groceries. We decided there was plenty of both. Heaving in unison, we dragged the skiff aboard and stowed it on deck, then pulled the anchor and got under way.

Outside Holkham Bay, Stephens Passage was peppered with whitecaps. Green swells pushing down from the north rose and fell in orderly rows. Near the middle of the channel I could see a tugboat shouldering its way north, throwing up fountains of spray. I felt a bit smug when I turned the *Swift* downwind; she runs beautifully in a following sea. After settling on a course of 140 degrees, I eased the throttle forward until the *Swift* was running at the same speed as the waves.

---

45. Low-pressure systems rotate counterclockwise in the Northern Hemisphere, and high-pressure systems move in the opposite direction. Thus, the leading edge of a high-pressure system spinning from west to east across the gulf is usually heralded by the arrival of a north wind, and on a low-pressure system the wind will be from the south or southwest. There are many exceptions to this, of course, but it is a useful rule of thumb.

Thistle Ledge was breaking a half mile to port. I nudged the helm a fraction to steer well away, then nudged it again to avoid running too close to Hobart Bay. I think it was Aldo Leopold who said that once you begin caring about the environment, it's like living with an open wound, and the sight of the massive clear-cuts that sprawl across the shoulders of the mountains on both sides of Hobart Bay are guaranteed to make me feel like I'm bleeding. Steering away put us on a course to run south along the shore of Admiralty Island, to Point Pybus, just south of Gambier Bay. At Pybus, we would alter course again to head southwest, where if we were lucky, I reasoned, we might find calmer water in the lee of Admiralty Island.

The *Swift* rose and fell with the waves, throwing off glittering arcs of spray. A Bonaparte's gull in winter plumage made a pass at the bow, found nothing of interest, and peeled away.

An hour later the wind began to die as we approached the passage between the Brothers Islands and Pybus Bay—a sprawling inlet that was once the site of several fox farms, where the animals were raised in cages for their fur. According to Native legend, the bay is home to a race of invisible dwarfs with a penchant for helping humans in trouble, but in 1924 they weren't much help to a fox poacher named Billy Gray: a posse of fox farmers hunted him down on a small island near the mouth and killed him while he slept in his tent.

Frederick Sound was calm when we hove to off Eliza Harbor for lunch. I broke out the binoculars while Michio pasted together sandwiches. We sat on the foredeck to glass the coast while we ate, the *Swift* rocking gently from side to side on the remains of the northern swell. The sea was pale gray. Smoke pouring from the funnel of a ship passing far to the south drew a low smudge along the horizon.

After finishing the sandwich, I wiped my face with a paper napkin, went back in the wheelhouse, and flipped the radio to the weather station. We were too far south to pick up the broadcast from Juneau, but I thought on such a clear day we might still be in range of Petersburg, which was only fifty miles away.

The ether crackled, shattering the broadcast into static. After ten

minutes of trying to decipher the electronic voice from the atmo-
spheric hiss and chatter I gave up, went back on deck, and eyed the sky.

"Still looks good," I said. Gauzy fingers of white were reaching
into the sky from the southwest. The rest of the sky was powder blue.

"Nice light," said Michio. "Now all we need is whales."

We drifted for another half hour, watching the horizon for spouts.
The light felt good on my face and it was peaceful to sit and watch the
world revolve around us.

"High tide in another couple of hours," I commented. "Maybe
when it turns we'll have some luck with the whales." It was a wild
guess, more hopeful than realistic, but there was a slim chance that a
change in current direction would have some effect on free-
swimming feed and thus bring about some activity from the whales—
if there were any around. The twenty or thirty square miles of ocean
visible from our position seemed as empty as the sky.

We idled, moving a mile or two before shutting down the engine,
then taking turns on watch and napping. Off Chapin Bay, a harbor
porpoise puffed to the surface a few meters from the bow and
snatched a quick breath before disappearing again. A handful of storm
petrels flicked by, skimming low across the water, and overhead a lone
eagle drew a helix in the air.

The next time I woke up from a snooze the sky was no longer
blue. The gauze-colored fingers of cloud had turned pearly gray, and
the *Swift* was rolling harder, rocking from side to side with a snap that
rattled the coffee cups on their hooks.

I glanced at my watch: it was after three o'clock. The tide had
turned more than an hour ago, in another hour it would be running
at its peak. The roll, I thought, must be from the increasing current
as it heaved and boiled over the bottom.[46]

46. The rise and fall of the tide can be plotted as a bell curve, with the greatest amount of
change occurring during the middle. To calculate the speed with which the water level is
changing during a given period, divide the distance from high tide to low tide by twelve.
During the six hours of a diurnal change, $\frac{1}{12}$ will occur during the first hour, $\frac{2}{12}$ during the
second, $\frac{3}{12}$ during the third and fourth, $\frac{2}{12}$ during the fifth, and the last $\frac{1}{12}$ during the sixth.

I checked the fathometer—we were in a hundred feet of water—then snatched a loose book as it made a dive for the floor. The kettle slid across the stove and clanged against the rail. I grabbed up all the loose objects on the countertop and stowed them in the sink just as the next roll began.

"Let's get under way," I hollered at Michio. "I don't like the look of the sky." A cloud bank the color of a bruise was approaching from the south, a streak of water at its base black with wind. My stomach did a slow flip as I realized the swells rocking the *Swift* were not the product of the tide but the pulse of something ugly and powerful spinning our way.

I flipped a chart out on the table and fingered our position. We had drifted and idled southwest until we were nearly to Yasha Island, only a few miles from Point Gardner at Admiralty Island's southern tip. The coast nearby was littered with harbors and coves, but they all faced to the south and offered no shelter. Security and Saginaw Bays on the opposite shore of Frederick Sound were ideal for riding out a southerly, but when I looked in that direction, they had been obliterated by the fast-moving front.

A puff of wind slipped in the open window and fluttered the corner of the chart. The top of a swell broke into a small patch of white—then behind it another and another, and within a minute or two the seas in every direction were crumbling.

A gust of wind shoved the *Swift* broadside to the swell, and I spun the helm to bring the bow into the waves. Michio looked at me for reassurance; I motioned for him to check that the cameras were safely stowed and to put his personal gear away.

"It's okay," I said, steering with one hand and jabbing at the chart with the other. "It's only about nine miles across Chatham Straits to Warm Springs Bay."

Thus, on a moderately high tide, say eighteen feet, the water level will rise or fall by four and a half feet per hour during the middle of the tide, which also makes the current during that period the strongest.

Warm Springs is what fishermen call a "bulletproof" harbor, protected on all sides by towering mountains. The entrance is narrow, and at the head of the bay is a well-maintained dock. Warm Springs Bay once sheltered the village of Baranof, a small settlement that lured passing fishermen with the promise of a bath in a natural hot springs nearby. Once the fishermen had soaked away the aches and pains of their trade they could stop off at Sadie Fenton and Fred O'Neal's general store to pick up mail, supplies, and the latest gossip for Chatham Straits.

By the time I first visted Baranof, the general store was abandoned and collapsing in disrepair. The only full-time residents left were Fred Bahovec and his wife, Chlotilde. She was seventy-eight, he was a hundred, and he was writing a memoir he had decided to call *The* First *Hundred Years*. Fred had been a fox farmer, he said, and yes, he had had trouble with poachers now and then. It seems doubtful that a soul as engaging as Fred would have had a hand in the Billy Gray affair, but if he did, he kept it to himself.

Michio brightened at the mention of Warm Springs Bay. When we first visited Warm Springs together in 1991, Fred had passed away (much to his surprise, I'm sure) and Chlotilde was still grieving, but we took her for a ride, anyway, running the *Swift* down Chatham Straits until we found a pod of whales that sent her into spasms of rapture by lolling on their backs less than fifty yards from the boat and waving their giant fins in the air. By the time we returned to the dock, she and Michio were solid pals. I didn't mention that she had recently been hospitalized in Sitka for cancer of the throat. That could wait, I figured, until we were safe at the dock.

"It'll be a downwind run," I said. "We should be there within an hour."

I sounded cockier than I felt. The seas weren't that bad yet—they were running between four and five feet—but the ebb was running at its strongest and flowing against the wind. Two thousand square miles of water was moving south in opposition to a rampaging air mass that was probably the size of Tennessee, in a combination that could only agitate an already-churning sea. When I remembered that Sadie Fenton had sold the general store in Baranof and moved on because Fred O'Neal disappeared—presumably sunk and drowned—after heading out into Chatham Straits in weather much like this, the *Swift* began to feel the size of a gnat.

Although it was not yet four o'clock, the light outside had a gray, gloomy weight, and when a gout of spray rattled across the windows, I flipped the switch for the windshield wipers and thumbed the radar on.

We idled, jogging into the chop while I considered what to do. From our present position a straight-line course to Warm Springs Bay would take us across an area of shallow water between Yasha Island and Point Gardner that is subject to ferocious rips; otherwise, we would have to head southwest, into the seas, until we could clear Yasha, then come around 120 degrees. This would entail some heavy pounding and add another half hour or more to the time it would take to reach Baranof; we might not reach shelter until close to dark.

Another bucket of salt water broke against the windows; I tightened the dogs on the door. On the radar screen, the coastline was blurred by the scatter of breaking waves, and when a smear of green fog appeared, I knew it meant heavy rain.

I spun the wheel, corkscrewing the *Swift* around, and settled on a course for Point Gardner. A downpour heavy enough to obscure radar also meant nightfall was coming early and running in the dark is fraught with risk: industrial-scale logging has littered the waterways of Southeast Alaska with thousands of abandoned logs, and striking one at night could be fatal.

I eased the throttle forward, pushing the *Swift* until she was running with the waves. The seas were running about five feet, with every so often one pushing six.[47] Quartering the seas was almost exhil-

47. Judging the size of waves is very difficult, and most estimates can be cut by a half to a third. However, for small craft the height of a wave is not as critical as its "period," or the interval between two waves. Twenty-foot rollers are not as dangerous as six-foot waves that are steep and closely spaced.

arating, with the *Swift* rising over one wave and surfing down its face, then powering to the top of the next. Michio braced himself against the table and stared over his shoulder at the waves.

"It's liable to get a bit rougher up ahead," I said, staring at the radar. There was something on the screen I had never seen before: the area between Point Gardner and Yasha Island was writhing like a green snake.

A knot formed in my stomach when I realized what it was: the tide pouring out of Stephens Passage and Frederick Sound was boiling up over the shallows and hurling itself headlong into the flow from Chatham Straits. What I was looking at was an area of steep breaking seas spaced so closely together that the radar was seeing it as one wave.

"Brace yourself," I said. I tried to sound calm, but spoke too loudly; I was wondering if it was too late to turn around.

It was. There was nothing to do but hang on.

12 ⟫ Storm

THE *SWIFT* DROPPED OFF the first wave and plunged into the trough, then clawed its way back to the top. Waves charging madly in every direction slammed into each other, erupting into pointed peaks. Green water foamed over the rail.

Blowing scud quickly overpowered the windshield wiper, and I was reduced to peering through the streaks. Somewhere ahead of us a steel buoy marking the end of a reef extending north from Yasha Island was bobbing and ducking in the boiling water, and if I missed it, the *Swift* could be swept into a patch of submerged boulders and torn to pieces.

A drawer leaped from its tracks and crashed to the floor. "Leave it," I barked when Michio made a move to pick it up. Water sloshing across the deck was seeping in around the door, making the cabin sole slippery. I didn't want him getting thrown and hurt.

"We'll be through this soon," I said. "The tide will flush us out the other side."

I risked taking one hand off the helm to adjust the radar screen and realized I was clenching my teeth. The chaotic wave train and blowing spray were overwhelming the radar's performance, making it difficult to discern water from land. All I could do was guess at a rough heading, try to hold it, and pray we could claw our way toward deeper water before we were pushed across the reef.

The noise was fearsome. Spray rattled off the windows like falling gravel while waves sledgehammered the hull. The beating seemed to go on and on, banging and tumbling the *Swift* until it felt as if she were falling down a flight of stairs.

"There!" Michio shouted, pointing off to port.

I caught a brief glimpse of red as the missing buoy bobbed to the top of a wave. A few minutes later the spray eased for a moment, and the long green finger of Point Gardner appeared on the radar screen. We were less than two miles away, with the buoy passing astern, and as I watched the depth sounder flash from twenty fathoms to forty and on down to fifty, I knew we had been swept past the reef.

"We're almost out of it," I said in an effort to reassure Michio. "This'll get better as soon as we clear the point."

I couldn't have been more wrong. It had taken us nearly half an hour to work our way through the tide rips, and in that time the wind had doubled. The waves were stacking up, beginning to climb one atop the other, and breaking for a hundred feet along their crests.

"Jesus," I muttered. My heart was racing. My breath was coming in pants. The *Swift* is a light shallow-draft boat, and the cabin creates a lot of windage. Warm Springs Bay lay west by north, on a magnetic bearing of 285 degrees, but to reach it without being blown past I estimated I would have to steer off by at least 40 degrees, which would mean "crabbing" across the wind, running broadside to the waves.

"We can't make it," I told Michio. He didn't say anything, just stared at me with his mouth open wide.

"We'll have to run north up Chatham Straits," I said, "try to find shelter on the Admiralty side." The *Swift* plummeted into the trough between two waves.

I pointed the bow downwind and gripped the throttle. One virtue of a gasoline engine over a diesel is the faster response to the throttle, which simplifies running in big seas. Faster acceleration gives the operator thrust on demand, and with a bit of experience most small-boat skippers develop a sense of timing that makes knowing when to power up the back of one wave and when to idle back to surf down the next an almost instinctive interaction with the rhythm of the moving water. After that, it becomes a matter of keeping a close eye on the pattern of the wave train to pick the safest course through the swells.

Conditions were now far beyond that, and as if to accentuate the severity of our situation, the next wave to pass under the *Swift*'s keel exploded in an avalanche of foam. We dropped like a falling elevator, smashed into the trough, and slewed sideways to the top of the next swell. I jammed the throttle forward, powering the bow around before the next breaker could roll us. We pitched, plunged, and rolled; a heavy duffel bag thumped to the floor.

"Get everything down," I snapped. "Put it all on the floor."

I felt bad about barking orders, but moving the gear and heavy camera bags off the bunks and shelves to the floor was a measure of how desperate things were becoming; shifting two or three hundred pounds would have only a minimal effect on the *Swift*'s overall balance, but if we were broached and flung sideways by a large breaking sea, lowering the center of gravity by even a small amount might make the difference between being rolled over and staying upright.

A little more than a year before, a boat similar to the *Wilderness Swift* had flipped during a salmon opening near Haines. The skipper of the *Tammy Kay* managed to swim free and was rescued, but a deckhand was trapped inside the overturned hull. After severe icing conditions forced a Coast Guard rescue helicopter to turn back and divers attempting to swim to the trapped man were stymied by a tangle of nets and lines, the crews of the half dozen boats that responded to the *Tammy Kay*'s mayday call were forced to listen to the muffled thumps of the sixteen-year-old crewman trying to free himself until he drowned. The night the *Tammy Kay* flipped, she was in the middle of the fishing fleet and the wind was blowing thirty knots; now the weather was much worse and the *Wilderness Swift* was alone. There was not another vessel in sight.

I risked a quick glance at the chart. Eight miles to the north, Wilson Cove formed a shallow indentation in the coast, but it was studded with rocks and too open to offer much shelter from the storm.

Seven miles farther, Whitewater Bay promised excellent shelter, but a reef that has been claiming boats since the Russian occupation blocked the southern half of its mouth. Clearing the reef would mean running *past* the bay, then doubling back in a risky maneuver that would put us broadside to the waves.

Another breaker hissed under our keel and dropped us into the void behind it. The best I could do was throttle up to gain speed in the trough, then idle back to avoid skidding out of control down the face. The waves had grown so large and steep I was worried we might drop off the face of one, burying the bow. If that happened, the next wave might throw us end over end.

Every fourth or fifth wave was a monster, a slick gray animal that rose so high it seemed to block the wind. I was sure it was only a matter of time until one fell on top of us and drove us under.

"Sixteen miles," I whispered. "Might as well be a hundred."

I didn't want to think about it. If we didn't make Whitewater before dark, it was another four miles to the next harbor. Chaik Bay had no threatening reef, but I figured every additional mile we had to run in the dark doubled our odds against making it.

"Is it getting worse?" Michio asked. He was wedged into the corner of the galley table, bracing himself against the bulkhead with one hand.

Don't let him see how scared you are. I swallowed and tried to lick my lips.

"Don't worry, Michio. The *Swift*'s a good boat."

He nodded, a little doubtfully, and stiffened as we hit the next wave.

When I glanced at him a few minutes later, his chin was tucked to his chest and his eyes were closed, his breathing regular and even.

Jesus, I thought, *he's fallen asleep.*

———————

HALFWAY BETWEEN Wilson Cove and Whitewater Bay the tide turned and brought with it an incremental drop in the wind, but even though the change took the frenzied edge off the seas, I was still too disoriented by the darkness and pounding to chance rounding the Whitewater reef. It took another long hour of running at quarter speed before I put the helm over to enter Chaik Bay. It was past eight o'clock before we tucked the *Swift* into an eight-fathom hole behind a small island, where the only sign of the storm was a gusty wind soughing through the trees.

I was numb, trembling with fatigue, and my shoulders felt like I had been beaten with a plank. By the time I got the anchor set and gathered up the contents of a cooler that had tumbled across the deck, Michio was breading cutlets and had a pot of rice on the stove.

I tipped a kettle of water into a bowl and gathered up a washcloth and soap. I was sticky, clammy with fear and sweat, and when I went out on deck and stripped off my shirt, the cool air felt good on my skin. Shivering more from the dissipation of adrenaline than the chill, I upended the bowl of warm water across my chest and let out a satisfied groan.

The smell of Michio's cooking mingled with the salty tang of seaweed and kelp. Blowing rain glistened in the light from the cabin. I felt safe, overwhelmed with sensations, and whistled as I toweled myself dry, thinking how good it was to be alive.

"Dinner ready!" Michio leaned his head out the door.

I snagged a beer from the cooler, slipped on my shirt, and went inside. Michio had performed his usual miracle, producing bowls of salad, rice, steamed beans, and a platter of pork cutlets fried to a crisp, golden brown.

I twisted the cap from the beer and the contents foamed over my hand. *I'm not the only one that got shaken up,* I thought, and grabbed for a napkin.

"Weren't you scared, Michio? When it started getting rough?" I was still amazed by how he had fallen asleep.

"Yes," he answered nonchalantly, forking a cutlet onto his plate. "But you said everything would be okay. So I go to sleep."

When I reassured Michio that he didn't have to worry because "the *Swift* is a good boat" I was dissembling, but he had accepted my words at face value. He trusted me, it was as simple as that, and as we worked through the meal I wondered how a person learns to trust like that.

In the past I had wondered at Michio's effect on other people, at how something about him seemed to inspire unexpected generosity and kindness, but now I began to understand that by simply *believing* in people, Michio's faith created its own guarantee.

You reap what you sow, I thought to myself. It's a common tenet of pop psychology that humans usually respond to the expectations of others by meeting them—treat a man like a thief and he'll steal, put him in a straitjacket and sure enough, he'll go mad—but the opposite is true as well, and to understand it I had only to consider the extraordinary heroism of the fireman or soldier compelled to act under life-threatening circumstances by (in addition to his training and own self-regard) the expectations of his leaders or society at large.

From there, it was a short leap to comparing Michio's outlook on life—that the world and its people were basically fair and good, and could be counted on to do their best—to my own, which was more like that of someone crossing a powerful river on a skein of thin ice.

I ought to be more like that, I thought, and made a halfhearted resolve to emulate Michio's unspoken faith that everything we need is at hand.

"Besides," Michio said, stuffing a spoonful of rice into his mouth, "if I don't go to sleep? I was getting *hakike*—seasick!"

13 》 Transients

TWO DAYS LATER Chatham Straits had settled down to a mild chop. A steady rain was falling when we cleared Village Point and turned north, as it had been since we dropped anchor in Chaik Bay. The horizon was a seamless shade of gray.

Behind us the peaks of Admiralty Island were lost in gloom. Native legend holds that people from the villages in the area sought shelter from the Great Flood on top of the mountains and were forced to erect stone walls to keep out marauding bears.

"Weather like this," I told Michio, "it's easy to believe in the Flood."

"Easy to believe bears, too," he replied, puffing out his cheeks to simulate relief. On the second day of lying at anchor in Chaik Bay, we had grown bored with waiting for the weather to break, gone ashore to explore a nearby creek, and come face-to-face with a grizzly in a patch of brush. The bear had done nothing but stare at us as if trying to figure out what we were, then put its nose to the ground and shuffled away, but with less than fifteen feet between us, looking into its black watermelon-seed eyes had been enough to leave Michio and me gasping.

Fifteen minutes later we were sitting on a stone beside the river reliving the encounter in that giggly, giddy-with-relief sort of way that separates hysteria from laughter (and celebrating the fact that even after years of watching and photographing bears at close range, the sudden appearance of one under such conditions remained as heart-stopping and exciting as the first time), when a sow and two half-grown cubs burst out of the brush a stone's throw away. The trio stampeded across the creek directly in front of us and disappeared into the forest on the other side at a dead run. The sow was far more concerned with removing her offspring from the reach of the first bear than she was with our presence, and neither she nor her cubs acknowledged us with more than a brief, wild-eyed glance.[48]

There are piles of stone on top of Table Mountain that are said to be the remains of the Natives' deluvian, anti-bear walls, and that—as Michio said after noting that we had just spent a week searching for bears without success, only to have four of them nearly run over us within the space of a few minutes—was easy to believe, too.

We were still more than a hundred miles from Juneau—too far to run in a single day, but Funter Bay was only forty-five miles away and we were making reasonable speed. "If the weather holds," I told Michio, "we might make it halfway."

For the first thirty miles it was just a matter of ticking off landmarks on the chart. We passed Hood Bay and Killisnoo, the site of a whaling station that operated until 1930, then the village of Angoon. Five miles farther north was Thayer Creek, named for a Forest Ser-

---

48. Half of all bear cubs die during their first year, and the primary cause of this mortality is male bears. Biologists surmise that this urge to infanticide is nature's way of increasing the chances that the genes of the largest, strongest boars will be passed on, since a sow that loses her offspring will enter estrus, or a period of fertility, sooner than one raising cubs, and choose to mate with one of the more dominant males in her area—a system that seems somewhat clumsy at first consideration, since a boar has no way of knowing whether or not he is killing his own cubs, but which in the long run gives preference to the fittest line of genes among the species.

vice employee killed by a brown bear shortly after he finished surveying a stand of timber for harvest, and a half hour later I pointed out
the flat at Parker Creek, where an exploratory party of sailors dispatched from the *Discovery* and *Chatham* by George Vancouver in
1794 had spent a miserable night in heavy rain.

"Popular experience," said Michio, giggling. Neither one of us had
felt dry since the stormy night on the mountain. But still, I said—
holding up my coffee cup to make my point—bouncing along in the
Wilderness Swift at twelve knots was a lot easier than manning the oars
of a longboat.

At Icy Straits the western horizon peeked under the blanket of
low-lying clouds and bathed the tumbling water in weak silver light.
The waves directly beneath the rift seemed to swell with an inner
emerald glow, and the contrast of that single streak of green against the
gloomy background of gray drew my eye like the vivid color of a
flower that insists on being seen.

A cat's-paw of intensely white foam sparkled at the top of a wave,
then burst into a shining black mound as a long dorsal fin sliced it
in half.

Michio shouted *"Shachi!"* at the same moment I hollered "Killer
whale!"

Michio put his face to the window while I eased back the throttle. The orca's blowhole puffed a jet of fine spray.

"Another one." Michio pointed off the bow. In less than a minute
we had spotted a half dozen killer whales scattered across our course,
moving slowly from east to west, in the direction of Icy Straits. The
Swift dipped and rolled as I came around on a heading parallel to the
whales.

"Killer whale" is a bit of a misnomer, not because the animals are
not killers—they are, and fantastically efficient ones at that—but
because they are not really whales at all. They are the largest member
of the dolphin, or *delphinidae*, family, and in spite of their size are more
closely related to the common bottlenose dolphin than to any of the
larger whales. With their high intelligence, close-knit family groups,

and longevity, they are more like humans than any other animal, and other than humans, they are the most widespread animal in the world. Killer whales inhabit every stretch of salt water between Antarctica and the Arctic Ocean, on both sides of the globe.

Shortly before Michio and I left on our voyage around Admiralty Island I spent the morning hunched over a cup of coffee in the Channel Bowl café listening to a friend from Cordova explain how researchers in Prince William Sound had recently become convinced that, like the carnivorous sundew plant, *Orcinus orca* occurs in two varieties: residents, who eat only fish, and transients, who roam vast areas and prey almost entirely on warm-blooded animals such as sea lions, seals, and whales.[49]

Diet is not the only thing that differentiates the two types of killer whales; each has distinctive physical traits as well. The tip of a transient's dorsal fin is falcate and sharp, like a mercenary's sword, whereas that of a resident assumes a more gentle, rounded shape. A subtle difference in the saddle patch—an area of gray skin on a killer whale's back—is more difficult to spot; on a transient, the patch is slightly longer. According to Lance Barrett-Lennard, a geneticist with the University of British Columbia who has made an extensive study of killer-whale DNA, the physical differences are the result of a separation between the two varieties that goes back hundreds or perhaps thousands of generations: transients and residents may share the same territories, but they never interbreed. Nor do they socialize or intermix in any way, and when the two meet, it is as if each is invisible to the other, with neither taking any notice of the other—rather like a band of motorcycle outlaws being snubbed by a bunch of farmers and responding with silent disdain.

More telling perhaps than the physical traits are the behavioral differences biologists see as a sign of separate "cultures." Residents tend

---

49. On at least one well-documented occasion a pod of transients also killed and consumed a moose swimming across Icy Straits, and I have heard anecdotes of a pod surrounding and killing a black bear swimming across a canal farther south.

to be more boisterous, engaging in lots of tail slapping, breaching, and splashing; transients are secretive and stealthy.

In the past Michio and I had had some fantastic encounters with pods of orca that seemed almost desirous of being observed, moving in steady, predictable patterns that made it possible to track carefully and politely alongside for a few photos. More than one curious orca has approached the *Swift* for a brief ride in the wake or to spy-hop alongside, standing on its tail and raising its head out of the water for a good long look.

Not so with this pod. There was something elusive in their behavior, something about the way they changed direction underwater and moved at different speeds that felt mysterious and evasive, like a sleight-of-hand trick meant to prevent us from guessing where they would appear.

They were running widely spaced, remaining submerged for long periods of time, in a long, wavering line sweeping west toward Icy Straits, leading me to believe they might be a hunting party of transients searching for porpoises or seals. But it was difficult to spot their black bodies against the choppy water and shifting curtains of rain, and when they surfaced, they were too far away for a clear view of their fins.

"If I drop the hydrophone over," I told Michio, "it might give us a clue." Resident orca use a chorus of clicks, squeals, grunts, and ratcheting birdcalls to communicate, but transients are completely silent as they hunt. For reasons I cannot name, this stealth sometimes creates an atavistic sense of menace that tingles up my spinal cord and draws me back to that place in the natural world where, for all our engines and electronics and opposable thumbs, humans beings are nothing but sacks of meat—a shivering reaction that is, of course, completely overblown; there is no record of a wild killer whale ever attacking a human being.

The tip of a fin cut the back of a wave, rose six inches above the surface, then disappeared. A moment later a second fin appeared close behind the first, swelling up from the water until it towered a full six feet above the surface before receding slowly out of sight. Until a few years ago, I believed that orca with large dorsal fins were the "herd bulls," harem masters that dominated a pod through sheer size. Now I know that some of the larger-finned creatures are female, cows that have lived long enough to assume the proportions of a male, and that the largest male in a pod is probably not a breeding bull at all but an elder son, because orca society (both resident and transient) is organized along strictly matriarchal lines, with dominant females sometimes living to be seventy or eighty years old, while her male offspring are lucky to reach fifty.

It is stretching things a bit to say that male orca are "mama's boys" who spend their lives tethered to their mother's apron strings, but to the best of my knowledge the majority do spend their lives swimming in their mother's wake, except for brief periods during the summer months when the disparate pods gather into large mating groups and they slip away for quick assignations with females from other pods.

So strict are the bonds of family among orca that each pod has evolved its own dialect—pod-specific variations in the killer whale's language of clicks and whistles distinctive enough to allow eavesdropping researchers to identify an individual's family and clan without ever laying eyes on the animal.[50] John Ford, head of marine mammal research at the Vancouver Aquarium in British Columbia and a man who probably knows as much about killer whales as anyone alive, believes the difference in dialects may serve to prevent inbreeding, with males pursuing females whose accents are the least like their own.

Another, more serious, parallel is the effect a few rampant individuals can have on an ecosystem. From the middle of the 1990s onward, the sea otter population in a large part of the Aleutian Islands fell by more than 90 percent, and according to James Estes, a biologist with the U.S. Geological Survey who is to sea otters what John Ford is to

50. A clan is a group of related resident pods descended from a single ancestral pod. It is not known if transient pods (being so silent, widespread, and therefore more difficult to study) are organized along similar lines.

killer whales, the dramatic decline may be the work of as few as three or four orca.

Prior to the Aleutian orcas' rampage, it was almost unheard of for *Orcinus orca* to prey on sea otters. But during the same period, the population of Steller sea lions in the Bering Sea and Aleutian Islands also plummeted by 90 percent (possibly as a result of overfishing by the fleets of factory trawlers that converge on Alaska every year), and it takes a lot of scrawny sea otters to equal the calories available in a single thousand-pound sea lion upholstered in thick layers of fat.[51] With the disappearance of the sea lions (the orca's favorite prey), Estes believes the Aleutian transients may have had little choice but to start hunting otters.[52]

Whether the finger of blame points at industrial fishing, a band of orca gone bad, or some other undiscovered cause, the damage reaches much deeper than the decline in otter numbers: sea otters eat a lot of sea urchins, which in turn eat a lot of kelp, which provides critical habitat to dozens of species of fish. Without otters to keep them in check, urchin populations can explode, denuding vast shorelines of kelp. Without kelp, there are fewer fish, and therefore less prey available to feed the Aleutian chain's bald eagles. Between sea and sky, the tendrils of disruption probably reach much farther than we can imagine, and it is not difficult to envision the entire ecosystem eventually slipping off its tracks.

Michio tucked his camera beneath his coat to protect it from a squall of rain.

"Too far away," he said, hunching his shoulders in resignation. The light was too flat and the orca too elusive to justify wasting film.

51. In spite of spending their lives immersed in frigid waters, sea otters have no insulating blubber like walruses or seals. Instead, they depend on their remarkably dense and luxurious fur for warmth, fur which in animals like mink or fox consists of between twenty and fifty thousand hairs per square inch, but in sea otters may contain over a million.
52. Another theory gaining currency is that the decline in otter numbers can be traced to pollutants sweeping north and east into the Aleutian Islands on the Japanese or Kushiro current, which circulates seawater from Asia clockwise across the entire North Pacific.

I spun the wheel, putting us back on course for Funter Bay. The sun was sliding toward the western horizon behind a veil of dark clouds, and I felt the gloom closing in around me. My self-respect, my ego—whatever you want to call it—was closely allied to my self-image as the guide who could always get a photographer something special, and when I considered that we were ten days and two hundred miles into the trip with nothing to show for our efforts but a few shots of blue ice, my mood began to slip, too. Michio was quiet, staring out the window across the rolling whitecaps toward a huge clear-cut on the slopes of Chichagof Island, and I wondered if his thoughts were wandering the same channels as my own.

The notion of transients as some kind of aberration kept swimming through my brain, forming shadowy gray shapes that slipped in and out of my thoughts like half-formed fears, resurrecting images of the human predators among us—Robert Hansen and others of his ilk, monsters like Ted Bundy or John Wayne Gacy, who linger behind shallow masks of civility, indiscernible from the rest of us by shape or form, hungering for warm meat.

Like the kelp beds, our cultural ecosystem is a delicate thing, and it doesn't require the presence of many aberrant individuals to throw the whole thing out of whack. A shrewd sociologist could probably trace a connection between our culture's serial killers and psychopaths, the cash-and-carry politicians in the pay of corporations that strip the meat from the planet's bones, and the cynicism of schoolkids who shoot each other down in the halls.

The propeller growled as the *Swift* rolled across the top of a wave. And me, I wondered, what am I doing? Living on a boat, wandering like a transient across thousands of miles of water every year?

Seven miles ahead, Funter Bay came and went in the mist, appearing and disappearing behind a shifting curtain of rain. A half hour later, when I nosed the *Swift* into a dock there and snubbed the mooring lines to a cleat before shutting down the engine, the uprooted sensation was still blowing through my chest.

"Grab your camera, Michio. There's something I want to show you."

Ours was the only boat at the dock. No one was watching as I led Michio across a beach paved in slabs of gray shale and swung into the forest at the foot of a bluff.

The understory was tangled and lifeless, a profusion of wrist-sized saplings vying for sunlight beneath an impenetrable canopy of even-aged spruce that had sprung up after the original old-growth forest was stripped away to feed the needs of a salmon cannery and gold mine operating nearby in the 1930s. The only sound was the rustle of our rain gear against the underbrush, the snap of brittle twigs, and the patter of rain dripping through the trees. Rusty orange water trickled along a shallow watercourse at our feet.

"Cholera water" a friend of mine called it when I was helping him build a small cabin nearby. "Drink that and you'll die." He was only half joking, as that was precisely what had happened to more than forty Aleut Indians interned in Funter Bay during World War II.

On June 7, 1942, a special task force of the Imperial Japanese Army invaded Kiska Island, one of the westernmost islands in the Aleutian chain. The next day, more Japanese units occupied nearby Attu. It was the first time foreign troops had occupied American soil since 1812, and in the turmoil that followed, U.S. troops evacuated more than 880 Aleuts from their treeless, windswept home and forced them into internment camps a thousand miles away in Funter Bay. While German POWs housed in well-built bunkhouses twenty miles west in Excursion Inlet organized orchestras and tried on warm woolen coats (courtesy of the Red Cross), the Aleut Americans were huddling in the dank, leaky remains of the abandoned cannery, dying of depression and medical neglect while trying to subsist on a meager diet of rice. The records of the sole harried doctor assigned to care for the declining Aleuts sometimes listed the cause of death as simply "pain."

Michio had always been deeply interested in Native cultures, possessed with an abiding curiosity about how aboriginal people related to each other and to nature, and it was this that I was considering when the impulse to show him the cemetery took me. I thought he might find the stoicism of the Aleuts and their courage in caring for one another under such adverse conditions as poignant and touching as I had.

I was well into a rambling discourse on the invasion and evacuation when the look on his face stopped me cold. Christ! I was mortified. Does he think I'm trying to blame the Japanese?

"Michio, I never . . ." I stumbled over my words, but he wasn't listening.

He stooped to rub the dirt from a headstone. "This was a baby," he said sadly, sweeping a litter of spruce needles from the grave. Alexey Kenneth Kochutin was three months old when he died.

Like Alexey's, the names on the rest of the headstones are rhythmic and poetic, full of czarist consonants that click on my tongue: Emanoff, Gustigoff, and Kochutin; Bourdukofsky, Tetoff, and Prokopiof. Many of the graves were marked with the three-armed cross of the Russian Orthodox faith, others with a simple slab of stone.

"This one," Michio pointed to a lichen-dappled tombstone, "almost the same age as my mother when I was born."

Women, old people, and children made up the bulk of the dead. During the summer of 1943, in spite of the fact that they had ostensibly been evacuated to protect them from the invading Japanese, most of the able-bodied men interned at Funter Bay were transported *back* to the Pribilof Islands to conduct an annual harvest of fur seals under the auspices of the federal government, leaving the women and children to fend for themselves.[53] While they were gone, epidemics of disease ravaged the camps. At times, virtually every Aleut in Funter Bay was bedridden with dysentery, influenza, or measles, and it was left to a handful of children to feed, bathe, and nurse the rest.

Several of the graves were decorated with seashells. The Aleuts were children of space and open water, masters of the lance-sharp boat made of bentwood and skin, which they called a *bidarka,* and I could

53. With the wartime boom in the price of fur, the seal harvest was phenomenally lucrative for the federal government. Nonetheless, the conscripted hunters were paid scant wages. When some of the younger men expressed their dissatisfaction, they were labeled as mutineers, and the cook received orders not to feed them.

imagine the survivors placing the cockle shells on the graves as a reminder of the endless sea and sky of their island home. It was painful to imagine women and children dying beneath the dripping canopy of the rainforest, longing for a last glimpse of the sky. The bare ground and mute, lifeless colors of the graveyard made me wonder how homesick a person had to be to die.[54]

Michio was having similar thoughts. "It must have been terrible," he said, "so far away from their own food."

It was a trenchant observation. Here in Southeast Alaska, where the Aleuts had not been allowed to fish or hunt, the prisoners must have longed with a hunger far sharper than the needs of the stomach for the fresh gull eggs and seal meat that for ten thousand years had formed their people's bones.

Michio knelt beside a headstone and peered at the date. "Nineteen forty-three," he said quietly. "It's only been fifty years."

The life span of an orca, I thought. With her keen acoustic perceptions, the matriarch of the pod we had just seen in Icy Straits might have heard the grinding of the USS *Delarof*'s propeller as the ship bearing the evacuees entered Funter Bay, or the rattle of the anchor chain and the splash of oars as the vessel's crew shuttled their human cargo ashore.

"My father was a soldier," Michio spoke in a low voice. "In China."

"Michio, I didn't mean—" I started to apologize again, but he forced his mouth into a slight smile that didn't reach his eyes, then shook his head to say no offense had been taken.

I tried and failed to imagine the father of one so simple and generous caught up in a war, then failed again when I tried to imagine Michio carrying a gun. But war makes no allowances for the limits of imagination. (After all, who, before 1942, could have imagined American citizens being torn from their homes by their own government and left to die of neglect on a remote Alaskan shore?) It was only an

---

54. In May 2000, the graveyard was repaired and restored by family members and volunteers working with Archbishop Paul Merculief, cleaning up debris and replacing the missing and rotting markers with new white crosses and a simple entrance arch.

accident of timing and circumstances, the difference of a single generation, that had made it possible for Michio and me to be friends
instead of looking at each other over the barrel of a gun.

IT WAS NEARLY DARK when we returned to the *Swift*. By the
time we sat down to dinner the weather had broken and a half-circle
moon was riding across the sky. Michio was silent. He had taken no
pictures and avoided my eye by looking out the window as we ate. I
was worried that in spite of his denial, I had somehow offended him
by marching him into the remnants of a tragedy linked to the war
between the Americans and the Japanese.

I probed his silence by asking for a lesson. "Michio, teach me
another word in Japanese."

He chewed for a moment before patting his mouth with a napkin
and reaching for a pen. Holding it carefully, he stroked a few lines of
hiragana onto a piece of paper and turned it for me to see.

"*Tomodachi,*" he said, pointing at the figures. "Friend." Then he
added a few quick strokes and smiled to clarify the adjective's meaning: "*Yoi-tomodachi,*" he said. "A good friend."

Home is not always a door at the end of a sidewalk. Sometimes it
is a broader place that holds the shape of the sky, the water we drink,
and the food that becomes the minerals of our bones. Sometimes it is
the sum of our experiences and memories, and sometimes it is wherever we happen to be—if we are with the right companion.

14 》 Miraculous Fledglings and Shape-Shifting Bears

IT IS JUNE as I write this, and the bay I am anchored in swarms with seabirds hovering and diving over a school of small, wriggling fish. The fish rise and fall in waves, peppering the surface of the water with eruptions of tiny ripples like those caused by a sudden rain and exciting a riot of fighting and diving among the flock of mewling gulls. It is warm out, almost balmy, and I work with the windows open, but when the odd cloud drifts over the sun now and then and the temperature drops a few degrees, I remember clearly how long and endless the winter following our voyage around Admiralty Island began to seem. All through November and December the sky over Juneau hung gray and wrinkled as an elephant's hide, dribbling snow that turned to rain as it fell, until by Christmas I was emphatically weary of the parsimonious light, tired of watching these same seabirds being tumbled and blown past my window by the wind, and had begun to pray for a rip-roaring northerly cold enough and strong enough to hurl the sun to its southern limits so it might return again sooner, full of spring's warmth and light. My father and mother had long ago traded in their winter parkas for the benign environment of a coffee farm in Hawaii, and I was eager to see them, but there are good years and bad years in the charter business, and the previous season had left no room on my credit card for a ticket to anyplace warm. Instead, I cranked the oil stove up another notch, pulled on a second sweater, and was halfway through February when Michio called.

"I've been in Tokyo," he said, "and I have big news."

Her name was Naoko. That much was clear. The rest was a jumbled explanation of how she was the daughter of his sister's best friend and he had had his eye on her for a while and she was perfect, really very perfect, and it just rolled into a big, babbling ball of enthusiasm from there.

I tried to wedge my way into the flood with a few questions, then jumped in when he paused for a breath: "Michio! Are you saying you've got a girlfriend?"

"I think we're getting married, Lynn. Getting married pretty soon."

THE REST OF THE WINTER was easy. It was as if some element of Michio's delight had flowed down the telephone line and spilled out into the confines of the *Wilderness Swift,* smoothing out the tedium of the season, promising an end to the unremitting night. I was still wearing two pairs of socks and a sweater to bed, but spring no longer seemed unattainable.

Things took another leap when I wandered into the local library, intending to kill some time in the periodicals, and picked up a copy of *Alaska Geographic* magazine dedicated to bears.

The cover shot was a picture of an irresistibly cute young brown bear at rest with its forepaws tucked under its chin. The bear was a well-known character, a habituated resident of the McNeil River State Game Sanctuary that has appeared in so many travel brochures, advertisements, and calendars that it has gained the vague familiarity of a second-tier movie star or model, so easily photographed that the cadre of professional wildlife photographers that make the circuit of Alaska's wildlife hot spots every year had given it a name. Otto was four or five years old when the picture was taken, and—like his human counterparts who model for print ads or appear on TV—it was just a matter of time before a younger, fuzzier, or more tolerant bear came along to displace him.

The photograph on the first page was even more precious—a pair of pint-sized polar bear cubs huddled in the snow, all beady black eyes and adorable button noses pasted onto cotton candy bodies. What the photograph didn't show (but was explained in the caption) was that the cubs were huddling in fear, clinging to each other for the reassurance of a sibling's touch while researchers manhandled their drugged, unconscious mother outside the frame.

I turned to the table of contents. It was illustrated with a half-page shot of a black bear munching a dandelion—a plant not native to Alaska, but which over the last half century or so has spread along highways and throughout urban areas, sprouting wherever human activity has disturbed the soil. The angle of the photograph made me think it was taken from slightly above. It looked like it was taken from a road.

I flicked through the magazine, fanning the pages back-to-front with my thumb. There were pictures of grizzlies in front of tour buses, black bears in garbage cans, and bears digging among the flames of a burning dump. There were pictures of bears being sedated and collared by biologists, and several of photographers taking pictures of bears. The text was informative and well written, but I was vaguely disappointed that it seemed to be more about bear-human interactions than about bears as an element of the wilderness.

I flipped back to the cover and settled into my chair. Might as well start from the front. After glancing at the table of contents again, I riffled to the first article ("Black Bears" by Bruce Baker) and opened the magazine across my lap.

My heart tripped a beat and stopped. I became acutely aware of the hum of a fluorescent fixture overhead, the in-and-out flow of my breath. On the verso page, opposite the article title, was a photograph of a silver-blue bear.

The stout, fully-muscled animal stood quartering the camera, pausing with one rear leg extended in mid-stride to stare into the lens. Each guard hair along the thick-set animal's back, head, and shoulders was the color of platinum, the photograph so sharp I could feel the fur under my hand. The undercoat—the dense mat of fine, tightly woven hairs that provides fur-bearing animals with insulation—was gray, perhaps black, and when combined with the silver guard hairs created an effect that made it easy to understand how a person trying to describe the color of this animal could arrive at blue.

I scanned the page, searching for a photo credit, and sat up a bit straighter when I recognized the photographer's name. John Hyde spent most of a decade working for the Alaska Department of Fish and Game as the state's only official wildlife photographer, until statewide elections catapulted a particularly rancorous and conservative body of legislators into power, and the department's budget was slashed, in part as punishment for the failure of biologists to endorse a powerful senator's desire to have an island near his home stocked with elk. Hamstrung by the budget cuts and disgusted by the venal politics, John quit and made the risky leap into freelance photography.

He's built like a fullback, with the sort of shoulders that can paddle a kayak into a stiff headwind all day without complaining or heft a pack without a lot of middle-aged grunts. When he laughs (which is often) his eyes squeeze down to glittering black points, and since going freelance, he has been a regular passenger on the *Swift*. Wherever he goes, John wears a clunky necklace of bangles and beads adorned with a small plastic whale—a talisman, made for him by his daughter, that never leaves his neck until he settles into his sleeping bag at night and goes on again as soon as he crawls out in the morning. He's a friend, but I knew that for John, whose family comes first, last, and always, asking for the how, when, and where of something so rare as a glacier bear in a business as competitive as wildlife photography would be like making a grab for his daughter's dinner.

The bear stared at me from the open magazine in my lap.

No way, I thought, settling back into the chair. Even asking would put John in an awkward spot. But the photograph was all the proof I needed that dreams, like Michio's fantasy of a family, sometimes came true, and that the chance of photographing a glacier bear was real.

⌃

JOHN LEANED one elbow on the table and stared at me sideways for a long second, covering his mouth with his hand in a kind of body language that said "I don't want to say this," but he did.

"Just don't tell anybody else, okay?"

It was early May. More than a year had passed since John's picture of the glacier bear had been published, Michio had gotten married, and the blueberry bushes on the hillsides above Juneau' were covered with flowers like translucent pink bells.

"Goes without saying," I replied, nodding. Michio murmured his assent, fingering a rough sketch that lay on the table between us. The drawing—a crude map of a deep bay—was an enormous measure of John's respect for Michio, one more piece of evidence to show how people trusted Michio because he trusted them. I was flattered, too. Sharing such information with a guide who makes his living off photographers was a generosity I never expected.

"Here." John touched the point of a pen to the coastline where a squiggled blue line made a river. "Take your rubber boots. It's a big tide flat, and you're gonna get pretty muddy."

We agreed. The pen fluttered, tapping a nervous rhythm in John's hand. "And don't tell anybody," he repeated. It wasn't just other photographers John was worried about. We all knew there were people around who would love to have a glacier bear skin on their wall. And we all knew how efficiently the "rainforest telegraph" spreads gossip through a town as small and tightly knit as Juneau. If I mentioned our destination to someone in the morning, by nightfall everyone from the governor's office to the rubbish dump would know.

"Thank you, John." Michio ducked his head in a tiny bow. "I think this time we will have better luck."

He folded the map, creasing the edges with his thumb before sliding it into a tattered notebook, then flipped back the notebook's cover to steal a quick glimpse of a photograph tucked inside. The photo was a simple one, a three-by-five snapshot of the sort churned out by Fotomats and drugstores—not the sort of artwork I expected from an artist of Michio's caliber, but since his arrival in Juneau, I had seen him slip it out of the notebook for a lingering inspection several times. In cherishing such a simple photo, it was as if he had shed his role as a photographer and found his prime purpose: the snapshot was a picture of his son.

THE FIRST TIME I met Shoma, Michio was vibrating with excitement, bouncing up onto his toes to peer over the crowd of passengers disembarking from Alaska Airlines flight 66. Stragglers were still streaming down the jetway when I spotted a slender Oriental woman wending her way through the knots of people, staggering under the burden of a large bag over one shoulder, dragging another behind. I started to point Naoko out to Michio when she paused to shift a blanket-wrapped bundle in the crook of her arm, but he was already gone, skipping and ducking through the crowd, edging sideways past a group of large men with fishing rods in their hands to snatch the parcel from her arms.

"My *aka-chan!* My baby!" Michio's face was ecstatic as he held the swaddled infant overhead at arm's length, lifting the child up like an offering to heaven, then lowering it to his nose. Shoma was only a few weeks old, still capable of the imperturbable sleep of the newborn, and the tiny red face beneath the blanket kept its eyes tightly closed.

Michio danced in a circle, chattering in a mixture of English and Japanese. Naoko was drooping, drained from the long journey and the ongoing surprise of being a mother, but somehow she managed to be radiant at the same time. Michio's infatuation with her was understandable: she's a beautiful woman, with the same wide-open face and kind eyes as her husband and a shy smile that says the world is her friend. I hung back as Michio turned to her and held out the baby—not for her to take, but as if offering her a glimpse of something profound—and something passed between them that made me think that this is the way people are *supposed* to be.

"This is my son, Shoma," Michio said, pulling me forward by my sleeve and bouncing the child in his arms. Naoko reached out and gently pried the baby from his hands, then laughed at her own relief at having the infant safe in her arms.

I held out a finger. "How do you do, Shoma?"

A tiny hand snaked out of the blanket, grasped my finger with surprising strength, and guided it into the tiny, sucking O of Shoma's mouth. For one flickering, timeless moment, I knew what it was to be part of something huge.

MICHIO HAD BEEN on top of the world ever since he became a husband and father. His work had earned him a show at the Carnegie Museum, his books were selling well in Europe and Japan, and his new family provided a pivot point, like the tip of a gyro, around which his life could spin. When I noticed he no longer fiddled with his tobacco and pipe, he shook his head seriously and said, "I give it up. I have to live a long time for my Shoma."

I was not doing as well. There were strains in my business, problems I did not have the heart to deal with because a love affair I had entered into with high hopes was splintering, leaving that organ feeling laid open and filleted. I had also spent most of the winter in Hawaii, on a chemotherapy ward with my failing father, and when Michio leaned over the table to dowse John's hand-drawn chart for bears, the arch of his back assumed that of my father's as he bent over the side of the bed to retch, and I was reminded once again of how there had been nothing I could do, no comfort I could extend beyond a hand on his shoulder or a damp cloth for his forehead, and when the doctors pronounced the daily blast of radiation and toxic chemicals ineffective, to help him onto a plane to Mexico, where a private clinic claimed to be curing cancer with an extract of apricot seeds.

"Can't hurt," my father's oncologist said with a shrug when asked about the Laetrile treatment. His was a humble approach to medicine—

no demigod status for him—but in acknowledging the possibility that other disciplines might offer hopes not encouraged by conventional medicine, he was also confessing his own impotence and proscribing my father's odds.

My father brightened under the new treatment and appeared to grow stronger until a day came when he felt well enough to go sightseeing in the countryside. It was a pleasant day, full of cactus-studded hills and green waves at the seaside, and when night fell he was in a good mood, trying out his limited Spanish, joking with the driver as we sped through a series of winding desert curves in a rented van. When a large owl flashed out of the darkness into the cone of the speeding headlights and exploded against the windscreen in a shower of feathers and broken glass, he sagged and went silent, undone by the omen, and reached for my hand.

After that he seemed to shrink, slumping into the wheelchair as I pushed him down the tiled hallways of the clinic, and did not want to talk as much or laugh, except to tell stories from his youth—stories of living through the Dust Bowl years in a canvas tent, watching through the flap as government agents slaughtered the family's herd as part of a depression-era program to drive up the price of beef. For the small-time Texas ranchers, the decimation was a horror, a heart-and-blood tragedy beyond any mere loss of dollars.

Nonetheless, the memory brought some light to his eyes and the glimmer of a smile to his face when he remembered his own father's rage toward an agent who—despite an explicit warning from my grandfather not to do so—had shot and killed his pet calf.

"Dad told the sumbitch to get off the place or he'd kill 'im," he chuckled, "and that peckerwood left pretty fast."

In telling the story, there was something on his face that was joyful and proud, as if the breaking forth of my grandfather's rage into a threat against the agent's life was remembered as the fullest possible proof of his own father's love for him, surpassing even the love a rancher holds for a herd nursed through years of drought. It was only later that I realized the story was my father's way of saying that he, too, would have done anything to protect my happiness as a child.

So it wasn't all bad. There were slippery moments of contentment, even humor, plaited into the general dismay. After the chemotherapy stripped away the remains of his thinning hair, we agreed that in some fiercely virile, like-it-or-be-damned kind of way, he looked good so thoroughly bald, and in a lighthearted moment accentuated the effect by the application of a (temporary) tattoo to his head. For a while after he returned home from the hospital he took great delight in donning a cap and setting off for his favorite coffee shop, where at an opportune moment he could casually doff the cap to run a hand over his nonexistent hair, then replace it, affording the other loiterers a brief glimpse of the black panther stalking across his scalp. (One speechless waitress nearly poured coffee in his lap, and when a witless wag at the gas station asked how he lost his hair, he cracked up the rest of the idlers by barking, "Standing on my head so people like *you* can kiss my ass!")

These are the things I hold on to, not the look of skin stretched tight over bones. I was explaining this to Michio as we slogged across the mudflat at the mouth of John's river. (He was right about the mud: we landed at low tide and twenty yards later were black to our knees.) A golden plover twittered away at our sucking approach, skittering across the surface of the mud with panicked cries of *te-teet!*

Michio reached down to tug his boot loose from the sucking mud, listening carefully as I recounted the details of my father's illness, then asked what a "peck-a-wood" was.

I had to think about it a moment. It seemed like too much to explain how the term had been coined by freed slaves after the Civil War as a reference to the "poor white trash" that continued to dominate their lives, or how it takes a swipe at the southerners' reluctance to change by alluding to a bird that spends its life banging its head against solid wood. I took the easy way out.

"It's southern slang, Michio. It's someone who doesn't know how to behave."

The plover ran back and forth along the edge of the water as if trying to find something it had misplaced, then stopped and began preening its breast.

"Plover," I said needlessly, pointing to the black-and-white bird. It was a male, in full breeding plumage. "Might've just flown in from Hawaii."

As winter slowly lifts its skirts to reveal spring, flocks of wandering tattlers, ruddy turnstones, sanderlings, phalaropes, and the awkwardly named bristle-thighed curlew (just to name a few) begin hopscotching up the Pacific coast from as far away as Panama and Argentina, joining more and more flocks along the way. By the middle of May, major staging areas like the mouth of the Stikine River see as many as three hundred thousand birds a day stopping over for a chance to rest and feed on their way to the Arctic, where they breed, raise families under the perpetual northern sun, and gorge themselves on the immense insect biomass that first turned Michio to his pipe.

The migration of any species is a marvel of navigation, but for sheer heart and endurance, few are in a class with the plover's. The elegant bird in front of us, now standing on one leg, head tucked to its shoulder, may have departed Hawaii as little as forty-eight hours ago, spiraling up into the thin, rushing atmosphere of the jet stream at twenty thousand feet, then turning north toward Polaris for twenty-five hundred miles of nonstop flying—an energy requirement that may reduce the plover's body weight by half. In autumn, this predicates that the adult plover's return to the tropics precedes that of its offspring by several weeks, since the adolescent birds are still learning how to feed and perfecting their ability to fly, desperately consuming insects, larvae, and everything else they can cram into their beaks in an effort to lay on the necessary store of fat, while their parents must increase their own chances of survival by leaving before the first snow flies. That the uninitiated young somehow find their way from the Arctic to the tiny, easily misplaced specks of the Hawaiian Archipel-

ago amid the vast sweep of the Pacific without benefit of their parents' guidance is surely one of nature's more remarkable feats.[55]

Admiring the delicate checkerboard of gold and brown across the
male's back, I couldn't help but wonder what percentage of his offspring would be lost to the journey, settling in exhaustion to the surface of the sea from which, not being equipped with the oily feathers
or webbed feet of a true waterbird, they would never be able to rise.
And—it frightened me just to ask—when the plovers return to
Hawaii, would my father still be alive? Or was he, too, about to cross
the tropic of Cancer a final time?

Michio crabbed sideways up a muddy slope, slithering forward one
foot at a time to avoid losing his balance in the slippery pudding. I followed, and at the top of the rise, where the mud gave way to grass,
turned to look behind us at the odd, monstrous line of our tracks
before digging in my pack for binoculars.

"It's paradise," I muttered. "A bear paradise." Before us, a narrow
valley curved out of sight to the left, creating a defile between two
timbered ridges. From the confluence of the shoreline and river, the
prospect was one of brilliant emerald green, as if God had decided to
plop his own private bowling lawn down on this remote spot, and I
did a quick calculation in my head: approximately a mile deep, three
to five hundred yards wide, knock off a little for the valley's taper and
the surface area of the stream—there were more than a hundred acres
of newly sprouted sedge grass in the valley, a lush pasture of every
bear's favorite food.

Michio pointed to a line of tracks meandering along the banks of
the stream. Another, larger, pair crossed the first at an oblique angle,
then faded into a patch of rye. For a hundred yards along the riverbank the luxurient growth had been cropped into ragged patches by

55. To my knowledge, the flight of the Pacific golden plover is exceeded only by that of
the bar-tailed godwit, a ten-inch-high bird with a jauntily upturned beak that leaves
Alaska every autumn for a nonstop flight to New Zealand—a distance of sixty-five hundred miles!

steady grazing, and as we moved inland I sorted out another half-dozen sets of tracks. One grizzly had crossed the valley from east to west, the rest of the tracks were made by blacks.

"So many." Michio glanced left and right. Both sides of the meadow were lined with a wall of alder dense enough to hide a dozen bears.

"Not just kuma," I said, stepping around a limp green coil of scat. Geese prize new sedge grass for the same reasons bears do, and the ground was peppered with their leavings. At the edge of a muddy vale, the tracks of an adolescent wolf skirted a pool of rainwater, doubled back to sniff at a stone, then padded off into a stand of trees, and as we hiked deeper into the valley, I could feel the weight of everything I had left behind in the city sliding from my shoulders—the pall of the sickroom lifting at the rise of a flock of robins, the bruising pain of the love affair fading with the pant of a raven's wing. Traversing the field was like freeing a snarl in a fishing line, the key to its undoing visible in the graffiti of the tracks, the yellow sprawl of buttercups, and the delicate, trembling poise of an eagle feather tangled in the lowest branch of a tree.

Michio pulled the feather free and slipped it into his cap, inserting the quill into the weave. I could hear the mumble of a small waterfall up ahead, and when a chorus of geese rose *whonk-whonk-whonk*ing into the air at the head of the valley I dropped to one knee, scanning the alder brush for the source of their alarm.

For a long moment, nothing. Then a branch waved and a shadow attached to the base of a tree became a bear. Shoulders glistening in the sunlight, it strolled out into the meadow, and when it stopped to paw at something between its feet, ripples of light played back and forth across its fur.

Michio slipped out of his pack, spread the legs of his tripod, and selected a lens. I did the same, balancing my pack against my legs. The bear stopped, lifted its nose, and tested the air for danger, then lowered its head and tore a mouthful of sedge from the ground. We were close enough to hear the *pop* and *crunch* of the grass as it chewed; Michio's camera whispered *chi-chi-chi* in return.

The bear ambled closer, its head swinging back and forth close to the ground as it paused between steps to graze. By the time it was thirty yards away I had gone through half a roll of film and could see the working of its jaws through the lens. At twenty yards, I finished the roll and groped for my pack, being sure to keep my eyes on the bear. I felt the pack teeter, made a grab, and heard it *whump* to the ground.

The bear exploded, spinning into a tight coil of muscles and black fur that unwound into a dead run. Mud and grass flew in every direction as it thundered down the riverbank, churned up the other side, and streaked for the far side of the clearing. Once across the meadow, it spun to face us, pausing long enough to stamp both forefeet and snort—*huff-huff*—before crackling away into the brush.

I felt bad about scaring the bear off its feed (and for blowing the photo opportunity), but tried to wave it off with a casual observation.

"See that, Michio? Like he was trying to tell us he wasn't really scared?" Like a bullied child, I thought, stopping to hurl names at his tormentors before diving behind a fence.

"I saw," said Michio. His face was drawn with concern. "He thinks we're peck-a-woods, Lynn."

IT WAS AFTER NINE O'CLOCK when we returned to the boat. The sun was going down and we were hungry. The sky was a soft baby pink. We had seen several bears, none of them blue, and the next two days were the same: row ashore early in the morning, while the mists still hung in the trees; find a vantage on a slight rise or knoll; then spend the next sixteen hours watching the show. It was rare for more than a half hour to pass without a bear in sight, there were often two or three, and once there were four, moving up and down the meadow like the electrons in an atom, orbiting each other in the slow, intricate dance of dominance and interaction that determines each bear's place in ursine society. Other than the bear I frightened, none appeared bothered by our presence, and on the second afternoon a large burly fellow sauntered up to within an easy stone's throw of my tripod, stretched out on the ground, and started snoring, as if trusting Michio and me to act as his personal sentries while he napped.

By the end of the second day we had begun to see the bears as individuals, each with a personality of its own, and to know them by subtle differences in their appearance. One had a tinge of red across its shoulders and back, as though it had been dusted with paprika; another, a handkerchief-sized blaze of white on its chest. It was as if we had slipped easily into their community, and as we grew better acquainted with the neighbors (and they with us) we grew content just to watch the drift of galleon clouds across the sky or—as the bears often seemed to be doing—to simply sit and watch the skunk cabbage grow, waiting for the glacier bear to appear. In the peace of watching, I felt myself emerging from the malaise I had brought aboard back in Juneau much like this glacier-carved valley had emerged from the ice—slowly, with an inexorable rise toward life, and a sense of relief that here, at least, things seemed to be working.[56]

But where was the silver bear? At night, Michio and I took turns staring at John Hyde's photo and scribbled map to convince ourselves we were in the right place. There was no doubt about it; the composition of alders and grass, the angle of light, the pattern of lichen on the trees—all were the same as in the photo, as readily identifiable as a face. I couldn't shake the notion that the blue bear might be a changeling, a Kushtaka creature that could be black or cinnamon colored one day and blue the next, transforming itself back and forth between the ordinary and the extraordinary on a whim.

56. During the Ice Age, so much of the planet's water was absorbed into ice that the weight of the glaciers compressed the land like a sponge. Now, with the ice in recession, the land is swelling with relief: sea level in some regions of northern Southeast Alaska is changing by as much as an inch and a half every year. Proof of this can be found in ancient marine terraces (escarpments cut by the pounding of ocean waves) located as high as five hundred feet above sea level. On a more recent, human, scale, the waterfront around Juneau (where rebound measures between six- and seven-tenths of an inch a year) is littered with rotting driftwood logs covered in lush blankets of salt-intolerant meadow-loving plants—a strong indication that the logs floated in when the land was much lower and have since risen above tidal inundation.

"Maybe," I told Michio as I forked another potato onto my plate, "we've been looking at the glacier bear all along. Maybe one of these bears we're seeing every day *is* the glacier bear and we just have to be here when it changes."

"And maybe," joked Michio, "you have been looking for a glacier bear too long."

He was right, of course. It was the sort of harebrained notion that would make any right-thinking scientist or biologist snort.

"But why not?" I argued. "Snowshoe hares change color. Ptarmigan, too."

Michio looked thoughtful for a moment while he spooned gravy from a pan to his plate. It was my turn to cook, and the gravy was full of lumps.

"Arctic fox," he said, holding the spoon like a wand, "and weasel."

I hadn't considered the short-tailed weasel (or ermine), with its white winter coat and ebony-tipped tail. I added marbled murrelets and pigeon guillemots to the list, then dismissed them; seasonal changes in bird plumage were too common to count. But the notion that a glacier bear might have something in common with the various mammals that undergo color changes was too entertaining to dismiss. Could the blue bear be a throwback to the Ice Age, when a similar mechanism would have provided protective coloration during the protracted winters? Was there some confused, vestigial gene that popped up now and then, transforming a black bear to silver and back to black? I was still thinking about it when I crawled into my sleeping bag that night. Short of following a lot of bears around for a very long time, there was no way to know.

15 » Wildfire

BY MORNING the sky had turned rotten and started to fall. With sheets of rain rattling across the cabin top, Michio threw a coat over his head, wiggled deeper into his sleeping bag, and mumbled something about sleeping until noon. The morning broadcast from the Coast Guard station in Juneau had warned of a gale moving in from the gulf, then asked mariners to keep an eye out for a sailboat reported overdue. It wasn't a suitable day for photography.

That evening the Coast Guard repeated the request for information on the overdue boat and upgraded the gale warning to a storm.[57]

By midnight the wind had become an animal, a bully with a grudge, repeatedly tearing the anchor loose from the bottom and driving the *Swift* backward toward the beach while Michio and I hauled the cable in hand over hand. For the next thirty-six hours, we never dried out, dashing in and out of the cabin through rain falling

---

57. Winds between thirty-four and forty-seven knots are classified as a gale; anything greater is a storm.

so hard it stung against our skin, frantic to get the ground tackle aboard and reset it before being blown ashore. By the time the wind started easing, we were exhausted, and when it left, neither of us regretted seeing it go.

The rain, however, stayed. The next day it was still pouring, with no sign of letting up, and we had to admit we were licked. I had to get back to Juneau, where a German television crew was waiting for me to help them get footage of spring grizzlies. Michio was disappointed. He had been hoping to recover some of his expenses by selling a story on the glacier bear to a Japanese magazine, but had other obligations, too.

"Maybe," he said, summing up the futility of our efforts, "maybe not finding a glacier bear *is* the story of the glacier bear." Then he shook his head ruefully before dismissing the idea as "too Zen."

THE GERMANS got their footage and paid me—and that was as good as that summer was going to get. The headlines in the local newspaper continued to offer up the usual refrain of wars and disasters as my father's cancer spread to his brain and the relationship that had kept me stumbling through much of the winter and spring continued to decline. It was becoming more difficult every day to remember that the planet was sailing through space without missing a beat in its orbit around a bright burning star or that the salmon would arrive at their appointed time.

On the third of June (the height of pupping season for sea lions and seals) a traveling exhibit devoted to the Tongass National Forest opened at the Alaska State Museum. *The Tongass: Alaska's Magnificent Rainforest* was a collaborative effort between a number of like-minded photographers and the Smithsonian Institution that did a fine job of capturing the beauty of the coastal rainforest, but it fell short in its efforts to describe the impact rampant clear-cutting was having on the land, skipping lightly across the decimation of wildlife populations, the ruination of salmon-spawning streams, and the trainloads of toxic waste being dumped into the water around the mills. Nor was any mention made of the more than $50 million a year the federal government was squandering in subsidies to the bloated timber industry. There was talk that the exhibit as originally planned had addressed some of these issues, but after Alaska's congressional delegation threatened to wreak vengeance on the Smithsonian's budget, a sanitized version was released.[58]

With an afternoon to kill before my next clients arrived, I had time to wander through the exhibit, stopping now and then to look over the shoulder of a tourist or student before moving on to the next portrait of an eagle or a deer. The prints were magnificent, table-sized panels of extraordinary clarity, and I paused to appreciate the way the needles of a near-life-sized spruce tree seemed to stand out of the wall before strolling into the next room.

The wall opposite the entrance to the second half of the exhibit was dominated by a slab of wood sawn from the diameter of an immense spruce tree, exposing a pattern of growth rings that had been flagged with historic events—the Magna Carta, Columbus in America, that sort of thing—up to the day the tree was felled.

I stepped past a middle-aged couple counting backward from *A Giant Leap for Mankind* to the husband's birthdate, glanced at a mural of a grizzly in a stream, and stopped. Mounted on the wall beside the silvan calendar was a four-foot-high print of a glacier bear.

It's hard to catalogue the emotions that swept across me at the sight of the photo. Envy, frustration, elation, astonishment—all had their place in the soup. I must have started muttering to myself, because a pair of teenage girls lingering nearby clutched each other and exchanged knowing looks when I bent to read the caption, then fled when I laughed out loud.

I laughed because I recognized the name of the photographer as that of one of North America's most prolific, a Seattle-based artist

---

58. Alaska's two senators and single congressman receive generous campaign contributions from the timber, mining, and oil industries on a regular basis.

whose work could be found on the spine of a whole shelfload of books. I laughed because it was mislabeled as a grizzly.

It wasn't possible that the photographer did not know what he had. He's reputed to be a meticulous planner, and no photographer of his caliber and productivity has the time to stumble around in remote areas without knowing exactly what subjects might be available to his (or her) camera.

No, I told myself, the mistake was made somewhere along the chain of people handling the print through the process of organizing the show. That the personnel of an institution so prestigious as the Smithsonian had not recognized a glacier bear (and perhaps had never even heard of it) only served to confirm how rare and remarkable the photograph was—a point doubly emphasized by the fact that the error had slipped by the staff of the Alaska State Museum as well, in the heart of the glacier bear's range.

On close inspection of the background in the photograph, it was obvious that it had been taken very close to John Hyde's. It was a different bear—a bit creamier in color, not quite as steely blue—but that only meant that somewhere within the warren of bays and inlets west of Juneau the genes of the Ice Age were percolating to the surface, rebounding after the recession of the ice like the land, and that my odds of eventually finding Michio a blue bear had doubled. When I walked out of the hushed atmosphere of the museum into the summer sunlight and the sounds of traffic, I was already planning our return.

Maybe in September, when the salmon are still running . . . set up a blind near that waterfall when there are fish in the pool . . .

❧

DAD WAS HAVING TROUBLE following the ceremony. My younger sister was getting married, standing at the altar in a church built of cobblestones on a small island north of Juneau, and as I sat behind him in the hard wooden pews I could see him tremble when he slipped away, then awoke with a start and stared around in confusion as he grasped for his bearing among the crowd of strangers. The long flight from Hawaii had been exhausting, both for him and for my mother, and when the priest asked, "Who will give away this woman?" he had to wait for an answer while Dad was helped to his feet and fumbled for the simple words of a father's acquiescence. The knot in my throat was as much for the rheumy-eyed confusion of this man who only a few short months before had been able to do complex sums in his head as for the hope and love inherent in the wedding.

Off the tip of the island a lone humpback jackknifed into a dive and disappeared, leaving nothing behind but the lamentations of sea-gulls and a fading ripple in its wake.

AUGUST CAME and Canada was burning. Three hundred miles north, a plague of wildfires swept through the forests of the Yukon and the Northwest Territories, throwing a pall of muddy smoke into the air. Michio was late, distracted by the demands of an overseas edi-tor and a looming publication date, and after three days of waiting, John Hyde and I left without him. The forecast said a high-pressure system was moving in, bringing with it clear skies and calm weather—boating and photography conditions too good to miss.

"Catch the mail plane to Kake," I told Michio. "Get somebody with a radio to call us and we'll come in." Like most villages, Kake is so friendly that he would have no trouble finding someone to help him locate the *Swift*. It would be relatively easy for him to fly into Juneau, catch a ride on one of the small floatplanes that make the 180-mile round-trip to Kupreanof Island every day, and join us for a week of photographing whales.

The plan worked, and when I took the *Swift* out of gear and coasted into the dock to retrieve him, John and I had reason to chide his tardiness: on our second day of searching we had located a single whale blowing and diving around a school of herring. Ten minutes after we arrived on the scene, the whale had begun breaching, throw-ing the full length of its forty-ton body into the air and falling back with a thunderous splash that was surely meant as a signal to rally the troops, because within minutes whales were steaming toward us from every point of the compass, appearing out of what had until then seemed an empty sea. Before it was over, the pod had decimated the herring and John had captured it all on film.

"He breached fifteen or twenty times, too," John said, jiggling a plastic bag of exposed film in Michio's face. Michio slapped himself on the forehead, feigning consternation, but was unable to hide his delight. We wasted no time running north again at full speed, hoping to find the humpbacks before they dispersed.

Four hours later it seemed our fortune had failed. The same high-pressure system that gave us the calm weather was also sucking smoke from the wildfires in Canada across the icefield and spitting it out over Alaska. The pall was growing worse by the hour, and as we searched for the whales smoke blurred the horizon and threatened to block out the sun. By the time we finally found the whales, everything was wrapped in a pale, muddy light so lifeless and depressing that neither Michio nor John bothered with a camera.

Twenty-four hours later I was toying with the idea of quitting. There were reports that the fires were getting worse and the world looked diseased through a haze of yellow smoke.

"It's a waste of gas," I argued. "And the weather forecast says it could last for days."

Michio looked up from a new lens he was cleaning, a 500-millimeter "mirror" lens that magnified via a finely polished parabolic surface instead of a series of glass elements. He considered my argument, then shook his head. "Nothing to photograph in town, Lynn." Earlier he had shown me how he planned to use the curved surface of the mirror to create "doughnuts" of light from the sparkles of sunlight on the water—an effect, he said, that was necessary for an image in his head.

"It could be beautiful," he said, drawing the arc of a sounding whale's tail with his hand. "In sunshine, the water running from the tail . . ."

Two or three times since leaving Kake a whale had swum near the boat, but never quite close enough or positioned as precisely in the track of the sun as Michio wanted. And with the flat, ugly light, I reminded him, the odds of translating the image from his imagination onto film were terrible.

I was wrong. And as the sun fell it became more and more evident how wrong I was. The changing angle of light through the smoke turned the water first softly golden, then orange, then scarlet, and as the sun reached the horizon its track wrote a blazing, inverted exclamation mark on the sea. More whales appeared—porpoises, too—and from that convergence of events came a photo opportunity more remarkable than anything I could have imagined.

Michio and John never stopped shooting, reloading, and shooting some more. Whales rose blowing to the surface all around, taking deep barrel-chested breaths before diving again. I had my hands full, kicking the *Swift* in and out of gear, spinning this way and that as I maneuvered to position the boat at the proper angle to the sun. When a whale erupted to the surface a stone's throw from the bow, Michio leaped into position, focusing as he knelt, and captured the alignment of the animal, the sun, and its blazing track in a shot that transformed the whole of that horrible smoky day into a flawless instant.

At anchor in Gambier Bay that night, I scribbled in my journal, "All hell breaking loose on the other side of the border today—and somehow it ended in beauty."

"NOT THIS YEAR," Michio said when I suggested we plan a September search for the glacier bear. "I have to make my plan for the Chukchi."

His interest in aboriginal people had recently taken him across the Bering Strait to Siberia, where nomadic reindeer herders still live a wandering life in tents. Now all of his immense passion and imagination was focused on spending a full year documenting their lives. What excited him most, he said, was the possibility of taking his wife and baby along. "Shoma and Naoko with me. It would be the best experience of my life."

Tall words, I thought, for someone whose life is already so rich.

"But maybe spring?" he countered, appending a warning. "If we are not with Chukchi, that is."

A small void opened up inside me, a feeling that loomed like the smoke. I knew we would never quit searching for the blue bear until we found it—after all, hadn't Michio refused to quit just because the smoke made getting the image seem impossible, and hadn't he been working on his caribou book for more than a dozen years? But suddenly the idea of reaching our goal carried a whiff of threat—accomplishing it might mean the end of our trips.

I was happy for Michio, with the tremendous possibilities of his life, but with the changes inherent in having a family and traveling overseas more and more every year, it seemed the links we had forged might fade. I didn't want to see the friendship change, wasn't ready for the "letting go" that would entail; I was already being forced to let go of too much.

ANGER WAS MINE. A toxic, red-eyed madness beyond anything I had ever known. Between trips I had been doing some minor remodeling to my lover's apartment—installing a desk, building a bed for her child—and she drew back into a corner of the kitchen while I ranted and threw my tools in a bag. Someone once described love as "that wonderful, weightless moment at the top of the swing," and after months of suspecting that every time I took her son for the night she was using the freedom to pursue another man, the moment had passed—and the plunge begun—when I arrived unexpectedly and found "him" hurrying down her stairs.

Everything boiled over. The overtaxed credit cards; the pain of the affair; the friend hired to act as a relief driver on the *Swift* who quit without warning, leaving me with no option but to cancel thousands of dollars in already-booked trips and nothing to say to the clients who called, outraged and screaming at the sudden reversal of their plans. I stuffed a drill in the bag, counted my chisels, and slammed out the door. I had to get home, had to pack a bag with dark clothes. There was a funeral in Hawaii to attend.

"YOU SHOULD COME as soon as you can." My mother's voice was steady, a rise in pitch the only sign of strain.

"How's he doing?"

"Not very well. Your brother will be here tomorrow morning."

Not very well. We were still moving around the truth, trying to act like the smell of it wasn't in the room. I tried not to let my voice crack, but after I said good-bye I lay on the floor and cried.

"They say no more than four drops every two hours." The hospice worker tilted her head back to demonstrate how I should administer the morphine with an eyedropper under my father's tongue, then gave me a look that said, "That's the official line; now do whatever you have to do."

"How will this go?" I asked. She knew what I meant and answered with a concise description of how the kidneys would fail, resulting in a buildup of fluid in the lungs.

"You'll hear it. There may be some difficulty breathing . . . we call it the 'death rattle' . . ." She paused to hand my brother a list of funeral homes. "His heart will stop when the strain becomes too great."

I wondered if she was aware of her slip, of how she had exchanged the practiced, professional remove of using "thes" and "its" to describe my father's organs for the humanity inferred by referring to his heart as "his." He was lying on his side, the glint of unshaven stubble like sand on his cheeks, covered with a sheet. His eyes were closed—they had been all day—and I wondered if he could hear what we were saying. When I arrived at the farm after the long flight from Alaska to Hawaii, he was in the same position, and when I leaned over to tell him I had arrived I received no response.

Mine is a family uncomfortable with touch, but when everyone else left the room I lay down beside him, fit my chest to his back . . . *once muscled, now bone* . . . buried my face in his neck . . . *when I was a child he always smelled of cigarettes* . . . put my arms around him, hugging him to me as if I could keep him from leaving, and whispered, "Please, Daddy. Don't go."

THEY SAY the soul leaves the body at the moment of death, rising up like a silver balloon. I watched carefully and saw nothing, but did feel something wrench from my own chest, a tearing of membranes, ligaments, and veins that broke ribs on its way out, leaving a chasm behind that would forever divide life into before and after: before, when there was the comfort of a father, and after, when there was not.

16 ⟫ Kamchatka

TWO DAYS after my father died the staff at the museum took down the photograph of the glacier bear and packed up the show. The last cruise ship of the summer went south, bruising the sky with its smoke, and two weeks later a sharp freeze cut the leaves from the trees. Five hundred miles north, a flock of juvenile plovers fled the onset of winter.

In December, snow fell from a sky the color of wood smoke; in February, the aurora curled across the sky like steam. By March the wind was pregnant with spring, and when Michio called to say he was too busy for the glacier bear, I was disappointed, but took it in stride.

"How about later this summer?" I asked, and spelled out my idea of setting up a blind near the waterfall in John Hyde's valley.

"I don't know," he said, then explained that he was planning to spend part of July and August (the peak of the salmon run) in a place that was fast becoming a mecca for anyone interested in bears—Kuril-skoya Lake on the Kamchatka Peninsula, twenty-five hundred miles away in the Russian Far East.

The Kamchatka Peninsula hangs below the fist of Siberia like a

seven-hundred-mile-long thumb thrust between the Okhotsk and
Bering Seas. It is a land of smoking volcanoes, dense forests of golden
birch, and rivers teeming with salmon. In the south, near Kurilskoya,
the peninsula supports a population of grizzlies as dense as any in
Alaska. Kamchatka first appeared on a map in 1665, when a Russian
cartographer named Semion Remisov penciled an approximation of
the rumored land onto a sheet of parchment. It took another thirty
years for the first Russians to reach the peninsula and until 1725 for
rumors filtering out of the vast, rich land to inspire Peter the Great to
appoint a Danish sea captain as head of the First Kamchatka Expedition. Vitus Bering's instructions were to map the peninsula, then keep
going west until he proved Asia and the New World were separate
continents. After spending three years hacking his way to the eastern
edge of Asia, Bering built two ships and blundered northeast into the
fog long enough to discover the strait between Alaska and Siberia that
now bears his name, but under a plague of foul weather, incompetent
officers, equipment failures, and a near-mutinous crew, he was forced
to abort the voyage without ever having actually seen the New World.

It took Bering three years to convince the emperor to give him
another chance, but in the end he must have been magnificently per-
suasive. When he departed Saint Petersburg in 1733 he marched at the
head of the greatest army of exploration the world had ever seen, with
orders to find the west coast of America and investigate it as far south
as Mexico. It took the ten thousand men of the Great Nordic Expedition seven years just to reach Kamchatka and build the city Bering
named Petropavlovsk after the *Saint Peter* and the *Saint Paul* (his two
ships), but by June 15, 1741, he had managed to sail east far enough
to sight Mount Saint Elias near Yakutat before being beaten back by
the unrelenting storms of the gulf.[59]

---

59. On July 31, the *Saint Peter* touched at Kayak Island near Cordova. Bering himself
never went ashore, but among the party of officers and men he sent to the beach was a
German naturalist named Georg Wilhelm Steller. While on shore, Steller, who had studied John James Audubon's catalogue of birds from the New World before leaving Europe,
recognized a bird flitting among the spruce trees as a cousin of the American blue jay—

Sick and exhausted, Bering wrecked his ship on a small island off the coast of Kamchatka while trying to return to Petropavlovsk and died. His crew survived the winter by clubbing hundreds of nearly tame sea otters for their meat and wrapping themselves in the pelts. After being rescued, a few of the survivors returned to Saint Petersburg dressed in otter-skin cloaks, and the sight of the dark, lush fur was enough to send a wave of promyshlenniki fur hunters swarming across the Bering Strait and into Alaska. It took less than a century for the brutal gold rush to exterminate the sea otter across most of its range, but once that was accomplished and Alaska sold to the United States in 1867, Kamchatka faded from the collective consciousness of the West. After the Bolshevik Revolution, the entire area was closed to outsiders—Russians and foreigners alike—until the Soviet empire disintegrated in 1990.

In 1990, the owner of a Juneau-based adventure company searching for new additions to his company's catalogue flew to Chukotka in Siberia to paddle the coast in an *umiak,* an Eskimo skin boat, and after hearing about the remarkable number of bears in the preserve, returned the following autumn and hired a Russian army helicopter to fly him in. When Ken Leghorn returned to Juneau, his stories confirmed that the Khakeetsin River, running plugged with salmon and surrounded by bears beneath a smoking volcano, was the sort of raw, primordial place I had always dreamed of exploring.

"It was incredible," Ken told me. "We hiked for four hours up a small creek and counted fifty-six bears." They were charged twice, once dodging away down a twist in the trail, the second time diffusing the charge by rattling branches and yelling.

When Michio asked, "What do you think, Lynn?" I knew he was working his way around to asking me along. Over the years, he had invited me on adventures to an island off the coast of British Columbia to photograph the ruins of Native longhouses, to Manitoba for

---

the expedition's first tangible proof that they had indeed reached the New World by approaching from the west. The cobalt blue bird with the raucous call and characteristic flap-and-glide flight pattern is still known as the Steller's jay.

polar bears, and to the Arctic National Wildlife Refuge to witness the migration of the caribou herd, but the pressures and commitments of my guiding business had always prevented me from joining him, and a glance at my calendar showed that once again I would have to decline. I was booked for the weeks he would be in Kamchatka.

"But can you come to Juneau in September?" I asked.

He hesitated before answering. There was so much to be done, what with his projects in Africa, Siberia, and Alaska. And finding time to spend with his family was a priority.

"Tabun," he said. Maybe. "I'll try to call when I come home."

JULY STARTED OUT as if it was blessed. Evelyne R., a semiprofessional photographer from Switzerland, pointed at a blue iceberg drifting near the mouth of the fjord and said, "I vant an eagle on zet." In less time than it takes to tell, a bald eagle stroked out of the forest, flared its broad wings, and settled on the ice; three motor drives whirred, and Evelyne's considerable bulk jiggled with excitement as she and her husband exchanged astonished looks. For days the weather had been perfect, with clear skies and water like glass, and every time one of my passengers said "I want to see a . . ." (killer whale, porpoise, bubblenet feeding, or what have you), the wish had been fulfilled. Orca swam in our wake, porpoises paced off the bow, and humpbacks and sea lions fell asleep beside the hull. This was Dominik and Evelyne's third trip to Alaska, and they had come to expect plenty of photo opportunities, but for Gary, a photographer from Utah, it was the first, and he was wide-eyed with astonishment at our luck. Perpetually good-natured, with a bushy mustache that is nonetheless inadequate to cover a permanent grin, Gary is the sort of client a guide is happy to have, and it wasn't long after he slung his gear aboard the *Swift* and started cracking jokes that I decided I was dealing not so much with a customer as a friend.

Our luck held on a rambling ten-day course that took the *Swift* south down Stephens Passage, across Frederick Sound, and north into Chatham Straits, with everything we could ask for falling into our hands.

That changed when we pulled into Kake.

WE NEEDED FUEL, our water supply was low, and after an extended period within the confines of the *Swift*, there was tacit agreement that more than food, water, or gasoline, what everyone needed most was a shower. From the harbor in Kake it is a short walk to a combination hotel–grocery store–café, where three bucks will get a traveler a sliver of cheap soap, a clean towel, and an unlimited supply of hot water. Dominik went on ahead while Gary and I fueled up the boat, and after topping off the water tanks, it felt good to stretch our legs on the dusty road between the harbor and town.

At the hotel, Gary fed change into a pay phone while I ordered cheeseburgers and made a quick pass through the store.

"They've got ice-cream bars," I said, dropping a plastic bag of groceries on the floor beside Gary's table. His hair was wet from the shower. He looked pleased at the prospect of a treat and when I asked, told me everything was okay at home.

"They're hell-raisers, man. Especially my daughter." The way he shook his head was full of pride. As best I could tell, there was little in life Gary didn't enjoy, but mention of his family always turned on an extra light. Of his wife, he had said several times, "I couldn't do anything without Lillian. She's the reason I'm alive."

I looked around for the waitress and asked for a Coke. Through the service window into the kitchen I could see the cook frying something at the stove.

"I've got time to check my messages," I said. A pay phone hung on the wall a few feet from our table, a rack of newspapers at its feet. I played a musical score on the Touch-Tone buttons, waited for the automated operator to answer, then punched in the code to access my phone. The first message was from a British producer, wanting information on a film we had been discussing for a year. The second was a telemarketer trolling the services of yet another credit card company, and as I hit the delete code I looked over my shoulder to see if the burgers were coming.

"Hello, Lynn? It's Clara." The soft female voice floated out of the past. It had been nearly a decade since we first met, me with a twisted coat hanger, a screwdriver, and a strong desire to be a hero to the beautiful, soft-spoken chemist who had accidently locked herself out of her car, she with a boyfriend seven hundred miles away in Fairbanks. And, through one of those odd little overlaps that are so frequent in Alaska, a mutual friendship with Michio between us. She knew him from his studies at the university when he first moved to Fairbanks more than a decade ago. Since she had moved back to Fairbanks to teach and be near her boyfriend, our contact had been limited to the occasional letter or card, and my pulse quickened when she said, "I had to call."

The pause that followed was long enough for me to wonder why, and a wave of knowing that this message was either about something very good (was she moving back to Juneau? were she and John getting married?) or something very bad. My pulse quickened further when I heard her recorded voice take a deep breath.

"There's been an accident," she said. She struggled with the words. "An accident with Michio. He's been killed by a bear."

I think I dropped the phone. I remember hearing my own voice say, "Oh my God," and the feel of cool metal against my forehead from leaning my face against the phone. I could still hear Clara's voice on the line.

I fumbled with the cord, pulling the phone back to my ear in time to hear her say something about Russia . . . in Kamchatka, and how sorry she was.

The next message was the from my sister: "I just heard about Michio," and after that, a Japanese voice I didn't recognize saying, "Lynn-san . . . so very sorry . . . Hoshino-san dead from bear."

One after another, the messages beeped in from Germany, Japan, California, Fairbanks, and Juneau—friends and acquaintances from around the globe, all aiming the same horrible blow at my gut: Michio was dead, pulled from his tent by a bear.

Here are the circumstances as I know them.

MICHIO ARRIVED at the Kurilskoya brown bear refuge on July 25 in the company of a three-man television crew from Japan, arriving, as do many of those who visit the refuge, by chartered helicopter.

Theirs was the first photography or film group to obtain a permit to enter the refuge that year, timing their visit to coincide with the return of the salmon. Waiting at the refuge to assist them were Igor Revenko, Russia's foremost brown bear biologist, and his brother Andrei. I had met Revenko two years before, when a group of friends involved in brown bear conservation brought him to Juneau to present a slide show and talk on the Kamchatka bears. Within minutes of meeting the stocky, carefully spoken Russian with the quick spark of intelligence in his eyes I knew that he was someone I would feel comfortable following in bear country, and as a scientist, someone whose work I would trust. Andrei, who is somewhat less fluent in English, is reputed to be much the same.

The camp at Grassy Cape is a simple one, consisting of a single rough cabin just large enough to hold six people and their gear; a smaller, metal-roofed shack that serves as a food cache; and an outhouse. A third of a mile away on the Khakeetsin River is an observation tower, a small enclosure atop twenty-foot stilts situated so as to offer a clear view of grizzlies fishing in the river. On the opposite shore, near the outlet of the river which connects the lake with the Sea of Ohkotsk, is a fish weir and base camp which at the time was occupied by a few Russian fisheries specialists, a University of Montana graduate student named Bill Leacock who was cooperating with Revenko in a study of Kamchatka's bear population, and his family.[60]

At some point before Michio's party arrived at Grassy Cape, a large boar had broken into the cabin, ransacking the interior and leaving the

60. A fish weir is a picket line of stakes across a lake's outlet designed to funnel migrating salmon through a "gate" where they can be counted. Leacock's bear population studies were critical because no one, including Igor Revenko, knows how many there are. Since the disintegration of the Soviet Union, rumors of rampant poaching in Kamchatka have become common, and during his visit to Juneau in 1994, Igor estimated that as many as two thousand to twenty-five hundred bears had been killed that year alone. In addition to illegal trophy hunting, one of the direst threats to the world's bear population is China's insatiable appetite for bear gall, which is used as an ingredient in traditional medicines. Numerous tests have proven this application ineffective and invalid: bear gall has absolutely no therapeutic qualities, other than those of a placebo.

deep gouges of its claw marks on the walls. After boarding over the broken window and patching things up as best they could, Igor instructed everyone to burn all edible garbage and bury everything else. The salmon run was late—there were no fish in the river—and allowing the hungry seven-hundred-pound boar that had vandalized the cabin to associate humans and food would be a dangerous mistake. With that caveat, the crew moved into the cabin—all except Michio, who for as long as I had known him had preferred being outdoors to the confines of a cabin. Even when it was just the two of us on the *Swift,* with the comfort of running water and heat, he sometimes chose to roll out his bedroll on the foredeck or retreat to the cabin top with a book—acts I never interpreted as an effort to escape my company or that of other humans, but rather as showing his preference for the smells and sounds of the open air. In Kamchatka, he chose to sleep in his tent.

On Saturday, July 26, a thirty-two-year-old American photographer based in Anchorage arrived at Kurilskoya. In an interview with a writer from the *Anchorage Daily News,* Curtis Hight explained how he, too, pitched his tent a few feet from Michio's after Igor had told him there was no more room in the tiny cabin, presumably because the television crew's gear filled every available space.

By nightfall the weather was changing, with a heavy mist blowing in, and Michio crawled into his tent.

"Wake me if a bear comes," Hoshino said softly as he turned in.

"Excuse me?" Hight asked.

"Wake me if a bear comes—near the tent," Hoshino said again.[61]

[Two and a half hours later],[62] Hight woke sharply to an explosion of noise. . . . It sounded like it was coming from the food cache, about [fifty] feet away.

61. Excerpted from an article written by George Bryson for *We Alaskans,* an insert magazine in the *Anchorage Daily News.*
62. In my correspondence with Hight, some discrepancies between his account of the incident and that published in *We Alaskans* came to light. Where applicable, I have inserted Hight's firsthand corrections and clarifications into the article's text, within brackets.

Slipping out of his tent, he tentatively began to investigate, carefully circling around the cabin toward the cache. A large brown bear was jumping up and down on the metal roof of the food shed, apparently trying to break in.

Hight yelled and clapped his hands. The bear looked at him. He yelled again, . . . [wondering why] no one else in camp had bothered to get up. Slowly the bear moved away, circling behind Hoshino's tent.

Hight yelled to Hoshino, who stuck his head out the flap. "There's a bear—about 10 feet behind your tent!"

"Where?" Hoshino asked, squinting into the darkness.

"Right there!" Hight said. "Should I get Igor?"

"Yes, get Igor," Hoshino said.

The cabin was locked. Hight began banging on the door, yelling that there was a bear outside.

In a few moments, Revenko stepped outside with a can of pepper spray.

There were no guns in camp; they weren't allowed. So Revenko, Hoshino and Hight tried their best to run the bear off by yelling and banging pans. It didn't work. Finally, Revenko pulled out his bear spray. Approaching within [eight to ten] yards, he pointed and fired.

Watching from a right angle, Hight saw how the sparkling white plume of atomized pepper shot through the air, then balled up just shy of the bear's nose. The spray settled to the ground. Leaning forward, the brown bear sniffed it in the grass. It didn't seem to faze him.

He was a mature boar, Revenko decided, maybe 600 or 700 pounds with a distinguishing red wound across his forehead. [Hight explained that the estimate of the bear's size came after the bear was shot, not from Igor that night.]

For about a half-hour, the men tried to [drive] the boar out of camp. Each time, it veered up the hillside, then veered back down. Finally, it seemed to leave on its own accord.

The next morning Hight decided to sleep in the observation tower. Revenko thought the wound in the bear's forehead might have been caused when it smashed through the cabin window, and he thought he would be safer off the ground. Michio elected to stick with his tent.

The following day Andrei Revenko took Michio and the television crew across the lake by boat to scout for an alternative filming location. With the salmon run so late, the number of bears congregating around Grassy Cape was low, so they needed to explore other options. On the same day, the owner of a Petropavlovsk television station flew in aboard his personal helicopter and preempted Curtis Hight's claim to the tower. Rather than sleep on the ground again that night, the photographer spread his sleeping bag on top of the cabin, above Michio's tent.

The next morning, Hight reported, the owner of the telvision station did something so outlandish I have difficulty believing it is true: he placed human food on the lakeshore to lure the bear into range of his camera, then videotaped it consuming the food.

"[He] obviously didn't feel very guilty about it, because in their televised report they show that footage," Hight said. "Everybody in camp watched this happen—saw this bear come down and start [eating the food]."[63]

I feel a twinge of bitterness when I remember that the Russian also left a wooden box filled with loaves of bread in his helicopter. The boar ripped the windows out of the helicopter to get inside, and the damage was done: in his willingness to take a shortcut to filming the bear and by being so careless with the rest of his food, the television executive had reinforced a dangerous link in the animal's mind between humans and food. On the night of August 2, Igor was again forced to drive it from camp with his spray.

Day after day, men and bears waited for the salmon to arrive. Night after night, the Revenko brothers faced down the hungry boar when it invaded the camp. On August 6, Igor reported, he urged Michio to move inside, but Michio still preferred his tent. On August 7, the

63. From the Bryson article.

fish arrived in droves, and Hight reports watching the boar work the shallows with some success—but for Michio, the run had come too late. In a translated report, Igor Revenko detailed the tragedy that followed:

[It] happened at 4 A.M. I woke up by call of (Japanese) cameramen. "Tent! Bear! Tent!" In two seconds, I and my brother and the rest of the crew got out and heard Michio's cry and bear's growl. It was dark and we flashlighted the tent being destroyed and bear back in the grass 10 meters away.

Immediately we started to yell enormously but the bear didn't even rise a head. I found shovel and metal bucket and started to bang, three to five meters from bear. Bear rised head once very shortly, then took Hoshino's body by teeth and disappeared in the darkness.[64]

The *We Alaskans* account goes on to state that

Events after that blurred from one to another. Igor Revenko took the Japanese TV crew to the science station across the lake. Bill Leacock was there and radioed for help. The party returned to the camp with guns. Searching around the cabin in daylight, they saw the bear had taken Hoshino's body into a thick forest.

At [one o'clock], a helicopter arrived with a professional hunter and special forces officer. Revenko boarded the aircraft and soon pointed out the large boar. The pilot flushed it out of the trees. Now the bear was running back toward camp. The helicopter followed in pursuit. Walking along the beach behind a ridge, Hight saw the helicopter coming directly toward him.

"I was about 300 yards from camp," Hight said, "and the bear started heading toward the beach, coming straight at me . . ."

The helicopter veered in front of the bear and turned it

64. Ibid.

around. The special forces officer and the hunter shot it several times from a few dozen feet overhead.

Heading toward the fallen bear, Hight saw the helicopter land, and simultaneously saw the bear stand back up. It was still alive— running now at full speed toward the forest.

The helicopter rose off the ground once more and quickly swept back overhead. The special forces officer fired again. The bear crashed to the ground. Hight reached the site just as the helicopter landed. The hunter stepped out and shot the bear a final time. . . .

Instinctively, [Hight] took the bear's picture.

BACK ABOARD the *Swift* again, I was experiencing the strange sensation of watching everything I did from some place outside of my body. I was numb, I suppose, and functioning on autopilot as I ran through a safety check, started the engine, and took in the mooring lines. Gary was solicitous, offering to make coffee and watching me from the corner of his eye, but my Swiss passengers showed no reaction when told of my friend's death.

I have no memory of the long run north toward the top of Frederick Sound other than that of slick gray water beneath a cloud-dotted sky. I presume I was in "guide mode," the outer fringes of my brain scanning the horizon for the orca or humpbacks my clients wanted to see, but inside I was battling a delirious rage, irate that the circle of the seasons had seduced me into believing that Michio and I would always have another chance. Somewhere near the Brothers Islands I reined myself in, tied the shock and disbelief into a knot, and pushed it deep inside. I'm working, I told myself. I've got things to do.

To the west, the sun pulled moisture from the blanket of forest draped across Admiralty Island's shoulders and threw it up in clouds. At eight o'clock a whale rose a half mile from the bow and I cut the throttle, bringing the *Swift* to a halt.

We drifted, rocking gently in the silence as the sonorous *paah!* of the whale's breath echoed around the compass. The sun hid its face behind the clouds, spread its silver wings, and sent shafts of light spearing down from the sky. The whale swam closer, turning slowly left and right, then arched its back and sounded.

Imagine a great silence, as crisp as mountain air, broken only by the piping of seabirds. Waves chuckle against the hull. Beyond, an arrangement of islands and mountain ridges recedes into the distance in a series of pastel colors that deepen from gray to blue.

Now imagine a forty-foot whale bursting from the water, rising dead center in the scene as it throws itself upward in an explosive breach. There is a report like artillery as the whale spins and falls on its back, and a heartbeat later, the sound of the splash.

That is what happened, not once but fifteen times, as if the whale, having evolved from a land mammal into a creature of the sea, had decided to become a bird by throwing itself again and again toward heaven.

The first breach took us by surprise, the second left us astonished. By the third, the anticipation was electric, and by the fifth, all thoughts of Michio and tragedy were emptied for a moment from my mind, for that is the nature of such beauty—that it draws us outside of ourselves to a place beyond memory and thought, and in doing so makes us whole.

By the fifth jump, joy of a bright and tentative sort flooded over me, the flight of the whale reminding me of so many similar moments with Michio, when the ecstasy of nature's power had lifted us up on adrenaline and awe, and in some way a part of me became convinced that the whale *was* Michio, come to say good-bye.

My transport didn't last long. By the end of the display the light had gone, leaving the water and sky a weak shade of gray, and as the whale dove a final time—a waterfall sheeting from its flukes—the memory of Michio lifting up his camera in gratitude to the whales on the first of our many trips tied my tongue. Gary and the others were still chattering with excitement, but I put the engine in gear and steered the *Swift* toward shelter in silence.

Inside Gambier Bay the water was the color of smoked glass. After dropping anchor, I pulled a beer from the cooler, mumbled a few words to the others, and retreated to the foredeck. Lines of mew gulls stroking by in ragged formation called out to each other in soft voices as they flocked to a roost for the night.

Gary stuck his head out the door: "You okay, Lynn?"

I kept my back turned and lifted the beer to say thanks for his concern.

"Okay," was all I could mumble. The mountains turned to silhouettes and another memory of Michio slugged me in the gut. Gambier Bay was the last place we had anchored together, on the night Canada was burning. For a moment, I thought I heard him humming in the cabin and it hurt to swallow when I took a sip of beer. I shut my eyes and squeezed my chest to keep from sobbing.

When I opened my eyes again it was dark.

17 》 Primary Colors

I DON'T KNOW WHY I missed Michio's memorial service in Fairbanks. I was probably already booked, committed to guiding someone for something, but who, I cannot remember, and for what, I apparently did not care, because I stopped keeping notes or making entries in the *Swift*'s log, took no photographs, and left the pages of my journal blank. A friend told me later that the service took place on a crisp autumn day, with the birch trees around Fairbanks plumed in gold. More than two hundred people crowded into the Dog Mushers' Hall to hear numerous speakers praise the memory of the man many of them referred to as "my best friend." Running throughout the service was a theme of wonder, awe at the dark poetry that had led Michio, with his great love for all things natural, to death in the jaws of a bear; of questioning—and accepting—that although the event and the loss were horrible to contemplate, in another sense it was somehow right. Nick Jans, a schoolteacher from a small village near the Arctic Circle who is also one of Alaska's most lucid and poetic writers, spoke for everyone when he said, "I forgive the bear that took Michio from us."

Then as if still not quite believing it had happened, "He must not have known who Michio *was*."

A friend mailed me a program from the service. In it, three paragraphs from one of Michio's essays had been translated into English, a hundred words on his thoughts about bears and fear. "If there wasn't a single bear in all of Alaska," he wrote,

> I could hike through the mountains with complete peace of mind. I could camp without worry. But what a dull place Alaska would be!
>
> Here people share the land with bears. There is a certain wariness between people and bears. And that wariness forces upon us a valuable sense of humility.
>
> People continue to tame and subjugate nature. But when we visit the few remaining scraps of wilderness where bears roam free, we can still feel an instinctive fear. How precious that feeling is. And how precious these places, and these bears, are.[65]

The friend who sent me the program had also scrawled a message across it in a looping, feminine hand: "His ashes will be scattered in Alaska, some in Japan."

I had ashes to scatter, too. For thousands of years, the people of the Pacific Northwest coast have thrown a "one year party" to honor the dead, and my family was unconsciously incorporating that tradition into mourning my father. On September 15, the anniversary of his death, my mother returned to Alaska with his cremated remains.

---

65. Translated by Karen Colligan-Taylor, a close friend of Michio's for many years. Karen first met Michio in 1979, the summer of his first visit to Southeast Alaska, while she and her husband, Mike, were building a small cabin near the entrance to Glacier Bay. After finishing a dissertation on Japanese environmental literature and obtaining her Ph.D., Karen moved with her family to Fairbanks, where she established the Japanese studies program at the University of Alaska and continued to reinforce her ties with Michio as he bought the land next to hers, built a home, and settled down. This essay also appeared in Michio's *The Grizzly Bear Family Book* (New York: North-South Books, 1993).

Since his death, Karen has taken early retirement from the university to work on her own writing and to edit an anthology of Michio's photographs and prose.

We drove a hundred miles south of Anchorage on a road paved with restless autumn leaves that rose up in golden swirls at our passing. The sky was a giddy autumn blue, and where it poured over a bed of green and white stones, the water of the river we gathered beside was clear as air. Sockeye salmon dressed in the scarlet colors of spawning filled the pools.

Red fish and yellow leaves beneath a blue sky—the scene blurred into a mosaic of primary colors through my tears as I stepped to the edge of the river, the surprising weight of my father's ashes in my hands. The ashes hissed as they entered the water, the heavier bits sinking immediately to the bottom beneath the salmon, settling into the gravel amid clusters of freshly spawned eggs; the lighter, powdery material clung to the surface, drifting in ribbons and patches through rafts of golden leaves. A trace of fine dust rose from the empty bag like smoke, twisted on the breeze, and dispersed. The last physical trace of my father was gone.

The next morning a small notice appeared in the Anchorage paper:

A memorial service will be held for Michio Hoshino at the Alaska Christian Church at 2 P.M.

I should have expected it, should have realized that Michio had enough friends in Alaska's largest city for a second memorial. I hesitated before picking up the phone book—*I don't think I can do this two days in a row*—then ran my finger down the listings until I found the address.

The chapel was spare, without the ostentation of excessive stained glass or hardwood pews, and when I walked in, Naoko was straightening a row of metal chairs.

"How are you?" I asked. She was surprised to see me.

"I'm . . . okay." She forced a small smile.

She looks stronger than I feel, I thought. Shoma, now two years old and still too young to understand his loss, scampered by in a pressed jumper and new shoes, ducked beneath a table arranged as an altar, and peered into a vase of flowers. The altar was a simple one: a clean cloth over a folding table, a brace of candles around some flowers, much like a similar one my sisters had arranged for my father in an equally simple church. (My contribution to that altar was one of Michio's books, propped open to a photograph of sunrise above Teklanika, in Denali National Park.)

"He's grown," I said to Naoko, nodding at Shoma. I couldn't think of anything else to say.

After exchanging a few words with the various photographers and biologists I recognized in the crowd, we settled into the uncomfortable chairs. There was a slide show of scenes from Alaska, followed by a period of silence, and afterward the audience took turns sharing memories and stories about the deceased.

I've always avoided public speaking. My face burns and I tremble, sweat pours from my hands. But for Michio (and for Shoma and Naoko) I had to do it, had to try to say how I felt. I scribbled a few notes on a folded program to avoid going dumb, swallowed and took my turn at the podium. Instead of following my notes, I found myself trying to describe how Michio had once flown to Juneau and forgotten to bring any clothes; laughing through my tears as I related how after a quick shopping trip, he had emerged wearing a brand-new pair of jeans, and how three days later the manufacturer's cardboard label was still attached to the hip pocket of the pants. I wanted to illustrate not how absentminded Michio could be, but rather how little ego or self-absorption he possessed, and how his attention (unlike that of most people) was always focused outside himself.

I'm not sure the anecdote translated well. Two middle-aged Japanese women in the audience exchanged puzzled looks, then small frowns, as if they thought I might be mocking the dead, and I hurried to reassure them this wasn't so by stumbling into a description of how on the evening I heard of his death, the whale off Gambier Bay had leaped repeatedly into the shafts of silver light.

"Just breaching and breaching," I said, choking by now: "The whale . . . the kujira, I mean . . . it was like Michio. . . ."

I wanted to say how I felt his presence, that somehow he was there in the whale and the glorious light, but the words wouldn't come. Instead, I finished by reading a sentence I had scribbled on my program.

"As a photographer," I read, "Michio taught me how to *look* with my eyes—but as a friend, how to *see* with my heart."

FOR TWO WEEKS after the memorials, the weather was sullen and gray. In Juneau the gutters ran like creeks and the citizenry disappeared from the streets. When a north wind finally moved in and blue repossessed the sky, I loaded a borrowed canoe on the *Swift* and without saying a word to anyone about where I was going backed the boat from its slip.

Wind whistling down from the icefield heaped the waters of Taku Inlet into boiling waves, pitching the *Swift* onto her beam and throwing cold showers of scud across the decks. Small boats usually avoid crossing the inlet when the outflow winds known locally as Takus are blowing—they have been known to capsize small ships. But that day conditions were merely ugly, not truly dangerous, and I didn't really care. The studied concentration of steering through the waves, bracing myself for the next shuddering slam, was precisely what I was seeking, the edge where the immediacy and demands of the physical world served to block out all thought. Since the memorials, I hadn't wanted to see anyone or talk; as a friend later put it, I wasn't being very "nice." When the granite fingers of the Devil's Paw came into view I turned the helm a quarter of a turn to starboard and put the seas on the stern.

The next thirty miles was a downwind run, sledding in the grip of the wind with showers of sparkling spray flying up from the bow. When I turned into Holkham Bay, the waters of Soun-doun were so calm and green that the mountains reflecting from the surface seemed painted on.

A burr of metal on the keel of the canoe gouged a scratch in the cabin top as I lowered it over the side. It was a workhorse, dimpled and dented, its aluminum skin painted with splotches of duck hunter tans and greens. I wasn't interested in aesthetics—it was the concen-

tration and rhythm, the sheer *effort* of a canoe I required. It didn't matter that the paddles were mismatched and too short.[66]

All that first day I paddled with the sun at my back while rounded
hills and abrupt, forested headlands passed on both sides. The cut-
water whispered and chuckled through the water as I reached out
with the paddle, spearing the sea and pulling it toward me with my
arms. Stroke after stroke, feeling the burn of unused muscles spread
across my back and the sting of rising blisters on my palms. At one of
the salmon streams where Michio and I had waited for the blue bear
to appear I pulled ashore, scouting for tracks. Finding nothing, I
returned to the canoe, where a twist of the blade at the end of each
stroke kept my course straight and true.

The fjord bent north, then east, then north again, and with every
mile I moved inland the forest rose higher and steeper until slope
became wall, incline became precipice, and centuries of rainforest as
thick and moss-bound as any Amazonian tangle began to give way to
patches of cliff-hugging alder and willow.

The first night's camp was beside the fallen trunk of a hemlock tree
with the girth of a rhino. On the second day the icebergs grew more
numerous and I began to wend through alleys and windrows of ice
that threatened to close behind me at the change of the tide. Brash ice
grated and rang against the aluminum skin of the canoe as I poled
through the thicker patches, hissing and popping like a brushfire at my
passing. The second night it was difficult to find a clearing among the
alder large enough or flat enough to pitch the tent, until I settled in a
patch the size of a billiards table. That night the ground beneath my
sleeping bag was lumpy with roots and stones.

On the third day the rain came as a drifting mist so thick that
swinging a cupped palm at arm's length gathered a handful of water,
and I kept the dark loom of the fjord wall close at hand, leery of

66. While standing, rest the blade of a paddle on the ground and hold the shaft to your
chest; the grip should reach between your chin and your nose.

becoming lost in the gloom. The dragon-scaled cliffs rose black and glistening, straight up into a low sky the color of ashes. Cold water minnowed under my collar, trickled down my back, and when my morning coffee caught up with my bladder, my hands were cold and clumsy at my fly as I knelt in the floor of the canoe.

Paddling on, the upstruck angle of the granite walls eased, tilted back to level, and a valley appeared, the roar of a rain-swollen river running through its center coming from the mist. According to the chart I carried folded in a plastic bag, the river drained a high mountain basin before falling two thousand feet through a gorge. The sound was preposterous, altogether too loud for any phenomenon short of a volcano, and when I dragged the canoe ashore, the sound of it clanging against the stones was lost beneath the bellowing of the river, which ran the color of cement, leaping and boiling over boulders the size of small cars.

When a glacier retreats, it begets rock as barren and bald as the moon, and now all the world seemed to have turned to angry water and stones. I knew that for a while—say ten or twenty years—life would remain an exceedingly small idea in this neighborhood; only lichens, moss, and a few other simple forms of life capable of grasping a living from the minerals in the stones and the gases in the air are able to colonize such sterile rubble.

In time, however, the slow accumulation of organic material among the cracks and declivities would form something of a poor soil where seeds and spores borne in on the wind or clinging to the feet of birds would start to grow. After a few spare pilgrims of grass and other flowering plants took root, more stingy soil would be formed, and after a half century or so, thickets of alder shrub would take the neighborhood by storm. Alder contributes a rich detritus of rotting leaves and fixes nitrogen in the soil, enough so that after a few decades more, the seeds of trees would begin to find their way in, take a firm grip, and send down roots to suckle at the soil. If the seedlings survive, they rise into the light, exclaiming themselves above their brushy neighbors, until on a hot summer day a cloud of yellow pollen bursting from the ripened sex glands of distant kin drifts by on the wind and embraces the young tree. Within days, seed cones clinging to its branches grow swollen, pregnant with the possibility of a forest. Squirrels and jays move in, cutting, picking, digging, eating, shitting, and scattering the gravid cones from hell to breakfast. More seeds sprout and more seedlings live, rising up to become saplings that eventually grow tall and large enough to touch branch tip to branch tip, casting a shadow over the alder, which then withers from the lack of light and dies.

Spruce needles are highly acidic, and for the next hundred years, those falling at the feet of the trees slowly alter the flavor of the soil from the alkaloid dullness of lime to a sharp, bitter tang. Ironically, spruce is acid-intolerant—it has no taste for its own waste—but hemlock and cedar are not. These interlopers gradually mix and meddle with the hegemony of the spruce until they grow tall, rot, and are thrown to the ground by fierce winter storms. When spring comes, sunlight streaming in through the resulting holes in the canopy ignites a riot of blueberry and dogwood. After a gestation of centuries, a mature, proper forest is born.

As I labored, packing in relays all of the necessities of life to a high shelf away from the clamor of the river, I thought about the intelligence behind this process, of how it will continue without end throughout time. The mist closed in, erasing the valley, and when I hurled a fist-sized stone into the rain it disappeared into the vapors as if flung entirely free of the world. For a moment I considered the possibility of running across a glacier bear, then dismissed it. There was little chance of seeing anything in the rain.

THE SOGGY WEATHER held for that day and the next, falling thick and solid as if the contents of the oceans of heaven were being drained and flung to the ground. I feared wandering too far from the tent, lest I be unable to find my way back, and so ate and read, napped and read some more, then lay on my back and memorized the pattern of stitching in the nylon panels of the roof.

After forty-eight hours the rain stopped, the clouds lifted, and the air in the valley hung without moving. In the distance, the broken stele and columns of the glacier dangled down from the clouds, top-pling slowly, one after the other into the fjord. Above the glacier a series of immense peaks appeared, ribboned in cascades, sidestepping away into eternity. The river continued to roar but lacked the threat-ening, monstrous presence it had held while hidden by the storm.

I felt diminished by the sight of the glacier and all it had accom-plished—carving mountains and valleys with its comings and goings, rearranging entire worlds made of stone—and all of the epochs that seemed to stretch out before and behind me, the geologic periods and eras that render the strivings of our lives no more consequential than the names and dates on old tombstones, which must eventually disap-pear under the gentle, insistent friction of the rain. And feeling this, I also felt a great contentment warm my blood.

When a warbler trilled nearby and terns and gulls began to appear, I put hiking boots on my feet, water, food, and binoculars in a bag, and began climbing. I glassed, watched, and listened as I climbed. A quartet of goats browsing the shoulder of a mountain above the valley watched in their turn, until they became used to this slow-moving creature and allowed me to wander among them, only occasionally rising up to snort in suspicion when a clumsy stone rolled away from my feet.

After a few days of this, the food sack grew light and fuel for the stove was running low. I stayed one more day, then slid the canoe across the moss-slicked boulders and paddled away in the direction I came, leaving the roar of the river behind.

Down-fjord, the water was choked with the spawn of the glacier. Harbor seals by the dozens lay outhauled on low table-topped bergs floating among more massive bits the size and shape of wrecked build-ings. The timid ones flinched at the sight of the canoe, abandoning their ice floes with panicked, inchworm wiggling; the braver ones slid away more reluctantly, only to pop up behind the canoe and follow, bug-eyed with curiosity, until I turned to watch and they dove.

An eagle perched on the peak of a pyramid-shaped berg crouched at my approach, spread its wings, and dropped out of sight behind the ice. A paddle stroke eased the canoe around the lip of the berg and revealed three eagles—two of them mature and white headed, the other a mottled brown youth—tearing at the carcass of a seal. The immature bird tugged at a limp, pink cord protruding from the belly of the corpse, while the hooked yellow beaks and talons of the adults ripped the flesh of the body. A second, larger, seal, shoulders and snout flecked with blood, lay some distance away at the edge of the berg, frantic with fear, torn between flight and what I presumed was maternity.[67]

The eagles startled at my appearance and I froze. The tableau was so close I could see the fine detailing of the raptors' feet, the ivory and lemon color of the skin, and the long, deadly curve of the spur. Normally, eagles are quite shy, flapping away at the first sign of threat, but the largest bird stretched its neck, turned its head, and pierced me with a stare, and the challenge in the reptilian yellow eye shot a shiver of apprehension up my spine. It was sharp, unblinking, and fearless, and some ancient animal gland deep inside me seemed to recognize that the huge bird was, at that moment, purely a predator and appraising me coldly, as if measuring the effort required to taste my organs and my eyes.

The alien, lizard-blink snap of a nictating membrane flickered across the staring eye as if signaling a decision, and the bird dismissed me, lowered its head, and resumed tearing at the half-grown pup. In a flurry of wing beats, eagle fought eagle, and the youngest was driven back from the meal. The second seal abandoned the floe, rolling into the water with a gurgling bark, and disappeared.

The set of the current carried me closer and closer to the frenzy, until the smell of blood and offal was in my nose. I was afraid to move, suffused with an unreasonable fear of inciting a possessive attack.[68]

---

67. It is highly unlikely the eagles killed the seal. They may on occasion take a newborn pup before it can swim, but anything larger would be difficult unless it had already been badly injured, perhaps by a hunter or fisherman's bullet or an orca, perhaps by suddenly rolling ice. In this case there was no way to tell.

68. It is important to note that I have never heard of an eagle acting aggressively toward a human except in defense of a nest, and usually not even then. On another occasion, I drifted even closer to a group of feeding eagles on the *Swift*, with two photographers aboard, with no reaction from the birds. Nonetheless, after staring into that unblinking dinosaur-eye from the vantage of a canoe, my reaction did not feel so very ridiculous.

I tightened my grip on the paddle and shifted my weight, considering how to throw myself into the bottom of the canoe and slash with the blade, fearing also that doing so might result in an upset into the glacial water. But the birds continued to ignore me and concentrated on tearing at their meal. I was so close I could hear the grating of talons on the ice.

The remains of the seal disappeared in a tearing and gulping of fur and flesh. The immature eagle sneaked a hook into a loop of gut and gulped at the rope of innards. Its elders tug-o-warred with a long string of meat and soon only the hide, like an inverted sock, lay among the scattered blood and hair of the feast.

When the raptors gave a final war cry and rose into the air one by one, I slumped and leaned forward, letting out my breath, and rested the paddle across my knees. The glacier thundered in the distance and another column of ice rumbled into the fjord.

I was trembling. The brutality and finality in the consumption of the seal had unnerved me, the feeding so fierce and barbarous that the vision of it threatened to uproot and cast away as delusion all of the beauty I had found in the glacier's work and the elegance of nature's systems. The feeling of contentment I had found at the camp near the glacier was gone.

All of the past rose up around me, dense and murky as the silt-laden river. Listless, I drifted, making weak strokes with the paddle and listening to the sound of God heaving the ice about until the cold crept into my feet and urged me to paddle on.

Firewood was plentiful in the forest that evening, and I built a roaring fire to force warmth into my bones. The tide fell away, exposing a thick band of mussels, and the shadow of the sun's passing climbed up the distant walls. A small raptor of some sort drifted in and out along the edge of the coming night, hunting in silence for inattentive songbirds and mice. Through the darkest part of twilight I wrestled and brooded, desperate to solve the cipher of life, and failing, hungered for whiskey until I climbed into my wet sleeping bag and slept with my back curled toward the fire.

———

I ROSE ACHING the next morning and took two aspirins, drained and dressed the blisters on my hands, and took two more. Sleep had been a loss, paid out to dreams of yellow, blood-streaked eyes and climbing an endless muddy hill. My food was gone, with the exception of a packet of dried milk that had gotten wet and set up hard, but I bypassed the cove where the *Swift* lay at anchor and paddled on.

I hugged the shore at the mouth of the fjord, bucking the incoming tide, riding the back eddies and swirls that boiled behind points of land. It would have been wiser to sit on the beach and wait for the tide to turn, but I chose to fight the inflowing current a hard stroke at a time, chopping the paddle into the ripping current and pulling against the burning blisters. Eyes blinking back trickles of sweat, I made a half yard on each stroke, stalling and giving up six inches as soon as the blade left the water.

It took an hour to make a half mile and I was near to quitting, until at last I turned the point into Stephens Passage and felt the force of the tide ease, turn, and come behind. The expanse of water beyond Harbor Island lay still and silver as mercury, and across the straits the green spine of Admiralty Island reached as far north and south as I could see. With the current behind me, progress was rapid. At mid-tide-and-falling, an upflash of herring silvered the water beside Thistle Ledge, and a gull folded its wings and dropped, knifing headfirst into the sea just as the explosive breath of a whale blew a fountain of spray into the air. I backpaddled to a halt as another great darkness rose and blew, water sheeting from the immense curve of its back, and watched as another and another and another whale surfaced, spouting and blowing, until their number became difficult to discern in the wallow of tails and fins.

One by one, the whales jackknifed and dove. The leader, a matriarch with a tail fluke the size of a truck bed, sounded first, and the others followed, charging the fish in a rushing, slipstream formation. Moments later, a palpable tension rose, shivering and trembling the surface of the water like a pot coming to a boil, and the high, keening sound of a stun song began vibrating and ringing up through the aluminum skin of the canoe.

Bubbles *blumped* to the surface in an arching line a hundred feet from shore and stopped. A single herring jumped, then twenty more, until dozens and hundreds swarmed to the surface. In a rush like a breaking volcano, the pod exploded—mouths agape—to the surface, and a shout broke from my lungs at the sight of a ten-foot pink tongue. A surge of turbulent green water threatened to slop over the canoe.

I dipped and pulled, backstroking the canoe into reverse, away from the flailing fins and heads. Heart pounding with glee and fear, I shouted a wordless call to the whales, and in a great, fishy gasp of satisfaction, one rumbled a throaty call in return.

The pod made war on the herring for an hour, decimating the school with a rhythm that was steady and precise: dive, circle, and bubble, then surge upward into the light, sweeping mouth-first into the ball of swirling silver before lolling a bit on the surface to catch their breath, then sounding again.

The sun settled into its western quadrant. The sea sparkled with fish scales and oil. At low tide the pod scattered, drawing exclamation points on the horizon with the plumes of their breath as if declaiming their fortune at living a life so replete with plunder.

I made camp early that night, gathering a fistful of narrow brown leaves from a muskeg beyond the fringe of the trees and using my knife to pry a handful of limpets from a rock. While I waited for the Labrador tea to brew, I steamed the meat from the limpet shells and ate them one by one. The meat was rubbery and difficult to chew, but rich with the flavor of the sea. Still unsatisfied, I poked into the understory of the forest for wild greens, but the season was advanced. The salad of twisted stalk, fiddleheads, and beach greens I envisioned was either nonexistent or too fibrous with age to enjoy. From the canoe, with a stick and a paddle, I carefully snagged a small Dungeness crab that had overestimated the ability of its coloring and shell to camouflage it among a shallow bed of seaweed and stones.

I killed the crab, broke it open and wrapped it in kelp, then put it on the fire to steam while I dug a handful of black lily roots for a starch. Finding a comfortable seat on a large stone, I cracked the crab from its shell, sucking the legs for slivers of sweet meat between bites of the crisp ricelike roots. The blisters on my palms stung in the salt water when I washed my hands in the sea.

The power in the whale's feeding frenzy had moved me; the eerie soprano of the hunting song played over and over in my head. The vibrational frequency of the song is said to resonate with the bodies of the herring to stun and disorient them, but after hearing and feeling it at such close range, humming through the skin of the canoe, I was more certain than ever that it was as much a song of joy and exultation as it was a tool of the hunt, a singing that celebrated the unity of the clan.

It had been a beautiful experience, in an inexorable, powerful way—so much so that it was hard to grasp the measure of death it entailed. A hundred tons of small silver lives had perished in the feeding, yet it was patently a fair exchange, this trade of small lives for large, just as consuming the limpets, lilies, and crab that made up my dinner was nothing to regret. The eagles, too, had been doing the same, taking the life of the seal for the sake of their own.

The image of my father's ashes drifting down into the clear water among the spawning salmon played across the screen of my mind. I counted off all the deaths I had seen, the tally of which remarked upon the fate of all living things, which is to be eaten, whether by whales, eagles, bears, or the microbes of the grave. But this is part and parcel of the continuation of life, I told myself, of the translation of bodies into more bodies, and life into life. The litter of shattered crab shell at my feet gave brilliant red testimony to how death becomes life, is *necessary* for life, and this being so, is beyond being labeled as good or bad.

In the journal of his voyage to Alaska in 1786, Jean-François de Galoup, Comte de La Pérouse, wrote that "nature is sublime only in the great; in the minutiae of things it is negligent." He could as easily have been writing about the nature of human life: often difficult or terrible in the details, but nonetheless part of a grand and unimaginable scheme, a tapestry of which I felt privileged to be a part, whether out in the wind and the rain, among the icebergs and the forest where each and every living element has the job of nurturing or consuming another, or in the company of someone like Michio. The idea of my father's remains now being part of the food chain that nourishes the salmon and all of the sharks, porpoises, killer whales, eagles, bears, and humans pleased me a great deal.

Gathering up the fragments of shell, I cast the scraps of my meal back into the water and thought about how those remains, too, would give up their molecules and minerals to the chain of life.

Nothing is wasted, I reassured myself. It's all an exchange.

TWO DAYS before Christmas, the temperature in Anchorage was hovering near zero. In the nearly thirty years since I first set foot in the city it had matured into a cosmopolitan arena of four-lane streets and national retail chains, but when I drove across town to join a friend and her partner for dinner at a Thai restaurant, the trees still glittered from head to toe in a white raiment of frost.

Jo was one of the first photographers I met through Michio, in the second year of our friendship, when she came to Southeast to join us for two weeks on the *Swift*. She's blonde, persistently creative in her photography, and has the sort of cheekbones and soulful eyes that make it hard for me not to stare. Since that first trip she had returned to Juneau several times, and because sharing the confines of a small boat with another person for days or weeks on end is guaranteed to either bond or alienate any but the blandest of personalities, Jo had become a trusted friend. After the last round of pad thai and skewered shrimp she suggested we move across town for dessert.

"He was friends with everybody, but I always felt there was some-thing special between you two," she said, speaking of Michio. She had lived in Fairbanks before moving to Anchorage, and it was she who described to me how beautiful the autumn day of his memorial service had been and how many people started their eulogies by saying, "He was my best friend. . . ."

Talk like that embarrasses me, and I started making small talk with her partner—a neatly bearded botanist with a quick wit with whom I had immediately felt comfortable the first time we met—while Jo excused herself from the table and disappeared. I enjoyed the way Rob doted on Jo, the way his eyes followed her as she wove away through the aisles of the bookstore we had chosen to visit for dessert, one of those chain outlets that cultivates an air of coziness with over-stuffed couches and an attached espresso-bar café. I think I was commenting on how good the chocolate cake with raspberry sauce was when Jo reappeared, took her seat, and slipped a thin gift-wrapped package onto the table in front of me.

I thanked her, then tugged at the wrapping and sliced a piece of tape with my thumb, taking my time to extend the pleasure of the surprise. Peeling back a corner of the blue paper revealed the spine of a children's book; unwrapping it farther exposed half of the title and the author's name.

I ripped the rest of the paper away and ran a hand across the glossy dust jacket and the simple lettering that said, *Nanook's Gift* by Michio Hoshino (translated by Karen Colligan-Taylor for Cadence Books). I tried to think of something to say, but it hurt when I tried to speak. Instead, I just turned the pages, scanning the words of Michio's final book.

Nanook is the Inupiaq Eskimo word for polar bear, and in Michio's last work he had conjured a children's story of a young Native boy, the grandson of a hunter, who while wandering through an Arctic storm is instructed by the bear's spirit in his coming responsibilities and duties in life. The lump in my throat eased a bit when I read:

> *"Boy, we are eaters of seals. Ring seals pursue cod, and cod swallow smaller creatures living in the sea . . . We are constantly reborn in new forms of life.*

"Hunters thrust their harpoons into beluga whale: whales catch salmon and salmon swallow herring . . . We are constantly reborn in new forms of life.

"Wolves pursue caribou, and caribou browse on lichen. Foxes hunt the eggs and chicks of nesting birds, and those birds eat small insects . . . We are constantly reborn in new forms of life.

"The wind that carried away your grandfather's last breath gave it to a newborn wolf as its first breath of life . . . We are constantly reborn in new forms of life."

A chill spread across my skin when I read the next words, an eerily prescient summation of all that the spirit of the polar bear had explained to the hunter-to-be, a boy eager to take his place in the world:

"We are each an expression of the earth.
When you pray for my life,
you become Nanook,
and Nanook becomes man.

Someday we shall meet in this world of ice.
When that happens, it does not matter
whether it is I who dies or you."

In slightly more than five hundred words spaced between twenty-nine photographs of polar bears and their cubs striding, wrestling, eating, and sleeping amid the blues and whites of a world that is neither water nor land, Michio had said everything that I have used a hundred thousand words to say in this book.

⟫ Epilogue

THE BEAR CAME OUT of the alders and took a few strides toward the beach. Pausing, it lifted its nose and sniffed at the air, then stood without moving as it interpreted the breeze. The tide was low, and the smell of bladder weed and kelp filled the air. A raven *klok-klock*ed from the trees.

One of my passengers raised his binoculars. I followed suit, adjusting the focus to bring the bear into relief. The sun was soft and gray behind a veil of thin clouds, and as the lumbering animal lowered its head and took another step toward the tide line, a question began to form in my head.

There's something different about this one, I started to say, but held my tongue; I didn't want to say anything until I was sure. With me were two photographers I had never worked with before: W., a tall, balding ex–big game hunting guide with an encyclopedic knowledge of Alaska's wildlife, and D., a younger photographer from Wyoming who hung on everything W. had to say.

During the winter following Michio's death I had sent invitations to several photographers I knew only by their reputations to join me on trips in search of new images and experiences, offering my services at a price that did little more than cover my costs. I rationalized this otherwise unsound business tactic by telling myself it was a way to expand my client list while exploring new areas, but in retrospect, it seems my true motive was probably a subconscious wish to fill the gap left by the loss of Michio by prospecting among others in his profession for new friends.

The impulse clearly wasn't working. The chemistry between my passengers and me was all wrong, and the atmosphere aboard the *Swift* had been awkward since W. and D. came aboard. W. appeared to be struggling to conceal a contempt for my opinions beneath a studied humility, betraying his disdain through a repertoire of fractional chin lifts, long stares out the window in lieu of answering questions, and animated conversations with D. that ceased as soon as I entered the room.

W. grunted as he stared through his binoculars. "This could be it."

For three days we had been in the bay, an east-facing harbor entered via a tidal channel in the shadow of the Chilkhat Mountains.[69] During that time we had seen numerous bears (both grizzlies and blacks) as well as several moose and the tracks of a foraging wolf. Although the bears had given us several opportunities for some first-class photos, including one sumo-weight grizzly that displayed the species' extraordinary strength by using one paw to shift aside an immense slab of stone to slurp up a few worms underneath, part of my effort to re-create my connection with Michio had been to continue the search for the blue bear, and my passengers and I had been sitting on the deck for several hours that morning, scanning the shoreline for a glimpse of gray fur. The bay branched left and right inside the entrance, with a small mudflat and creek at the head of each arm. Anchored near the center, we had a clear view of the coastline—a

69. As I explained before, photographers can be quite possessive, and a promise was made to D. and W. not to reveal the location—a secrecy motivated by both the desire to maintain the exclusive nature of our photos and the concern that naming the site might lead to illegal poaching.

more effective way of watching a large amount of territory than wandering along the beach or climbing a mountain.

Now it seemed the strategy was paying off. Sunlight burning through the gauzy layer of clouds sparkled off the shoulders and guard hairs of the bear. My heart quickened. W. grunted again. I still wasn't sure if the bear was silver or if its color was just a trick of the distance and the angle of the sun, but as I continued to stare through the binoculars, I was more sure with every passing second that if the animal wasn't blue, it damn sure wasn't black!

"Let's go," I said, and began readying the skiff. D. and W. scrambled to organize their gear, pausing now and then to snatch another glimpse of the bear as they packed their cameras. After mounting the outboard and putting an uh-oh bag, a coil of line, and an anchor aboard, I did the same. In recent years a few of my photos had won various competitions or received some other form of prominent display, and photo agencies had begun to contact me with offers to market my work. I was hesitant to accept, largely because doing so would have put me in direct competition with clients I considered my friends, but as an alternative, I had decided to begin experimenting with digital video. Now, in addition to my twenty-year-old 35-millimeter camera gear, my pack held an expensive new Japanese video camera and all of the spare batteries, tapes, lens adapters, diopters, and gizmos it required.

The little outboard muttered to itself as we eased away from the *Swift,* moving slowly and carefully toward the shore. W. and D. kept an eye on our quarry while I studied the pattern of the currents and the direction of the breeze, looking for a place to land that would not disturb the bear. Halfway between the boat and the beach, W. peered through his binoculars for a moment and gave a single emphatic nod of his head.

This was the bear we were looking for, the animal I had been seeking for so long. Energy pulsed through my body, sending a wave of elation through my veins. As rapidly as it peaked, however, my euphoria faded; never have I felt the absence of another person so intensely as I felt that of Michio when I reached into my pack for the video camera, zoomed in on the bear, and saw the pale shine of its fur.

The outboard sputtered and vibrated as I slowed to an idle. The viewfinder jiggled, capturing an image of the bear that staggered like a drunk. Beside me, I could hear D.'s camera snapping off frames. The glacier bear lowered its head, raised it again to stare in our direction, then took a step to the side and stopped. W. snapped a picture, then jerked his head toward the shore. The blue bear was too far away. Getting a decent shot would require setting up a tripod on the beach to support a large telephoto lens.

Barnacles scraped against the hull as I killed the outboard and tilted it up to let the inflatable drift ashore. Once in shallow water, D. and W. shouldered their packs and stepped over the side, then began moving up the beach, taking a few slow paces at a time whenever the glacier bear lowered its head to graze. I stayed behind, carefully balancing the anchor on the edge of the skiff after tying it to the bow, then giving the skiff a firm push out into deep water and jerking the anchor free with a coil of line arranged to pay out smoothly from my hand.[70]

The bear raised its head at the splash, stepped back, and stared in our direction. I froze. W. and D. did the same. After a long unblinking gaze, the bear lowered its head again to tear at a mouthful of grass, turning broadside and revealing the length of its body. I gasped and touched my chest with my hand. Its fur was the color of burnished metal, or of the sunlight that flickers along the rim of a storm at sea.

For the next twenty minutes the bear worked back and forth within range of W.'s and D.'s telephoto lenses, alternately grazing and sniffing the air. After taking another long look at the three odd creatures scuttling slowly along the beach a hundred yards away, it moved back to the edge of the brush and began marching deliberately back and forth across a line of small saplings, straddling them as if scratching its belly.[71]

I pulled my own camera from my pack and tried to focus on the

---

70. Even at the moment of fulfilling a decade-old dream, the rise and fall of the tide must be considered. At the rate the water level was falling, if I hadn't reanchored the skiff in deeper water, it would have been stranded in minutes.

71. This is a bear's way of leaving scent marks, or signposts, within its home range—a way of saying, "I'm here—and not leaving."

bear, swinging between a trembling excitement—*at last, at last*—and a small, awkward knot of resentment at the thought that although I was finally seeing a blue bear, I was doing it in the company of people with whom I had no hope of reaching a connection.

It wasn't supposed to be this way, I thought, and a muscle-deep memory of the odd, affectionate frustration I sometimes felt toward Michio for his somehow endearing habits of tardiness and single-minded forgetfulness swept through me until I almost laughed out loud. *Michio, where the hell are you, now that we've finally found the bear?*

I steadied the camera, adjusted the shutter speed, and snapped off a few frames, then gnawed at my lip in frustration. The distance was too great for my lens.

Dropping the still camera into my pack, I snapped the video camera onto the tripod, screwed a telephoto adapter onto the lens, and pressed the start button. The bear was sauntering back and forth with a muscular strut, rolling its shoulders and hams. As the camera rolled, it gave a small, abrupt shake of its head and, in the manner of a man who has suddenly remembered he has somewhere to go, lifted its nose to the breeze and strode deliberately and rapidly into the forest, vanishing behind a wall of thick brush.

SUNSET, and the light was fading. The tide had fallen, risen, and begun falling again while we waited for the bear to reappear, but the shoreline remained lifeless and empty. Back on the *Swift,* W. and D. hadn't responded when I remarked on how seeing the bear had stirred me, how after so many years of searching it had seemed a spiritual moment, and as dinner simmered on the stove, we took turns watching the darkening stretch of beach where the bear had disappeared.

"He's back," W. said as he rose from the table, pointing. On shore a pale shadow drifted out of the alder and blended into a patch of grass.

D. shook his head, dismissing the bear's reappearance as of no value. "It's too dark for photos."

I hesitated, the deep-seated impulse to do what was best for my clients (which was to leave the bear alone and hope it would reappear tomorrow) battling with the excitement of seeing the bear until I finally gave in, grabbed up my camera pack and dropped it in the skiff, saying, "It's light enough for video."[72]

In truth I wasn't that interested in getting video of the bear. What I was after was a chance to see the bear—no, to *be* with the bear—without the distraction of other people or the desire to turn its image into a commodity; to listen to the sound of it chewing or perhaps catch a faint whiff of its wet-dog-and-cow-parsnip smell. In short, what I wanted was an intimate moment with the bear, but as a man and a bear, not as a bear and a guide, and to imagine how it would have been to see it with my friend.

The outboard started on the first pull and purred quietly as I pulled away from the *Swift*. It was that time of evening when color flees a landscape, when a forest is more gray than green, and the water grows a shade darker than the sky. The bear had settled down to graze, moving back and forth a slow step at a time. Behind me, I could hear the faint mutter of the tide pouring around the rocks at the harbor's entrance; from the trees ahead, the buzzing note of a varied thrush.

The current was strong, and I steered the skiff at an angle to the beach, crabbing sideways on a course for the bear—not the best stalking technique, but for reasons I cannot name I felt I should approach openly and slowly, with no effort to hide, and no move toward subterfuge or deceit.

At fifty yards the bear looked up and gazed directly at me—an ash-colored phantasm in the gloam. At forty it turned sideways, revealing the deep blue-gray of its back and side. At twenty yards it lowered its head and resumed grazing, throwing sidelong glances at my approach.

Fifty feet, forty-five, forty—I cut the outboard, slipped an oar from its lashings, and paddled until I touched bottom, then reached for my pack.

---

72. The technology involved in capturing digital images requires much less light than film photography, with some newer instruments capable of capturing images in near darkness (although not in color).

The bear looked up at the sound of the zipper, a blade of rye grass hanging from its mouth. Heedless of the weak light, with no thought of exposure, I raised the camera and pressed the shutter.

A full minute passed, then another, as we stared at each other; I could see the swell of its ribs as it breathed. When it lowered its head for another bite of grass, I could hear the grinding of its jaws. Pushing with the oar, I edged a few feet closer—closer than was reasonable or smart.

I'm not sure even now how close I would have gone, if I would have nudged ashore and stepped out, letting the skiff drift while I walked right up to the bear and placed my hand on its back to feel the hard muscles beneath its fur. I'll never know, because before I reached that final step I breached some limit it had set, some boundary of space, and it turned, quartering to face me. Shifting its bulk from foot to foot for a moment as if trying to decide what to do, the bear suddenly whirled and jumped, exploding into two long, bounding strides that took it into the forest.

I froze, listening for the crackle of breaking branches that usually follows a hasty retreat. I listened, but heard nothing; listened harder and heard nothing again. With nothing but the hum of my own blood in my ears, I began wondering if the bear had stopped a few feet inside the fringe of shrubs lining the beach and was listening in return, holding stock-still as it peered out from the swallowing darkness.

I'd like to report some deep revelation as a result of communing with the bear—how for one fraction of time everything around me seemed impossibly dark and light at the same time, as if I were seeing the arrangement of water and stone and all of the hundreds of life-forms that make up the forest and sea as a bright incandescence that was no product of light but instead a component of its own flowing brightly from one element to the next, flickering and shining like the fur of the bear—but I can't, because once the bear was gone, I was just a man sitting in a skiff in the darkness, and one who had drawn too thoughtlessly close to a peacefully grazing animal and frightened it, to boot.

In its flight, the glacier bear had shown itself to be like any other bear, with the same traits and reactions of any member of its species. It was, after all, just a common black bear, with nothing more obviously unusual about it than the color of its fur, and I realized it had probably never really mattered whether or not I ever found one and photographed it. What *did* matter, it was clear, was the experience of the chase and the company I kept during the search. What mattered were the things seen and done on its trail.

This was something I never fully understood until I sat down to write this story, to peel my life apart down to the final 1/60 of a second when the shutter fell and the image of the blue bear was captured. Until then, I never perceived how each and every event and encounter of an entire lifetime, no matter how enormous or small, leads from one to another, and that to the next, in a process as exact as a watchmaker's mind or the return of the salmon, that we might learn those lessons which show us our worth and our place at each moment, until this, the final moment when it is time to write,

The End

❯ Select Bibliography

Armstrong, Robert H. *Guide to the Birds of Alaska*. Alaska Northwest Books, 1990.

Baker, Marcus, and William H. Dall. *Pacific Coast Pilot. Coast and Islands of Alaska*. 2d series. U.S. Government Printing Office, 1879.

Bohn, Dave. *Glacier Bay: The Land and the Silence*. Sierra Club–Ballantine Books, 1967.

Conner, Cathy, and Daniel O'Haire. *Roadside Geology of Alaska*. Mountain Press, 1988.

Cutter, Donald C. *Malaspina and Galiano; Spanish Voyages to the Northwest Coast*. University of Washington Press, Douglas and McIntyre, 1991.

Dauenhauer, Richard, and Nora M. Dauenhauer. *Haa Shuka, Our Ancestors: Tlingit Oral Narratives*. University of Washington Press, Sealaska Heritage Foundation, 1997.

Davis, Neil. *Alaska Science Nuggets*. Geophysical Institute, University of Alaska, 1982.

Emmons, George T. *The Tlingit Indians*. Edited by Frederica de Laguna. University of Washington Press, Douglas and McIntyre, 1991.

Ford, John K. B., and Graeme M. Ellis. *Transients: Mammal-Hunting Killer*

Whales of British Columbia, Washington, and Southeastern Alaska. University of British Columbia Press, 1999.

Ford, John K. B., Graeme M. Ellis, and Kenneth C. Balcomb. *Killer Whales: The Natural History and Genealogy of "Orcinus Orca" in British Columbia and Washington State.* University of British Columbia Press, 1994.

Goldschmidt, Walter R., and Theodore H. Haas. *Haa Aani, Our Land: Tlingit and Haida Land Rights and Use.* University of Washington Press, Sealaska Heritage Foundation, 1998.

Henning, Robert A. *Admiralty: Island in Contention. Alaska Geographic* series, vol. 1, no. 3. Alaska Geographic Society, 1974.

————. *Alaska's Bears. Alaska Geographic* series, vol. 20, no. 4. Alaska Geographic Society, 1993.

————. *Exploring Alaska's Birds. Alaska Geographic* series, vol. 28, no. 1. Alaska Geographic Society, 2001.

Hilson, Stephen E. *Exploring Alaska and British Columbia.* Evergreen Pacific Publishing, 1997.

Jans, Nick. *Tracks of the Unseen: Meditations on Alaska Wildlife, Landscape, and Photography.* Fulcrum, 2000.

Morey, Walt. *Operation Blue Bear: A True Story.* Dutton, 1975.

Muir, John. *Travels in Alaska.* Houghton-Mifflin, 1915.

O'Clair, Rita, with Richard Carstensen and Robert H. Armstrong. *The Nature of Southeast Alaska: A Guide to Plants, Animals, and Habitats.* Alaska Northwest Books, 1992.

Olson, Henry, and Richard Bayne. *The Wit and Wisdom of Tiger Olson (Oldtime Alaskan).* Douglas Printing, 1979.

Orth, Donald J. *Dictionary of Alaska Place Names.* U.S. Government Printing Office, 1971.

Stewart, Doug. "Tales of Two Orcas." *National Wildlife,* December/January 2001.

Thill, Michael, and Mary Jo Thill. *The Aleut Evacuation: The Untold War Story.* Gaff-Rigged Productions, 1992. Videorecording.

Wickwire, Jim, and Dorothy Bullitt. *Addicted to Danger.* Pocket Books, 1998.

Wood, C. E. S. "Among the Thlinkit Indians in Alaska." *Century,* July 1882.

Young, S. Hall. *Hall Young of Alaska: The Mushing Parson.* Fleming H. Revell, 1927.